SLIDE 68

SLIDE 68

86 Your Current Life and Pursue
the Lifestyle You've Been Dreaming Of

ANTHONY VON MICKLE

iUniverse, Inc.
Bloomington

Slide 68
86 Your Current Life and Pursue the Lifestyle
You've Been Dreaming Of

iUniverse books may be ordered through booksellers or by contacting:

iUniverse
1663 Liberty Drive
Bloomington, IN 47403
www.iuniverse.com
1-800-Authors (1-800-288-4677)

ISBN: 978-1-4759-6518-6 (sc)
ISBN: 978-1-4759-6520-9 (hc)
ISBN: 978-1-4759-6519-3 (ebk)

Printed in the United States of America

iUniverse rev. date: 12/19/2012

Acknowledgements

My name will be forever credited as the sole author of this book, but I assure all who reads it that this is a team effort. With that, I thank God for introducing me to another of life's seemingly insurmountable obstacles with His specific intent to bring me out on top and placing me far ahead of where I would have been without them. I'm grateful for the perpetual prayers of Reverend Willie Kennedy and Nazareth Baptist Church of Cassatt, SC and Reverend Dr. Darrell K. White and the Bethlehem Baptist of Alexandria, VA both which are my church families. I'm grateful to my parents, Willie and Dorothy Mickle for always allowing me and my brothers Trent and Willie II (Squirt) to chart our own courses and never forcing us down paths that we didn't want to take. There are a host of other family members which are far too many to name on both my parent's sides so allow me to suffice it by saying thank you all. Due to the writing of my first book, Real Estate for Real People, our family was extended and now we welcome the entire Mickle clan from Gainesville, FL and Larry and Angela Knight Deskins (now deceased) from St. Louis, MO.

I'm grateful for all my kids, the two that are biologically mine and the host of others who have forced their way on me including the Belly Babies. That would be Quan (Pig Belly), Yasmine (Little Ole Fat Belly), Mia (My Rich Baby), Shamar (Ranky Belly) and Maya and my newest Triniti ;(Stanky Belly). If you have to traverse the globe in search of your wildest dream, do so, but ensure that you travel safely and have fun along the way.

There are far too many friends to list but I especially acknowledge my nonjudgmental homeboys that never failed me including Mike "Eff Yo Couch Darknesses!" Jenkins, Ken "What Up G" Curry, Cory "Let Me Hold Somein"Adams and my Citadel brother Sheldon Wilson. I can't forget my sisters including Tiffany Bell, Melissa "Go Steelers" Buckner - White, Angie Dickerson, The Amy Hymes Show, SSG Sholanda "Shalo" Scott, and my California girl Melanie "Beverly Hills Montage" Jackson. A sincere lifelong thanks goes to the Washington DC Area Citadel Alumni Association, Wharton and Harvard Business School Club's of D.C., The Investment Forum and all the readers of The Fleetwood, News That Makes You Move from The Investment Forum.

I'm grateful for all my educational institutions including Pine Tree Hill Elementary, Camden Middle School, North Central High, The Citadel, Harvard University's Ukrainian Research Institute, Keller Graduate School, Georgetown University, Harvard Business School, Tsinghua University, Argosy University and especially Dr. Frankie Felder and the Clemson University Diversity Initiatives.

Contents

PART 3:

PART 4:

PART 5:

PART 6:

Introduction

Life Can and Will Deal Us
a Bad Hand from Time to Time

In 2007, I experienced one of the most tumultuous times in my adult life both professionally and financially. When my financial losses reached $3 million, I simply stopped counting. When my operating income (salary plus investment income) declined 99 percent, I wondered how long it would take before it finally hit zero. I experienced what I'd read about many times, which is markets can bring you to your knees and test the very fiber you are made of. I'd turned an $8-an-hour part-time job into a multimillion-dollar portfolio only to have it all come crashing down. In addition, my career progression stymied in the face of jealousy, followed by the worst recession since the Great Depression. I wondered when I would recover. (I knew I would recover; I just didn't know when.) It was during that time that I felt like I was in the middle of a large body of water. I had two choices: (1) I could swim back to the simple, middle-class life I knew before any taste of the good life, or (2) I could swim forward and head for territory I had only slightly experienced that might hold promise of a better lifestyle in which I would hopefully never have to experience this hardship again. I chose the latter.

"Money doesn't buy happiness," they say, but a lack of it to take care of your basic needs can make you downright miserable. As I endured this experience, I occasionally thought back to the famous Footprints poem. The writer described how there were two men walking along the beach, in my case God and me, but there was only one set of footprints, as these were the times that He carried me.

The times were just tough for me, no doubt about it, and some days just plain ugly; but the beauty was I had been down a similar path before. I kept thinking back to the 1996 Olympic opening ceremony in Atlanta, when a large white curtain was drawn and all the athletes showcased their respective talents behind it. The audience saw no color, no country, no commercial or endorsement details, but just talent. The ceremony ended with a discus thrower beginning to launch his prized steel hundreds of feet across the field, but he didn't release it. He simply collapsed his chiseled frame and humbled himself to the ground so that his face was close to his knees, with his right hand clutching the disc at his feet and his left arm fully extended behind him. At that moment, the lights disappeared and there was darkness.

Many times I thought of that scene. I also thought of the story my grandfather, Reverend Ezekial Roseborough, used to tell me. He described the scene of a defeated Samson after he lost his strength. Samson simply had one more request as he stood between the pillars of the Coliseum filled with enemies; he cried out, "Lord, give me strength." With that, he pushed mightily with everything he had, and the foundation gave way, defeating his enemies with one powerful blow.

You may currently feel that the weight of the world is on your shoulders and you're looking for a way out. I understand. Nothing seems to be working or working fast enough. Still, I understand, and I've been there. What I can assure you is that if you follow the steps in this book and commit yourself to these principles, success can't escape you forever.

There Is Good News on the Way, as Seasons Do and Must Change

As someone with advanced degrees from top schools, in addition to years of experience as both very poor and very affluent, I can attest that your making a step toward correcting your life situation is more than many people choose to do. I can't guarantee that things will happen overnight, but with set goals, a clear plan, and a lot of faith, you can turn your life around.

As you read this book, you will find references to God; this is not an attempt to convert atheists into believers, but to assure you that fancy degrees and top networked connections can't do it all. You can have the best information in the world, but greed and gluttony can bring about the worst in people and you simply have to pray to God that people are telling you the truth. No Ivy League school can guarantee you that.

In our struggle, some may look to God for answers. I am not a biblical scholar, but I do go to church regularly, and thankfully I can tell you in the words delivered by Minister Flemming at Bethlehem Baptist Church on June 14, 2009, "Yes, there are answers from God." The minister gave example after example from various books of the Bible of how, at the seemingly worst of times when we look for answers to our most troubling problems, God will provide a word of comfort if we're open to receive it.

You Must Stay Committed

The first thing you must demonstrate is motivation; you must believe that the American dream is still alive, but most importantly that it is obtainable. I want to illustrate realistic time frames to dreams, not just examples of the whiz kids who came up with something one day in a basement and two years later they have a gazillion dollars. That's wonderful if it happens, but believing that will happen is a long shot, though it *is* possible.

Second, you must see the mental process along the way that must be had before things start to happen. This is clearly nonconventional schooling. Even an MBA probably won't teach you this. There has to be an insatiable desire for something that far exceeds your current resources no matter how much you have.

The third thing is you must be committed to the commitment. There is no easy walk and no instant answers. Sometimes you will have to endure a season of trials and that season may last a full calendar year before you receive one ounce of understanding, but it is that one ounce that may prove to be the missing ingredient or piece to your puzzle. Living the lifestyle you've been dreaming of is no roll of the dice. You can't simply forecast that if you plan and stay the course for some defined period, that surely you will have full success. There are forces working totally out of your control that have to occur before you can progress.

That being said, you have to stay the course, even if you don't know which way the paths are winding and you can't see up ahead. Just know that if you stay on course long enough, you will find yourself in the winners' circle. Chances are that with intense focus, once things start to happen, they will continue to happen faster than you ever imagined. The beauty is that once you really get into a groove, your mind can work more efficiently; you can ease up on the how-to but keep the hammer down on the execution. You just have to start where you are. If you feel you're at your wits' end, be like Benjamin Franklin: just tie a knot in the rope and hang on.

How the Book Is Organized

Each chapter provides real-life examples of problems that I have encountered en route to my dream life and what I did to overcome them. I want to demonstrate that my answers to my problems were not unique to my situation, but instead the mind-set that is required to overcome any obstacles. Periodically throughout the book are points that I want you to take away from each chapter; these are enclosed in the Slide 68 Mind-set boxes.

At the end of the book, I have included a number of actual newsletters that I send to my list of hundreds of subscribers, which are getting them real results. The newsletter is called "The Fleetwood" after the manufacturer of the new mobile home we moved to when I was in eighth grade. It was a time when I actively pursued a new image and new life for myself. When I did, I had the best start to the ninth grade anyone could have asked for. That was the launching pad to a highly successful high school career, one that would launch a wonderful new life not only for myself but for my entire family. Every now and then, we may have to reinvent a few things in our lives and that's okay, but when you do, be sure to pull from the most positive experience you can.

Disclaimer

The business and political professionals mentioned in this book are people whom I either know or have met from a business standpoint. I mention them because I am impressed by their business or political knowledge; I do not necessarily agree with any of their personal opinions and actions.

The information, ideas, and suggestions in this book are not intended to render professional advice. Before following any suggestions contained in this book, you should consult your personal accountant or other financial advisor. Neither the author nor the publisher shall be liable or responsible for any loss or damage allegedly arising as a consequence of your use or application of any information or suggestions in this book.

"He failed in business in '31. He was defeated for state legislator in '32. He tried another business in '33. It failed. His fiancée died in '35. He had a nervous breakdown in '36. In '43 he ran for congress and was defeated. He tried again in '48 and was defeated again. He tried running for the Senate in '55. He lost. The next year he ran for Vice President and lost. In '59 he ran for the Senate again and was defeated. In 1860, the man who signed his name A. Lincoln, was elected the 16th President of the United States. The difference between history's boldest accomplishments and its most staggering failures is often, simply, the diligent will to persevere."

Lincoln Perseverance Motivational Poster. Accessed January 1, 2007. Available at http://www.successories.com/products/Motivational-Posters/ Great-Leaders/20/3731/Lincoln-Perseverance-Motivational-Poster

PART 1:

Dealing with Life's Problems

From the Mobile Home to Where Moguls Roam, and Then Back to the Mobile Home: Outlasting Success's Fleeting Nature

Sprawling mansions in the suburbs, exotic cars with chrome wheels, private helicopter flight lessons, trips to St. Regis's Monarch Beach resort in Southern California . . . doesn't it sound like the *Lifestyles of the Rich and Famous*? I certainly thought so. What more could a young, thirty-two-year-old bachelor ask for? I suppose one could ask for more, depending on where you came from in life, but I was never expected to lead this kind of life. In fact, no one from my trailer park was.

We've all seen trailer parks portrayed in the worst way on the television cop shows, but as a former resident, I can assure you fact is stranger than fiction. On television, there's always someone who has poor grammar, a filthy living arrangement, and the trashiest American life possible. In reality, you may or may not have all those elements, but one thing I have found generally speaking is that people who don't live in mobile home parks tend to look down on those who do. Way down.

Perhaps I should not have felt so badly when my mom and I were walking in front of our mobile home park along the Route 1 corridor of Cassatt, South Carolina, in the early eighties when a carload of white men purposely took aim, readied themselves, and just as they got close to us, threw a bag filled with half-empty beer bottles right at me. They screamed racial epithets at the top of their lungs and sped quickly down the highway. Instantly, I was covered in blood, glass, and alcohol. At eight years old, what could I have possibly done to deserve this? My mom was furious! There was absolutely nothing we could do at that point. That could be one reason why I don't drink today, but I doubt it.

And then there were the kids, my school-aged peers, who lived in homes that were not mobile and were brutally demonstrative of their innermost thoughts; they let everyone know if they thought you were poor or on welfare. Thank God my parents never were. They simply didn't have the skills or rich mind-set to do much better, and they lived in a town where opportunities for advancement were few and far between.

So how did I escape? What was the one thing that put me over the top? Did someone see something in me, pull me aside, and invest in my bright future? Did I show superior athletic skills on the basketball court or football field? Was I deemed a child prodigy, who mastered calculus before age ten? It sure would have been nice if any of those things were true, but they aren't.

It really has more to do with the refrigerator—an empty refrigerator. I was tired of opening the door to find it empty, only to go back to it five minutes later to find it empty again. Certain that there must be something in there, I would go back five minutes later, hoping to find something that I'd overlooked the first time. That was enough to make me realize that I had to find a way out of this mess, this lifestyle of daydreams, where my friends and I occasionally sat under a tree saying, "What if we were adopted? What if some rich man came along and said, 'I'm your real daddy, and you can come live with me now'?" We could go to his house and he could show us the new motorcycle and racetrack and the new shoes like all the other kids got. As horrible as it sounds today as a parent that your children might think something like that, it is about as honest and innocent as any dreaming, less-fortunate kids can be.

Perhaps I made it out because I was the middle child; I read being the middle child deemed me the most likely to succeed among my siblings, according to the book *Secrets of the Millionaire Mind: Mastering the Inner Game of Wealth* by T. Harv Eker. In any case, that was the lifestyle I left before things turned completely around for the better. I came out of poverty thinking surely I'd never have to look back. But after twenty years, I began feeling like Humpty Dumpty—I had a great fall.

Spring couldn't get to Washington soon enough. We had been blasted by the worst winter weather in quite some time. I was looking forward to a strong second quarter because I'd been out of work for a while. Two job offers I received were looking like opportunities to do one at night and the other by day, which was going to provide a much-needed cash cushion to get back on track. In fact, combining the two six-figure incomes was going to put me ahead—way ahead. The ebb and flow of government contracts had simply grown old, and the supposed advantage of having a top-secret-clearance golden credential, which was once hailed as a meal ticket for life, had rapidly become a very unstable way to make a good living. As the barometer was beginning to rise, so was my motivation for a great next few months.

I recall having to go to my parents' house for a few days to take care of some business in late March, and for some reason, as my trip started I experienced a great calm. I'm not sure where it came from, but for whatever reason, I wasn't in a hurry; I wasn't anxious like I usually am to cover the nearly five hundred miles, and I just got the feeling that everything was going to be all right. I don't really understand it, but it was the most calming feeling, like the exotic weather that comes just before nature delivers an earth-shattering storm. It was a good thing I was calm, because what was to happen next was about to knock the wind out of me.

When I returned from South Carolina, I was out running some errands, and my son called and told me that the power was out. I was a little caught off guard as the bill generally came to me online, but I hadn't received an online bill in a while and was beginning to get a little curious about that. When I logged on to check the balance, it had ballooned to nearly $1200. It was at that time I thought back to a baby shower that my aunt persuaded me to give to one of her friends. I had figured a baby shower wasn't a big deal, but as the shower grew closer, I was beginning to get a bit concerned as the number of people coming to the shower kept growing.

I then began to ask questions about who the person was, even though I thought I might have met her once before. My aunt told me it was some of her African friends, and I later learned that African baby showers were major celebrations. I recall thinking to myself, *why don't you invite them to your house in that case?* I've been called softhearted and will say yes when others say no. I didn't say anything, however, as I was scheduled to be out of town. As the date grew closer, I decided to cut my travel short just to ensure how my house was being received. I knew my aunt would take the utmost care, but I was beginning to hear through the grapevine that my other family members were getting involved with major decorating schemes.

When I returned, I walked into my kitchen to find that my house had been taken over and transformed. They had decorated the entire living room and basement, and I have to admit it was very striking. I was told at first it was going to be just the basement but I knew that wasn't going to work so I didn't mind kitchen use, but I never expected them to go to the extreme decorative levels. The thing that I was concerned about the entire time was the amount of utilities they were using. They had every light on in the house and all types of items plugged in. Furniture had been moved, and I was thinking about the utility contribution amount they could afford being insufficient.

For those who have never attended an African shower, let me assure you they are major family events. Men and children come out, and timeliness isn't really in their scope. People were asking for directions at 10:00 p.m. I was thinking this was an experience I would think twice about in the future, and I was wondering how much of this my aunt knew beforehand.

At any rate, we were all having a good time, and the family showed a ton of appreciation to me for opening my doors. Many of the teenagers in the family had really taken to me for some reason. Perhaps it was my relative youth, appearance of wealth, and ability to identify with them. They surrounded me in a corner and began to pour their young souls out. They told me all about their concerns, their problems, their desires, their futures, and so on. I had never experienced anything like it and was simply honored that they were sharing this with me and not some gangster on the streets, who could have easily taken advantage of their honesty and openness. Still, I had to think about the utility bill that was mounting. I allowed it to subside in my mind and just enjoyed the moment.

The reality of what I was thinking caught up a few weeks later when the bill came. They had used easily $300 worth of gas and electricity that day, which was substantially more than I ever use at the investment forums I do when I choose to hold them at my house. So when I got the call that the lights were cut, I thought about the partial payment I had made weeks earlier. I could have paid the entire bill but just wanted to prolong my cash cushion throughout the layoff. Add that to a bill that probably landed in my junk mail items, and it became a large bill.

When I arrived home to deal with the bill, I received a knock on the door from a strange old man asking me if I was aware that my house was about to be sold. I told him I wasn't, but I recalled receiving a letter from a law firm several days prior.

So now all my job offers were just hanging there, awaiting executive decisions that were not about to happen due to the record losses, and I was rapidly running out of my savings.

Getting the letter wasn't a shock, as I had been working with my bank to refinance my mortgage under the new programs for underemployed workers. The bank seemed willing at first and sent me a new agreement with new payments. I was pleased and looked forward to somewhat easier mortgage terms. I signed and notarized the contract and sent it back. Soon after, I began receiving letters from attorneys asking me if I wanted to file bankruptcy to save my home. I called the bank to inquire about the matter, and I was told by their customer service reps not to worry. So I didn't. This became a monthly matter. Each time I called, I talked with another set of reps. They were never able to find anything of significance regarding my account, but generally after about an hour, I would have assurance that everything was fine. For months, I went through this without any real concern, so when the stranger knocked on my door, I pretty much dismissed him.

I Just Bought Your Mansion; Now Get Out!

The next day, I received a handwritten letter on the door with a guy's name on it saying he'd purchased my house and wanted to negotiate a move-out date. I thought to myself, *those idiots at the bank lied to me for months, taking my money as if everything was fine, and then they sold my house right out from under me.* They then lied about having any knowledge of a new contract and claimed they couldn't find any record of it.

This wasn't the time for me to argue this point with the guy who purchased it at the auction for nearly $850,000 less than I paid; this was time to go. I didn't even have time to focus on the financials of it all because completely out of the blue, I lost four people I knew that same week. I wasn't able to make any of their funerals. Talk about a week of being tested. Still, here was this guy who had just bought my house right out from under me. I couldn't get mad at him. I did question the business ethics of the guy who purchased it sending someone else to my door. I really wondered, *how could the bank make such a stupid deal?* If they were willing to give that much of a discount on my account, surely they could have given it to me. It's probably because of all the TARP money they'd collected from the taxpayers, which allowed them to write off the mortgage and then sell it again in another transaction to someone else, in this case, the man who purchased it.

I will defer to Charles Gasparino's opening chapter of his book entitled *Bought and Paid For: The Unholy Alliance Between Barack Obama and Wall Street.* He does an award-winning job explaining exactly how the nation ended up in this housing and mortgage crisis mess, working his way all the way back to the Clinton administration and cutting no one any slack. If you lost money in the real estate market and ever want to figure out why everything tanked so fast, this is an excellent piece of work that answers tons of questions and provides you insight into a whole lot more.

Two of my neighbors told me of similar stories when they found out what had happened. One said he'd even seen a special on TV from a former mortgage executive, who said the banks were never willing to give new deals and couldn't care less about the homeowners. At the moment, that seemed to be the case, but for now it didn't help me in terms of saving the house.

I can easily make my case for the bank giving me substandard loans that I should have never had when I made enough money to be given better terms. It was ugly evidence that the racial economic divide was as wide as the Atlantic Ocean and growing. I perpetually tried to close the gap on economic empowerment in the years preceding the recession by hosting events from the Investment Forum, but the banks had a much louder voice and one that was backed with an unlimited checkbook. As much as I could and probably should focus on racial inequality, at least to a greater degree than I will in this book, I'd rather focus on more positive concepts. Blacks and other minorities are not the only people being affected in the current financial catastrophe, so I'd like you to focus your attention on getting past barriers, regardless of what they are or who you are.

To make matters worse, the guy who bought the house kept sending that annoying old man who knocked on the door the first time, and he was really starting to irk me with his stupid comments. Normally I respect elders and try not to talk badly to them, but this guy had pushed his limit so I let him have it. I wasn't mean to him but certainly wasn't welcoming, because he was being really inconsiderate by repeatedly showing up. I could have easily argued or made their life difficult and refused to move until the authorities got involved. I could have torn holes in every wall and painted the carpets and totally trashed the place, but what good was that really going to do?

I chose to go ahead and leave without any force because I was ready for change. I wanted to downsize in three months to a townhome closer to the city anyway in order to begin setting things up financially for my dream house and land purchase down south. In my eyes, this was simply a bigger kick-start toward my future. If the bank were found at fault, they would have had to repay me; but with the turmoil they were in, we knew that wasn't about to happen.

I'm sure some are thinking, *that's what people get for buying these oversize homes*. The reality is it doesn't matter if your house costs a million dollars or a hundred thousand. When your income stops and you go through a recession that eats away all of your funds, the end result is the same. I'm certainly not about to live life scared to death of getting laid off or losing assets. There are plenty of people who live in much less home who brag about how small or nonexistent their mortgage is; and as long as they are happy, that's great.

It was a good thing I kept my part-time new home sales consultant job over the past decade. It allowed me to see what others were doing, both those who were successfully managing to keep their homes as well as those who had fallen on hard times and lost their homes. I have to admit that there is some comfort in knowing that you are not alone when things don't work out so well. What I've found from working part-time for a decade in new home sales is that people say publicly that they would never spend that kind of money or they don't need all that space of a new home. The reality is when they come into the models, their expressions tell a very different story. They all *want* a new home; they're just too scared to sign up for it. In addition, some ethnic groups live in different styles than others. Some races can live with two or three families under one roof and tag team the mortgage. I have no desire to do that for an extended period of time, but have done it in the past. Yes, it does work, but eventually you move out and are on your own.

If losing the roof over my head wasn't enough, dealing with my employment situation also became very annoying. Because I had great credentials and a strong track record in spite of a deepening recession, I knew I'd be able to grab another $9-to-10k-a-month gig until I could really get back into the game. Unfortunately for me, changing jobs right at that moment was the worst thing I could have done because the government, without warning, decided it was time to do an updated background investigation on me; that is definitely not the time to change jobs. Depending on your clearance level, investigations occur in two parts, one being a polygraph test and the other a general check of your records. The problem was they had only completed my polygraph test by the time I left my last job, so my investigation was only partially completed. Because I was not actively working, they saw no reason to finish it. In my case, that left me with only half of my credentials, which is essentially like having none, so as the offers came in ranging from $150 to 200K, the only thing they were good for was really uncomfortable toilet paper.

I thought the background investigation problem would quickly be resolved once I could get the employers to understand what had happened, but to my surprise, it only got worse. The amount of red tape required to fix that simple problem turned out to be enormous in what I learned was a very broken government system. A problem that could have been resolved in weeks quickly turned into one that would last at least two years. So much for being squeaky clean enough to work for the government.

Life Will Happen;
You Just Have to Be Willing to Adjust.

In recessions, you have to be strategic if you want things to happen. The bank knew this, and so did I. They could have easily renegotiated with me, but they chose not to and they had their reasons. I could have easily become a pain in their necks, but I chose not to. My reason was that I knew the market trends better than the average consumer. The part-time real estate work I did with the model homes gave me insight to supervisory-level builders and developers with decades more experience than I have. As the recession began in 2008, we went through economic trends and studied the pricing of homes over the past hundred years.

Most of the economic housing cycles were roughly seven-year stints, with five years of expansion and two years of contraction. With the most recent market, we had nearly fourteen years of growth, and we knew that the contraction would last for about double the time, or roughly four years. That meant as long as I purchased another property within the next three years, or by 2015, I'd be buying at a great price. That was very important for the level of house I was building. Since it was the ultimate dream home, I had to buy at the right time and right price. Letting the current one go played to my advantage and left me better off because sellers were having a very rough time getting any buyers and the negative equity that homeowners had incurred was going to take decades to make up, if it was ever made up. Some people didn't know it, but they were stuck for life.

From an economic standpoint, I was feeling like I was actually the winner in all this. I paid a mint for the property, which had lost over half of its value. In order for me to at least break even, I needed the property value to increase 75 percent, which wasn't likely to happen even over the next twenty years. Add to that an increasing unemployment level, oversupply of housing units, banks scared to lend to people with good credit, and all the other factors of the economic depression. Basically, by the time this property would potentially rise in value to the levels I needed it to, I would be well into the dream home. So what seemed to be really bad from the outside looking in (and it was bad, no question) was a blessing in disguise.

Knowing this, I was able to strategize a great waterfront land deal. Since housing construction costs are pretty much what they are, you have to get the land for as low as you can get it; I was in a perfect position to be building a dream home and saving a lot of money in the process, although no money was going to change hands just yet. Still, the situation was pretty daunting, and business decision or not, some people simply can't take that kind of change.

The School of Hard Knocks

I spent the next grueling week showing my son the school of hard knocks. We lived a life without running water or power. We heated our water by the gas stove and worked hard during sunlight. Good thing it was spring, as the weather wasn't bad. Some days we worked almost twenty-four hours nonstop to unload what I was not willing to admit was a mansion. I wasn't a hoarder or junky person; the house was fully furnished and the rooms were big, so they contained big, heavy pieces of furniture.

These pieces were far too big to go to many family members, and I was working on a limited schedule. I could have done a massive yard sale, but I didn't want to lock in my losses to the public. I had a grand piano, and I wasn't going to put it in storage for the next three years and didn't want to allow an estimated $7000 loss to a stranger, assuming I could have gotten the market rate of $5000 for it. My aunt, who helped give me the oversize light bill, was yearning for it, so I gave it to her. I decided it was much better to give it to her than see it go to someone outside the family.

At that point, we decided to take everything out of the house in terms of appliances and fixtures. I gave every appliance to her, along with the piano, for easily a total of $25k in furnishings. I called my parents, told them what had happened, and told them their home was about to get furnishings like they'd never dreamed of. I tossed out all of their mobile home cheaper-than-cheap furniture and replaced it with plush leather couches, marble and oak wood tables, imported rugs, high-end lamps, new computing equipment, lawn tractors, light fixtures, ceiling fans, plants, landscape lights, and so on. They may be living in a mobile home, but theirs is furnished like no others. I called it Pimp My Trailer after the MTV show *Pimp My Ride*.

I then called my aunt in Alexandria and told her I was about to upgrade her chandeliers with ones that I'd paid thousands for, like those you see in hotel lobbies. I gave other beautiful light fixtures and candles and mirrors to cousins. I called my son's mom and told her I was about to do the same for her trailer. She now has a total home makeover. I then called one of my neighbors, who was also a real estate investor and motivational speaker, who'd agreed to loan me some storage space and upgraded her water filtration system. I also gave her thousands of dollars in wood blinds. This might have been a setback for me, but I was about to make it a step up for a ton of other people.

I gave my next-door neighbor my rarely played pool table and light fixture for pennies on the dollar, thanks to them allowing me to use their utility trailer to move my furnishings. Even after all those furnishings I gave away, I still had enough left to completely furnish a two-thousand-square-foot apartment with solid wood furnishings, but no place to put them. I ended up giving them to my cousin, who had just graduated from college and was starting her life with a great new career.

So much as it was a setback in so many people's eyes, it was clearing the way forward for my dream life. I have to admit, I thought back to Chris Gardner a number of times when my son and I would brush our teeth in public bathrooms while we were moving furniture. I continued to ask myself, *why is it that one has to fall so hard before his or her life turns to gold?*

I've read so many stories of people who have attained great success, and they all seem to have lost it all along the way somewhere. In some cases, they've lost it more than once. I'm not sure I wanted to keep going through this; one thing was for sure: this wasn't a lot of fun. This was another reason why having my material goals so precise was important. Working toward highly specific goals eliminates tons of wasteful decisions and especially purchases. Still, these moments test the very fiber of your being.

Can you look in the face of life when every chip you have is down and carry yourself toward the future with a great and positive outlook? That's probably a great question for so many firms on Wall Street. Look at the financial picture of firms such as Lehman Brothers, Bear Stearns, Fannie Mae, Freddie Mac, AIG, GM, Chrysler, and more, and try to determine how they will restore confidence to their employees and investors in the midst of such a storm.

The only thing I could do to keep my day moving along was to focus on what made me happy, which was designing my dream home. The Château D'Von was a French castle, complete with a helipad, dedicated Lamborghini Murcielago parking, two-level dining room, library, presidential suite, and more. I also focused on enjoying the good weather and thinking about how great my life was going to be when I got back on track. I hadn't ever fallen that low on the economic scale, and I certainly hope to not go back there again. As much as I felt that I didn't know what the next day would bring, I knew that I knew that I knew that I knew that God hadn't given me this insatiable desire for my dream life to dump me on the side of the road.

I knew I'd have greatness beyond anything I'd ever dreamed of, but wasn't sure when it was going to get here. In those moments, most would take the easy way out. They'd say get a job, live a life well below my means, and basically settle. Some of you may be going through the absolute worst of times as you are reading this, and you may even be spiritual warriors who are beginning to doubt God's ability to rescue you. From experience what I can tell you is life's most embarrassing, humbling, and terrifying problems all come with a deadline. That means your troubles can only last so long. After you have applied bandages to whatever you are going through and simply can't do anything more to free yourself from your situation, it is at that very instant that you must begin aggressive plans for your dream life, filling in as many details as humanly possible. Don't just take what life throws at you.

I will say, don't be mad or lose the faith if life starts to give you all of what you asked for by first taking everything you currently own. That was the case with me, and for the pain and agony I suffered, I sincerely hope you don't have to endure what I went through, but then again, maybe you don't want what I want. You can't have a full cup, request another beverage in the same glass, and get it without pouring out everything you have first. Something has to give, and we only get one cup. That was a very hard lesson for me to learn; it took many months of turmoil before I came to that realization. I was asking for life at a different level. In many ways, I felt like Danielson from the movie *Karate Kid*. A young Danielson wanted to learn from the master, Mr. Miyagi, and the master agreed. However, when the master began to teach him, Danielson didn't like the way the lesson was being taught. That's just it, though: when you come to the Master, He will give you what you ask for, just not on your terms. If you got it on your terms, you wouldn't need the Master, would you?

Turning My Situation on Its Head

I had to figure out what went wrong. Not a lot, but the few were very big and important. I didn't include my attorney and accountants in my last few transactions. Continued studies of the people I wanted to be more like showed that they got their investment advice from anyone but the salesperson. If you're thinking of investing in real estate, don't ask the realtor for advice. Along the same lines, if you're thinking of investing in a stock, don't ask a stockbroker. Attorneys and CPAs in top firms are aware of investment deals in businesses and real estate you may never hear of, and they can intertwine that information into your asset class and portfolio, which will help you make a smarter decision. At that point, you can use brokers for the transactions. That's what they get paid for anyway.

Deep down inside, I didn't want professional advice, because the markets had been good to me and I thought I could do it myself. Unknowingly, I was suffering from the rising tide that raised all boats, or in other words, the market was good. Had I gotten the professional advice I needed, I wouldn't have thought the loans that were provided to me were solid. The reality was they were from fly-by-night companies found online that didn't have a leg to stand on; and when the market tumbled, I was stuck holding the bag.

I was looking at timing the market just one more time and had gotten away from my plan. I made bad decisions and then prayed that God would save me, and I got mad when no life preserver was thrown my way. It took years for me to come to grips with the fact that allowing me to drown was the actual best decision. You don't want to have this happen when you get too far along and think you're set for life. I was focusing on a lot of little things instead of the main items I was trying to get. If you know where you want to go, go there. Don't stop at ten other locations along the way, hoping they will help you get there. That means if you want a Rolls Royce, save up and buy one. Don't buy a Lexus, then a Mercedes, then a Range Rover, thinking they will appreciate in value and make you smarter as you get closer to the Rolls.

I spent too much time investing in too many other products. I bought individual stocks and mutual funds in addition to real estate. That money could have been better spent investing in myself and my own talents. I was a gifted speaker, but I spent money learning more about investments via top schools. There is nothing wrong with that and I was at least smart enough to realize that I wanted to learn from the best, but I should have invested that money into training that would make me a better speaker. It's easy to say now, but it took me years to figure that out. Just because I am a gifted speaker doesn't mean I don't need additional training. If I had taken more speaker training, it would have helped me get more speaking engagements than I did with the investment training.

I first had to learn what true wealth was, and I learned that it wasn't just money. True wealth has a financial component, but it also includes time and other precious resources that simply can't be bought. A lot of things had to change in my mind to help my situation. Some people have learned to accept being poor, but I found that I wasn't interested in a poor lifestyle at any cost. In fact, I sucked at being poor, and quickly realized that being poor was a mentality, but darn it, so was being rich. A lot of my hardship came not so much from poor spending or investing habits as from where my money came from. I was spending many hours every day working for people who I no longer felt were worthy of the important benefits I could provide. They wanted me to do what they wanted done and weren't interested in anything more. That essentially put me in a box, and when I did perform for them, feeling it was a lower level for me, we had a major problem.

The most important things I could do at that point were to change the boss, the level of work, and most importantly, the income structure. I had to do things that I really liked doing and could do without watching the clock. I found that I didn't like doing just one thing either. When I was a network engineer, my main focus was ensuring that the networks stayed up and running. If I decided that I wanted to learn more about what type of tires the company was buying for its vehicles or if the HR department was saving money by ensuring employees got the best travel deals, management deemed this as totally outside of the scope of my job and would not allow me to do it. I didn't like that very well. What if I had a better travel process or knew someone who owned a travel agency, which it happened I did? My input simply wasn't welcome.

In addition, I worked for a negotiated amount of money, and for the most part at the end of every two weeks, that's what I received. To be honest, I didn't like that very much either. After I began advanced studies in financial planning, I especially paid attention to the portion that went for taxes. I really began to realize the differences in how income was taxed. I knew that estate taxes could be as much as 50 percent of your income, but long-term investment income rates of 15 percent were much better for the net worth I was trying to create. I realized that to get bigger returns, I either had to do a lot more deals or do bigger deals better, so I had to be willing to do twice the research I had done for previous deals and be more patient about pulling the trigger to make some of them happen. Some of the deals didn't happen, and I had to learn to be fine with that until the time was better. The beauty was I created a new level of mentorship along the way and expanded my circles of influence, which was priceless on many levels.

I began realizing that the company I was keeping were real gee-golly swell guys and gals, but they were mostly W-2 employees who earned between high five—and low six-figure incomes. My studies of the wealthy uncovered that my earnings were closer to my peers than I actually wanted them to be. I could certainly congregate with the people I was used to, but I'd better start getting closer to some more successful people. I'd heard many times when people would say, "You'll never get rich working for someone else," but that wasn't true. It depended on who you were working for and at what level. I was simply at the wrong level for sustaining the level of wealth I'd earned with dependence on the employer that was providing me the earning opportunity. The wealthy people I began congregating with gained massive amounts of wealth through leverage. I was leveraging all of my income to do greater things, but I learned you cannot leverage every penny you have all the time because if the rug gets pulled out from under you, you can quickly go under.

I learned that if I wasn't the least knowledgeable person in the group, then my growth was hindered, so I began attending events where most of the people had more education and expertise than I did. I wanted to be least smart person in the room most of the time. It didn't mean that I was dumb by any means, but I knew I needed to increase my knowledge on many levels. I knew the mind-set that got me into the mess I created would not be the mind-set that was going to get me out, and changing my foundation was immensely important even if that meant going to events where I didn't know anyone there. I knew I only needed a few close friends, and those would be the ones I would always have in my corner regardless of what I was trying to do.

As I began to change the basic fundamentals of my mind-set, I was surprised to realize I was spending a lot of time unlearning many of the things I'd diligently studied; I learned a new way of thinking. By 86ing the old way, I took the stench of a highly educated but poor level of results and replaced it with a newer, fresher, long-lasting scent of wealth. I began living the lifestyle that I was so desperately dreaming of. Once I got a whiff of a better life, there was no turning back to the days of old.

What I can tell you for certain is that settling is not what gets you to the dream-life level. People who settle tend to watch life from the sidelines. They can only wish it was them living out a dream. After taking a hard fall, the only way to go was up. I had to decide if I was going to live life or simply exist. So did I settle? Absolutely! I settled on not settling!

After my fortune collapsed, I had a lot of time on my hands. I saw it as a time of great reflection. It gave me the chance for a new start, and I yearned for new knowledge. Regardless of why I ended up in the situation I did, I felt that even more knowledge would be required to bring me out. Newfound knowledge is generally very expensive if we look toward paying tuition at schools, but there are other ways to get knowledge, especially in the United States—that's what makes this country great.

Almost every day, I went to local bookstores, where I would sit for hours and hours, reading and rereading the story of the great business leaders. Whether it was Warren Buffett, Ted Turner, or Robert Johnson, I read as much as I could get my hands on. I took advantage of newspapers, such as the *New York Times*, *Wall Street Journal*, and *Washington Post*, and read as many stories as I could read, garnering nuggets of information. Sometimes I would read six or seven hours a day and be the last one in the bookstore at closing. I can't lie: it was occasionally tough to think about the lifestyle that I had before, but I didn't dwell on it. I just wanted a new start, and until it came, I was in a passionate grind to soak up newfound knowledge. I'd visited bookstores before obviously, but I began to realize that even if a person was completely homeless, if that person had a passion for the latest and greatest anything, he could sit in franchise bookstores for ten hours and spend hours upon hours with business and political leaders every day completely free of charge. Fortunately, my situation was not exactly that bad, but it surely wasn't far away.

I had a laptop, and many of the bookstores I visited either had free Wi-Fi access or they were in shopping centers that were between other stores that had free Internet access that could be accessed from within the bookstore. That gave me tremendous power to instantly follow up on ideas or concepts

I'd never heard of before. I was able to attend local events at clubs that I still belonged to and fortunately had paid membership dues to years in advance. These corporate events were either free or of little cost, and that kept me in the faces of many of the moguls whom I looked up to for their business prowess, allowing me to ask very direct questions on a variety of subjects.

Due to a solid education, the success of my book *Real Estate for Real People*, and a lot of confidence, I was able to write the very book you are holding in your hands right now. I was learning and note-taking on the fly. In the meantime, I still was very noted within my circles, and many people had no clue what had happened to me; probably even if they knew, they wouldn't have had a ton of concern, thinking I would soon be back on top. Therefore, I met with many people at restaurants, private clubs, civic events, and so on. The reality is nobody knows your life is in shambles if you don't wear it on your sleeves. I wasn't interested in talking about the bad times anyway. My mind-set was always firmly planted on the future. My wardrobe was still very dapper, so only my closest friends knew the real story, although many times even they forgot due to how I carried myself.

I watched the economy get progressively worse under the Obama administration and knew it would be a long haul getting back, but reading the stories of the wealthy empowered me because I knew not everybody was hurting. There were still people who had multiple homes and would never need another dime. I watched a lot of CNBC titans to see what mistakes they made before finding the great wealth and success they enjoyed. I was delighted, yet surprised, to find that hitting rock bottom seemed to be very much a key ingredient in being catapulted to success. They had all fallen very hard and lost much more than I ever dreamed of having. That was the American dream still alive and well, regardless of what two straight quarters of declining gross domestic product meant—the definition of a recession, by the way. The dream life was a game of chance, will, and perseverance—mostly perseverance. I knew the second I gave up on my dream life, it was over, and that knowledge was the simplest way I kept it moving.

My schedule was set every day. I was either looking to gain new speaking engagements, in the bookstores, working very little as a new home sales assistant, or defining my dreams with as laser-like focus as I could. I used every tool in my laptop's program files, from Homestead web-design software to Microsoft Publisher to create documents. I raided the magazine racks in the bookstores, looking for pictures of everything I wanted. I completely designed my new dream homes by studying magazines such as *Christie's Great*

Estates and *Florida Design Architecture* to travel and leisure magazines. Each and every room, every floor, every ceiling, chandelier, column, paint color, and so on was designed or chosen based on magazine high-resolution photos and figuring out who created the rooms by going to the designer's or developer's websites. I raided E-Plans' 27,000 home plans to find the perfect vacation home for myself. I knew that once I returned to financial empowerment, I was going to have resiliency. That meant whether hell or high water came, if one home was taken away, I was going to go to another one. I researched helicopters, cars, trucks, insurance agents, tires, wealth management firms, and so on. You name it; if it came to my ultimate dream, I was doing homework while I had the time, as I knew that once the money came, it would be time to execute.

I continued to try and wait out the governmental job system, but after nearly two years and being told it could take another year, I decided that I had to look for other ways to generate income. *The system is wired in such a weird way*, I thought. The government knows I'm clean, but they won't provide me another $200k job; however, I can borrow 10 percent of that to go back to school and get more education and create more personal debt in a system that convinces the general public you are investing in yourself. Meanwhile, with colleges knowing the government will allow you to borrow thousands upon thousands of dollars to go back to school, universities raised tuition rates faster than the pace of inflation, knowing students would have a very tough time getting a job strong enough to pay the loans back. That was our American system, and sometimes you just had to play the game to eat. With that in mind, I decided I would finally commit to finishing a Doctorate in International Business (DBA). In addition, I figured why stay in Washington when I could just as easily study in much nicer, warmer climates, like sunny Southern Florida. So with that, I applied to a doctoral program where I could sit in class and start a new future elsewhere.

I learned a lot during my times of difficulty, as anyone who experiences hardship should. These times, whether they seem short to others or not, are no cakewalks; and the anniversaries of many events remind you of just how much time has slipped by. The bottom line is you have to focus on your future, not your past. If you desire the lifestyle you've been dreaming of, it takes more intense focus than money, I assure you. So spend this time wisely for study and counsel of the best in the most inexpensive way you can find. One of my best motivational and spiritual sources came from Angela Yates, a young lady who came late to one of my speaking engagements. For whatever reason, she added my name to her distribution list and sent me spiritual lessons each day. One of the most memorable and perhaps most important for these times was the one that follows:

> Trust in the LORD with all your heart and lean not on your own understanding; in all your ways submit to him, and he will make your paths straight. (Prov. 3:5–6 NIV)

To me that meant we don't understand why we are going through these difficult times and all the research in the world may never yield the answer, but trust that this too shall pass and don't spend a lot of time trying to use your faulty understanding.

Message

Do you think that you can do anything great without God's help? No way! It is impossible. You can never achieve anything with your own understanding. Even though you put in your hard work and use your intelligence, you will reach your goal only if you trust in God. Do not wonder why you face so many failures in your life. The answer is right here. Submit to Him and trust that only through God will you have success, strength, wisdom, and everything. God will guide you through all paths and will make your dreams come true.

You've Realized Something Is Missing: Smiling Faces Tell Lies and I've Got Proof

It's Monday afternoon, August 4, at 4:45 p.m. Technically, I could have left work hours ago because my company gives me the flexibility to come in at 6:00 a.m. and I take full advantage. However, I decided to stay late today; perhaps it would get back to my manager that I *really* am interested in this job and this field, about which I couldn't care less at this point. I'm not sure he would believe it, but at least no one could say I wasn't there.

Fairly relaxed from eating ice cream out of a plastic cup that they used to partially entice us to attend the meeting, I'm just trying to look interested. And then I get a text message from Toni Boykin. *Man, oh man, does she like this text messaging thing.* To be honest, her text messages have been my saving grace through a lot of dull, boring meetings. I can't believe I let her convince me to give Sprint some more of my money to up my plan to Unlimited Everything, but I use the darn thing so much I should be thanking her and wondering why I didn't do it sooner.

As I look around this room and ultimately this building, I have to think you really can't ask for anything more in terms of work environment. The inside of this building seems to be fairly modern. There are lots of copier rooms and kitchen areas. Most people have offices that they share, unlike today's cubicle nation. There are lots of conference rooms, and the majority of them are wired with high-tech communication devices, such as wireless microphones and remote conferencing features.

The screens are mostly retractable, so they drop down and disappear in their little hideaway havens with the touch of a button. You can easily tell the meeting junkies, because they can't wait to impress the unsuspecting crowd on how to troubleshoot the conference call that notifies us another caller is

21

on the line in another office but can't hear anything. If that's not enough, they have already arrived a few minutes early to suck up to the guest speaker and illustrate how they are experts in screen retracting and know where all the high-tech gadgetry is located.

The speakers look great today. They are well-dressed and eager to talk about their prepared slides, just as good consultants in a top-tier consulting firm are supposed to look. Their super-long PowerPoint presentations have lots of complex graphs and charts and bulleted points. Even to someone fairly tough to impress, each one of them would come across as real corporate bigwigs. I'm willing to bet that ten years ago, I would have eagerly listened to every word from every speaker and eagerly awaited my turn to ask some bull-crap question to try and impress the people in the room. A lot has changed in ten years, I can assure you, so today I'm perfectly content just sitting there smiling, looking interested, and returning text messages as my phone quietly, yet annoyingly, vibrates with each incoming summons to respond.

Me (4:27 p.m.): I am sooooo out of place! I'm just trying to hold on, but Lawd Jesus, it ain't easy.

Toni Boykin (4:28 p.m.): Where r u?

Me (4:29 p.m.) N a mtg right now but I'm not talking bout that. I'm in middle class america with a six figure salary 9 to 5 and I dnt belong here. A dream for many but . . .

Me (4:30 p.m.): I belong elsewhere and fitting n getting hard.

Toni Boykin (4:33 p.m.): I knew exactly what u were talkn about. U r doing something about it . . . do I need 2 tell u . . . sit back and look at da people n da meeting . . .

Me (4:34 p.m.): I'm lookin at em an they confirming that they belong here and I don't.

Me (4:34 p.m.): Yes I am doing a lot about it.

Toni Boykin (4:34 p.m.): How many people can say they have a published dvd and not to mention a book with rewards that haven't even touched the shelves . . .

Toni Boykin (4:34 p.m.): God put us n places where we think we don't belong for a reason and just for that season . . .

Me (4:36 p.m.): I know honey I know.

Toni Boykin (4:37 p.m.): yes maybe u don't belong but u have touched somebody n that office . . . this is just another chapter u can put on paper . . .

Toni encourages me to pay attention and tells me we'll text each other later. I agree and look back up at the slides. We are now on the third speaker, and I've surprisingly gathered about 30 percent of what was said even though I had no prior knowledge of the subject matter. As I read the slides, I gather that no one has told any of these people to put maybe four or five lines max on each slide; otherwise the slides are too busy and you'll lose people. At least that's what they told us in business school. To be honest, I don't care what's on the slides, as they are all toward the bottom of my priority list.

The guy who is speaking now may as well be saying, "Blah-blah-blahhh. Bla-blahh bla-blahhh bla blahhh." He's saying something about process and management; just a pile of gobbledygook to tell you the truth. Besides, I'm trying to figure out how much the electronic device costs that lights up with each pronounced syllable that the speaker feeds into the mic so I can get one of these things for my investment forum. In the background, I can hear the last speaker for the day saying, "If you look at slide 67, you will notice . . ." and once again I translate the remainder of his sentence into "Blah-blah blah . . . blah-blah blah-blah . . ."

Looking at my watch, I'm wondering how many people are thinking of other places they'd really rather be. I mean, are they that interested? This stuff is as dry as Idaho potatoes. On top of that, did he say slide sixty something? Surely you have to know you lost way too much of your audience with the numbers alone.

Maybe it really is me who can't seem to pay attention for the last twenty or so months. While their faces are showing genuine interest for the subject matter and they are enunciating correctly each syllable of every word so the conference callers on the phone can hear exactly what was said, my mind is embedded in the business section of the *Washington Post*. Their motto is "If you don't *get* it, you *don't get it*." Oh, I get it all right. I want to know how in the world are these businessmen and women profiting more off one private equity or leveraged buyout deal than I even have as a dream net worth?

Take This Job and Shove It

"Slide 68, you can see on this graph . . . bla-blahhh-blahh, bla-blahhh blahh blah." Enough already! I can't take another word of this today.

I grabbed my notebook, and with a look of where's the bathroom, I quietly exited the room, with no intentions of returning to hear the wrap-up. I went back to my desk and started banging away on the keys to document my frustration about where I was and where I was going to be. This real kick in the pants is what I call a Slide 68 moment and was the very reason I entitled this book *Slide 68*. Within weeks, I 86'd that job and began an even more passionate quest in search of something more important that would get me to the lifestyle I was dreaming of.

At the Citadel, the Military College of South Carolina, I learned that there was plenty to do outside of a life in the military. So many of the cadets had parents who were fully engaged in about every field imaginable, and some of the parents were doing quite well for themselves as it showed through their kids' vehicles. During my fast-moving life as a cadet, I was sure that I'd reach my high school senior yearbook goals, which I wrote on where I wanted to be in 10 years. I remember vividly that by 2001:

The Goals I Set

I wanted to be earning $2,000 a week ($104,000 a year, some number I logically crunched back then).

I wanted to live in Columbia, South Carolina.

I wanted to live in a nice house (something I assumed at the time would equate to about 2500 square feet).

I wanted to drive a Lexus LS 400.

I wanted to be more muscular.

I wanted to have a few dollars left over to help my parents pay some overdue bill or another without affecting my lifestyle.

I was encouraged to write all this down with a bit of influence from our caring JROTC instructors, and like magic, voila, there it was. In ten years, not only had I met every goal I wrote down, but I exceeded them. In some cases, I smashed them!

The Goals I Achieved

I went on to earn $160,000 a year.

I lived in Northern Virginia, which was a bigger and more exposed city than Columbia.

My house was 9600 square feet on ten rolling acres, with a stream on the property.

I not only had one Lexus; I had driven and given away two.

I was bench-pressing over 330 pounds.

Not only did I give my parents a few extra dollars, but I gave some other needy people down payments on homes.

I guess this is why they stress the importance of writing down your goals.

I had even amassed a very impressive portfolio of assets and had written an investment book. So if this was the case, why in the world was I sitting here in this meeting, feeling I wasn't happy with where I was in my career and my tangible possessions? This was pretty good by anyone's standards for a single guy who had just turned thirty-five. I was clearly a success story as a product of the great migration of those who had come from the more southern states to the Washington DC region for a better living.

I had read quite a few stories of megadeals in the local and national papers in addition to a lot of bestselling "here's how I made a fortune" books, and I was beginning to really, really believe in what I was reading. I mean, after all, this is America and I can have the American dream. I was already part of the way there. I spent time in the offices and homes of the most politically elite in Washington, as well as engaged in business discussions with some of the wealthiest African Americans ever.

They all worked; in fact, some of them worked more hours than many of the people in the offices I worked in, but the difference was that real work was actually being done, with very measurable results. A lot of the workers I saw were very good at faking their desire and love for what they did, when in fact, it was just a bunch of hogwash to make the manager happy. I cannot count the number of times I've heard people on conference calls talking extra loud to make others who are quietly minding their own business in the office believe they have so much work to do that they are too busy to die.

I've passed office after office of people who have mastered the art of minimizing game or Internet screens. You really aren't fooling anybody. The highly successful people weren't sitting in the office killing time just to say that they'd been there for seven, ten, or twelve hours. They were there and getting real results for real customers or themselves. When the office portion of their work was done, they were off to other things and didn't have to sit there and look the part. Around many of the big organizations I worked in, one could easily get lost in the shuffle because only 5 percent of the people truly knew what was going on. The others were just worker bees who wanted to earn a decent living and go home at the end of eight hours, with an occasional cost-of-living raise or annual bonus.

Before anyone gets the wrong impression, I commend people who want to make $75,000, $80,000, or even $100,000 a year, but I knew for the goals I was setting, which again were very achievable, that a nice $12k monthly salary wasn't going to get it. In my eleven years of working, I was absolutely convinced that expenses rise in direct proportion to salary, and that no matter if my raise was $2,000 or $20,000, I was simply going to keep upgrading some small part of my material life and would fall victim to the j.o.b. (just over broke) game for a long time.

Living Far Above Average

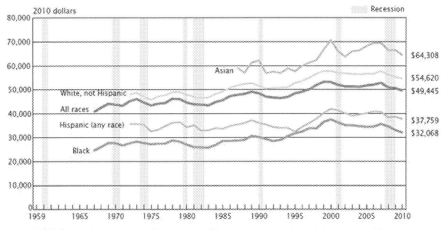

Real Median Household Income by Race and Hispanic Origin: 1967 to 2010

It is important that I paint realistic pictures for those who want to tackle the world and live life beyond your wildest dreams. It is possible? Yes, absolutely, but it takes tons of diligent, focused effort, and a little luck surely doesn't hurt.

The chart above (http://en.wikipedia.org/wiki/Median_household_income) illustrates the median US household income. I'd earned many times more than the $32K salary of average Black families, as well as White and Asian. Many people whom I've come across believe that there are thousands of millionaires in this country who live life with multimillion-dollar annual incomes, and there are. However, as a percentage of the population, those people are very much the minority. It is the images that we see flashed before our eyes so frequently that make us believe those people are out there by the thousands. I knew and understood this wholeheartedly, but I never allowed it to stop my vision of what I wanted. I had to accept that what I wanted was substantially more than what the average family was ever going to get remotely close to, and I was willing to work at it. Believe me, getting my head firmly around the concept of what the average family was earning took a substantial amount of time. I knew I was quite fortunate for what I had, but still my dreams were a much bigger motivator and attention grabber than the status quo was.

I wanted my money to come in chunks, like bloated income tax returns, and needed them to come more than once a year. I saw no reason why I shouldn't receive some type of monetary payment that could come in and make four mortgage payments in one month, and a very similar one that could come in the next month and fund the maximum annual retirement contribution the next. I knew it was quite possible, and I would not rest until I had it like that.

I had grown increasingly frustrated at work because I wasn't allowed to work around the portion of the business where I felt I could make the greatest contribution. I spent years of study at some of the finest schools learning about how to make businesses run more effectively. I wanted to spend my day doing work I considered important, such as adding to the company's bottom line. I was even told by my last employer that this was what they expected me to accomplish as one of my goals. Even in their management training, a director assured me that if I was adding to the company's bottom line, then the last thing I would have to worry about was being let go through any downsizing efforts.

Most of my colleagues only wanted to talk about what came on TV last night or some project they needed to finish around the house. I wanted to talk about mergers and acquisitions and making money. In one gut-wrenching interview as I looked for a new job, an executive told me, "You don't fit, and you stand out like a sore thumb." Blown away, I asked him what he meant. He said that the level of involvement that I wanted from the business side, such as M&A among other things, was not about to come my way. He said they didn't want you at the table as a low-level manager, and he was sure of it because he used to sit where I wanted to be.

He went on to tell me that those decisions were reserved for the VPs and above and that the last thing they cared about was the employees. They only cared about making money. I was clearly shaken, but felt I could still make a contribution. While he understood what I was saying, he still felt that I had seen too much from the outside to fit as a nice nine-to-five employee. He felt I belonged in the high circles I'd found outside of work and encouraged me to get out there among them. I didn't mind working my way up to the VP level, but there were many managers in front of me and the VPs that I knew best had over twenty years of experience. In addition, they were only making twenty to thirty thousand more than I was. I wasn't about to sit back and wait another fifteen years to make moderately more and still risk not being invited to the table. I wanted more out of my career, and I wanted it to happen a lot sooner than that. I knew it would require me to create opportunities on my own.

I felt more important and more engaged with the work I was doing with the Investment Forum, but I hadn't figured out a way to make a living from it. It was affording me the opportunity to move in circles with the top 1 percent of the success population. The goals of the Investment Forum were to expose people who were looking to make equity and real estate investments to better ways of making them. We periodically held forums, where I or invited guests would talk about an investment we'd made, what made us think about the investment, and what the outcome was. I gave pure unbiased advice so people would not fret that I was tied to some brokerage firm or another.

In addition, I became a noteworthy speaker and wrote a monthly newsletter that continued to expose people to investment concepts or provide further understanding about something that was going on in the investment community. In addition, they all wanted to stay abreast of who I was meeting with and what I was doing. The newsletter provided all this and then some, and the feedback was great. The issue was the forums weren't moneymakers, but my investments, books, and speaking engagements were. Since the money to fund the investments came from my nine-to–five job, I had to have them both for success.

Slide 68 Mind-Set

Taking control of your life is essential to living out your ultimate dreams. It is easy to get caught up in the day-to-day grind of the nine-to-five. In some cases, one may need to alter one's schedule to make more efficient use of the day. In other cases, it could mean eliminating some things altogether. In any case, people tend to know when things aren't going right in their lives. Our levels of efficiency, happiness, productivity, and so on are all out of balance, and until we sit down and recognize each problem that we are having, they will continue to occur.

You may find it helpful to discuss your problems with others, not always to get their advice on how to fix them but to hear how they sound to you. Many problems can be fixed not by looking for the right answers, but instead by asking the right questions. Those questions are only addressed when we carefully sound them out.

I thought back to a story I read in a book entitled *Put Your Dream to the Test* by international bestselling author John Maxwell. In the eighth chapter of his book, entitled *The Tenacity Question—Am I Moving Closer to My Dream?* he begins with this quotation:

> The mere possession of a vision is not the same as living it, nor can we encourage others with it if we do not, ourselves, understand and follow its truths . . . To be blessed with visions is not enough . . . we must live them!

Author H. Jackson Brown says in *Life's Little Instruction Book*, there are two rules of perseverance: "Rule #1. Take one more step. Rule #2. When you can't take one more step, refer to Rule #1." That's what it takes to achieve a dream: the will to take one more step, even when you're convinced you can't. People who live their dreams refuse to give up, knowing that if they keep chipping away, making whatever small progress they can every day, they increase the chance that something will happen in their favor. They answer yes to the tenacity question, which asks, "Am I moving closer to my dream?"

Money May Not Buy Happiness, but It Sure Makes Life a Lot Easier and a Lot More Fun

Money isn't everything; money isn't everything! How many times have we heard that statement? Have you ever wondered who's saying it? Do you know any broke people who aren't saying it or rich people who are? Do you know any wealthy people who are willing to trade places with the poor? Me neither, and yet we have heard this saying for years. Money is great at solving the problems it can and horrible at solving the problems it can't, but to suggest that it means little the way that I've heard people reference it is a bit over the top in my view.

I subscribe to Donald Trump's philosophy on this. In his video *Entrepreneur's Success Code*, he was interviewed by Jon Ward during the introduction of Trump University, an online learning center for real estate investing. Ward asked, "In the big scheme of things, may I ask you, Mr. Trump, how important is money to you and should money be the central focus when it comes to building success and wealth?" Trump stated that money should not be the central focus, which caught me off guard because of the wealth he has built and the lifestyle he lives. He said, "Money should never be the central focus. I think happiness should be the central focus."

I also like the saying by Thomas Friedman and Michael Mandelbaum in their book *That Used to Be Us*, when they said, "'Lots of things in life are more important than money,' goes the old saying, and they all cost money."

I agree with Trump's logic and understand where he is going, yet we live on an earth that requires materials. You don't have to have the fanciest of materials in everything you do, but there is nothing wrong with at least having the option to get a few really nice things in life. So unless there is someone still on the barter system, money is required. Many people have come to realize that, and to some, the talk of it is taboo; but the people who I have found that tend not to discuss it are the ones who have it by the boatloads or those who don't have it at all. The folks in the middle are the ones who seem to be the most conscious of it.

I always knew my take on money in terms of happiness, and I have found that when I have extra money, I feel very much happier than the times when I do not, so I can only entertain the "money doesn't buy happiness" conversation for so long. I've heard broke people say money isn't going to buy you happiness, but lack of a sufficient amount always brings unhappiness. I believe people have to understand that it is very much relative. If you get a brand-new Rolls Royce, you probably will only drive it on sunny days and won't allow anyone to even think of eating fast food in the backseat. However, after you've driven a Rolls Royce for ten years, it's just another car, albeit a nice one by even billionaire standards.

Trump talked about this very same issue during the recording. "I have found that over a period of time, money, it doesn't buy happiness but it makes life a lot easier. A lot of people without money like to say money isn't everything, money isn't everything, and they're absolutely right but it does make life a lot easier." I couldn't agree more. Money doesn't buy happiness, but it makes people who are already happy ecstatic! It also depends largely on where the money came from. I read many stories of sophisticated Wall Street investors who bet the farm against the subprime mortgage market, which in part created a lot of losses even for me; they made hundreds of millions, and in some cases billions, of dollars, but they didn't seem one smile happier than before the gains were realized. In one sense, a person could argue they were already filthy rich, but on the other hand, you have to look at the way the money came. The profits were made betting more people would end up in my situation, which is something that's very difficult to deal with even if it comes with a hefty sack of cash. I never wanted to get rich by deliberately putting another man in the poorhouse. It just is not a very nice thing to do, and eventually it will take all the money you made and then some to pay for it.

Slide 68 Mind-Set

1. **Love what you do.**

2. **Never quit.**

Trump mentioned two other very critical elements for success: (1) you have to love what you do, and (2) never, ever quit. These two points made a ton of sense and were primarily why I had fallen into such a rut. The never-quitting part was easy. I came from nothing and had obtained quite a bit, so it was never about quitting. The love-what-you-do part was where I was having a lot of trouble. Even my doctor had instructed me to find another job for life's sake during a routine visit. My nine-to-five was boring me to tears, but the work I was doing with the business I started on the side was the most fulfilling job I ever had. The problem was that the nine-to-five paid the bills, and the side job simply wasn't at that level for the moment as the economy had taken its toll. Although sometimes my side business paid more than the nine-to-five, I needed that performance more consistently in order to walk away from the day job.

To make matters worse, I had also taken a very large pay cut. Having a few small businesses and employees that you are responsible for isn't a great time to lose revenue. It's never a great time to lose revenue, but when you feel yourself falling into a rut on what you're getting paid for in a nine-to-five, productivity can fall substantially, as it did for me.

So many people who have made it tend to write their success stories after they've made all the money they want to make and now are just keeping score. What about telling the story while you're going through it? Do they not think anyone is interested while the trials are going on? I certainly am, and I know many other people who are as well. Maybe there is a fear of "what if I don't make it?" Well, then let the fear rest, but tell the story anyway. Besides, if mentally you are that sure you are going to make it in life, you probably are.

I believe the story is felt and told so much better in the heat of battle. You remember the details, the feelings, the pain, the small wins, and eventually the triumph so much better while you're living it. So why not tell it then? I can't take the credit for this idea, although it is one that I believe in. Instead, I give credit to a friend of mine whom I met at work, named Clint Ferguson. Clint was a smooth brother. He was always well-dressed and well-spoken. He was sharp, and he tended to remind me of R&B singer Morris Day. Anyone who knows Morris Day and the Time knows Morris was smooth. He was cool, and the ladies dug him. The only thing separating these two was that they chose different occupations.

Clint and I would talk about money, investments, politics, women, you name it. He always had good insight on things. He was also a very positive guy, and he believed in me and where I was going. That's one reason why I didn't mind shooting the breeze with him. One day in the parking lot, he and I were talking about my success, and he said, "You know, man, you should hook up with Tyler Perry and see if you can make a movie about your life. You should tell your story as it happens. Kind of like a part one you are here, and part two you are there, and so on." I remember his comments pretty clearly, even though that was spring 2006, which is also why I think he's right about telling your story as it happens.

His points were well taken, and while I simply haven't thought all the way through the super writer, actor, and producer Tyler Perry idea, writing the story now is good for several reasons. One, even if I do meet Tyler, he has to have something in writing. Beyond that, I think others will benefit greatly because I am more in tune to the story of the more common people now. After you're sitting on forty million, living in a mansion, and on the cover of magazines, you've lost the personal touch with the crowd that many can relate to. Sure, people have the ability to walk away and think a successful person was down-to-earth, but will they really identify with where the successful person is? I would tend to say no, because although this person may have problems, he or she has enough money to fix them or the right professional team in place to make something happen really fast. Of course, I say that regarding the problems that can be fixed with money. If you're a sad or depressed rich person, additional money does nothing for you. So from that standpoint, you really can't relate. I certainly thank Clint for dropping that seed on fertile ground, and I will make good on it as I'm making the climb as we speak.

My life in general is great, not just due to a healthy financial situation but through a wealthy mind-set and continuing to take interesting turns for the better; however, with a lost revenue source, I quickly realized how much misfortune can consume your mind. Nonetheless, there is always someone going through a worse situation than you. That's another reason why I'm writing this book.

People often operate as if they are the only one going through something, when just a little conversation with others will tell them otherwise. Nearly everyone I know thinks my life is filled with breakfast and lunch with the rich and all my days are filled with glory and prestige. Currently, they couldn't be farther from the truth. Granted, I do have some pretty spectacular runs, but they are mostly days that I create. I don't believe in the idea of people saying, "Have a good day." You may luck up and have a good day; otherwise, things will be pretty normal. You *must* create great days on your own. They don't just happen. In addition, I have some not-so-great days that just really aren't worth writing about. Not that I don't have bad news to share—I certainly have enough of it to pass around—but they are just normal days in the current time of my life. I'll add a few points of not-so-great days throughout the book, but only just a few. First, I don't have a lot of them, because I refuse to allow myself to have them. Secondly, I'm not writing a book filled with average, ordinary, or just bad days.

If I'm successful in writing my own future, which is a good way to make it happen, then by the end of this book, I will be living my life just how I designed it to be. The entire exercise of writing this book is just as much a journal and motivator for me as it is for you who are looking to gain something from it. A very important lesson I hope you will take away from this is to stay in touch with friends and colleagues along the path of any difficult time in your life. It is very easy to shut down on people when your good fortune changes because you don't want them to see you toughing it out. Staying in touch with others shows that you are not alone, and you may learn a few things along the way.

I stay connected with people at both ends of the success spectrum, regardless of what's going on. The poor and average guy wants to know what's going on in the mind-set of the rich. He wants to know what the rich person is reading, thinking, and doing. The rich guy has to keep a pulse on many who are not rich because chances are he is a provider and supplier to the average citizen. If he loses touch, then he immediately becomes a consumer and begins eating away at his wealth. At that point, he's only as good as his last success. I'm in tune at both ends, so I often see sides of both worlds. It gives me the opportunity to stay grounded, be the middleman, and provide insight to both sides. As much as I didn't care for growing up less fortunate, it gives me a lot of drive. Now that I'm grown, I can clearly see that the best way to help poor people is to not become one of them. My motto remains, "From the mobile home to where moguls roam."

A lot of people can stomach work that is okay, but a man who loves what he does will never work another day in his life. Show me a multimillionaire who hates what he does for a living, and I'll show you someone who just won the lottery and is currently drafting his "take this job and shove it" resignation letter. As I've studied the wealthy, one thing I see is they love what they do and wouldn't consider doing anything else. I have yet to find anyone who has total control over their finances and their lives and is just unhappy with their work.

I believe over time your interest may change, but no way are you going to gain any substantial level of wealth by just being okay with what it is you do. Too much time at the "Quick Pick" lottery counter only confirms you don't love and probably hate what it is you do for a living. That, and also you don't pay much attention to the concepts of probability and statistics.

Getting Rich Is a Proactive Science

One of the best books I ever read was *The Science of Getting Rich*, by Wallace D. Wattles; in it he talks about the importance of getting rich. He provides very thought-provoking philosophy on how you can't truly serve God to your potential unless you are rich, but most importantly how God will give you the treasures of your heart if you ask. The most important part is you have to be specific. This is where many men fall short. I meet with people all the time for breakfast, lunch, and dinner, and they are commonly in awe of what I have or what I've done; but I can attest that most simply say they want what I have and haven't a clue of what they really want. According to Wattles, "You must form a clear and definite mental picture of what you want . . . . It is not enough that you should have a general desire for wealth 'to do good with.' *Everybody* has that desire." If you give people a blank slate, in four hours the slate will be as incomplete as it was four minutes after you gave it to them.

This is why I felt justified after I created the $40 Million Dollar Dream Sheet. During a lunch break from work one day, I decided to drive through an affluent community, an enlightenment I routinely enjoy. I decided to drive down a street I had never driven down before and came across an 18,000-square-foot French mansion so magnificent that I had to have it. I went out and purchased a digital camera just to get a high-resolution photo of it so I could enlarge it, frame it, and place it on my wall. Within one year, I upgraded to a home much larger than the one I was in, but still far short of where I wanted to be. After three years, I wondered how in the world I was going to make the leap from where I was to where I wanted to be. Many of my friends were awe-inspired by the house and the concept. Each time I would give tours of my home, which was often, I would show the picture. Occasionally, I would mention a slight change that I might make if it were mine.

One day it finally dawned on me that while the front of the house was stately and magnificent and made the statement I wanted to make, I had no clue what the back looked like and never would because of how it was situated on the property. Then I began to ask myself what the foyer looked like and then the kitchen and master bedroom. Then I began thinking I didn't know what any of the rooms of the house looked like. For all I knew, I might have hated every one of them, and yet I was willing to release to God how desperately I wanted something I knew little to nothing about. At that point, I began searching for all the rooms I wanted through books, magazines, model homes, hotels, and so on.

Over the next two years, I began meeting and talking with architects, who I discovered wanted to charge me a mint (and they did) for what I was trying to build. They also proposed great homes of sizes that were a bit bigger than I had in mind. In short, I decided nobody knew what I wanted like I did. I took to the road, traveling frequently to various parts of Florida. Many of the magazines that I read had pictures of rooms that I liked the most, and it seemed almost all of them were found in some part of Southern Florida, from barrel-vault ceilings at Topia Fine Woodworking to fine French Chateau architectural design by John Henry AIA Architects.

I learned a ton of information about Florida that I otherwise wouldn't have known just by proactively conceptualizing a dream. For years, I looked at the Sunshine State as a place to vacation. When someone said Florida, I immediately had thoughts of Walt Disney World in Orlando or maybe Miami's South Beach. What I didn't know was the mega wealth found there. In Orlando, I found homes perched in areas that Disney vacationers would marvel at. One such community was Isleworth, which gained worldwide attention as being the home of the world's best and most notorious golfer Tiger Woods. It was there that Tiger's wife got after him for his exotic behavior off the course. While visiting the community, I learned that Tiger was just one of many high-profile residents. Other sports legends, such as the NBA's Shaquille O'Neal and Patrick Ewing, also lived there.

I found out how tremendously difficult it was to obtain entry into the community and just how much some of the privileged pay to live there. On the surface, it may sound like just an impressive place to visit, but when you're designing a dream house, you do have to have a budget in mind. It was there that I learned that I could subtract enormous costs just based on the price of the land. For some, keeping up with the Joneses is important, but not for me. I never desired to live next to Tiger, and avoiding so would take thousands of dollars a month off my mortgage payment, which more than paid for the price of all trips to Florida in my book.

I also learned of Weston, Florida, which was the suburbs of Ft. Lauderdale. There I went to visit a fine Spanish villa, with its own tennis court and koi pond. I also learned that if I had bought the home from the current owner, I might have gotten an occasional knock on the door from a very popular neighbor, famed quarterback Dan Marino. I spent many hours in this home with its owner discussing the finer luxury automobiles on the market, as he had just purchased yet another Rolls Royce, this time the Mulsanne. I was invited back to enjoy a night of fine dining on the rooftop terrace with the local symphony orchestra. To top it off, while there visiting, I received an e-mail from Tiffany, a great friend whom I call my little sister, who alerted me that I should enter a contest for top bachelors with *Upscale*, a fine Atlanta magazine. My experiences were apparently enough to impress them, and I was chosen as one of three in a nationwide search to be featured in a cover story. This wasn't a bad return on time invested just for a bit of proactive dream seeking. I was having a marvelous time along the way.

My frequent reading and studying on various home designers and builders substantially increased my knowledge of the world of the über-rich. One of the homes I visited next was on Millionaire's Row in Ft. Lauderdale. Not only did I learn where some of the most successful people in South Florida resided, but I also learned that just to buy a vacant lot in the community could cost as much as eight million dollars. Ouch! Can you imagine just how quickly you could blow through $40 million dollars when you spent 20 percent of it on just raw land? After the property viewing, I had an evening of fun on the *Jungle Queen*, a popular tourist destination that showed me the floating palaces, aka the multimillion-dollar yachts that cost as much as if not more than the mansions that they were docked behind. Should you decide to visit the area and take the dinner cruise, don't be alarmed to find out what some people say about the superrich is true. It seems that as you pass by their homes, if they're out enjoying the Intercoastal Waterways and meandering about in their backyards, they moon you as the boat passes by. How's that for predinner entertainment?

As I began to really get involved in red terra-cotta roofs, my travels took me to Palm Beach. After a day of land searching, I enjoyed a wonderful dinner in City Place, which has to be one of the most extravagant and beautiful places to enjoy fine dining and tasteful entertainment. Afterward, I enjoyed a casual stroll through the compounds where Rockefeller and leading American socialite Marjorie Merriweather Post commonly gathered. William Avery Rockefeller was the billionaire oil tycoon who would easily hold title to the richest man ever had he still been living, and Merriweather Post was once married to Wall Street financier E. F. Hutton; both had vast properties there. Today household wealth is held by real estate tycoons, such as Donald Trump, who, to nobody's surprise, bought Merriweather Post's property and turned it into the Mar-a-lago, an ultraexclusive private club, where he commands a reported quarter-of-a-million-dollar-a-year membership fee.

My patio and chandelier design led me to the West, where I would begin to meet even more impressive people and begin putting together the parts of my not-so-humble abode. I will discuss more about my West Coast visits later, but I think you begin to see my point about how being proactive in terms of going after your goals and dreams perpetuates a life of living, not mere existence.

I don't want to discourage those who may have similar desires by thinking just because I traveled to many fun places, it required a lot of money. Surely you can spend an enormous amount of money going to these places, but it is certainly not a requirement and I challenge you to try it and see. My goal was to design the most spectacular home I could build for myself and do it without spending a dime more than I had to. While I did have a lot of fun, I still had to translate all those nitpicky requirements into a document that the people responsible for building it could understand. That alone required hours upon countless daily hours of reading, writing, drawing, and research, not to mention two years of my life.

After delightful frustration and an insatiable desire to see what I wanted in 3D, I came across Chief Architect Software, which was a $2500, very complex program that would allow me to create what I wanted. The beauty was it would allow me to create and change my dream home as many times as I liked, whether it was 2:00 a.m. or 6:00 p.m., and I could easily be found designing it at both of those times. For an extra value-added treat, they provided a free thirty-day trial download, of which I took total advantage. After the download, I knew I was under the gun for time, so I worked on it for nearly fourteen hours straight, something I did every day for nearly two weeks. After brief breaks, I would go back into it for three or four additional hours. I was in absolute awe at the possibilities, and after twenty-five days, I built a website and included the 3D version with every room exactly how I wanted it. The website address is http://palatialdesigns.homestead.com should you decide to take a look at it and create something similar for yourself.

It wasn't until my trial period ended that I discovered *The Science of Getting Rich*, but the point is what was being said and what I was doing completely aligned with each other. Wattles went on to say, "You cannot transmit an idea unless you have it yourself. You must have it before you can give it, and many people fail to impress thinking substance because they have themselves only a vague and misty concept of the things they want to do, to have, or to become."

How Do You Predict the Future? Create It!

You *must* create great days on your own. They don't just happen. In addition, I have some not-so-great days that just really aren't worth writing about. No matter how much the great days cost, the fact remains they still come at some type of financial obligation, which goes back to the point that money makes life easier.

Slide 68 Mind-Set

I stay connected with people at both ends of the success spectrum, but focus much more on the success end. The poor and average guy wants to know what's going on in the mind-set of the rich. He wants to know what the rich person is reading, thinking, and doing. The rich guy has to keep a pulse on many who are not rich because chances are he is a provider and supplier to the average citizen. If he loses touch, then he immediately becomes a consumer and begins eating away at his wealth. At that point, he's only as good as his last success.

As much as I didn't care for growing up less fortunate, it gave me a lot of drive. Now that I'm grown, I can clearly see that the best way to help poor people is to not become one of them.

Lack of Money Never Stopped Me

When I graduated from North Central High School in May 1991, I had only recently been accepted at the Citadel, the Military College of South Carolina. I was very excited about the possibilities of going, but a little nervous at the same time due to its rigorous, regimented Fourth-Class System. The Fourth-Class System is the freshman year, designed to introduce the incoming class to the rigorous, disciplined life in a military academy. It is designed to be the worst experience one has ever encountered, so that if successfully completed, facing life's challenges after you graduate will be easier to handle. I would later find out that the Citadel is a good place to come from, but just not a good place to be.

With the acceptance letter came a request for a deposit of $150. That was a lot of money to ask of my parents during that time because it took everything they had to come up with it. My dad never had much college conversation for me, not because he didn't want me to go or didn't care; he just left my future up to me. He knew that I knew we didn't have the money for me to go. However, when he realized that I was accepted and they were requesting the $150 to hold my place, he made sure that my mom knew it was a priority.

I don't think any of us totally understood that the Citadel would cost substantially more than $150. To be quite honest, we never really knew how much it would cost. In fact, we didn't care. All we knew was that the Citadel would get the money and I would be there on the day we had to report.

All summer I was excited about my college decision and talked about it a lot. Many people gave me a pat on the back for stepping up big and making it happen. I was proud of the accomplishment. On the day before I left to go to the Citadel, my mom gave me all the money she had, which was $85. I figured that was good enough for me. Excited with a pocket full of money and knowing I wouldn't be able to have fun for a long while, I decided to call my ex-girlfriend Denise Parker and ask her to hang out with me that evening. There were two things I wanted to do before I went to college: skating and bowling.

Denise and I went out and had a great time. We went to Columbia, South Carolina, and went to the skating rink first, followed by McDonalds and then the bowling alley. We even ran across some other friends and family while we were out. We were having so much fun that we lost track of time and I ended up getting her home way too late, which her mom didn't really appreciate but she knew I was a good guy. More important than running short on time, I also nearly ran out of money. By the end of the night, I was down to my last $5.

I came home really late and snuck into the house to get a few hours' rest before our 4:30 a.m. departure for Charleston, South Carolina, which was about a two-and-a-half-hour ride. It seemed as if my head hit the pillow for no more than twenty minutes before my mom was coming in my room to wake me up. So there I was, exhausted from a great night of skating, bowling, and having fun, but with only $5 on the way to college. It just never dawned on me that I would need anything more if I would simply show up. And so it was that I reported to the Citadel with my trusty friend Abraham Lincoln.

I returned home four years later with dual bachelor's degrees. One was Modern Languages, French, and the other was Business Administration. In case you're wondering how I pulled it off, you'll have to consult the generous people who gave me scholarship money every year, including the Daniel Fund Scholarship, the Cadet Store Scholarship, and the Gift Shop Scholarship. Very generous loans were also provided from the South Carolina Student Loan Corporation, made possible by Hank Filler, the financial savior employed especially for guys like me, who had the potential to be there but not the money. Every time I needed a dime, they lent it, and the deal was I would pay it back six months after I graduated.

Because I was the first one in my family to go to college, I really didn't know much about what to do in terms of getting college money. In fact, I didn't know what to do at all. It was a mystery that I thankfully stayed ignorant of enough to not let it affect any of my decisions. Each semester, I would receive a letter from the financial aid office telling me I was short of money. It became so routine that I never thought much about it. It wasn't until the second semester of my junior year that I finally thought long and hard about it. At that point, I got scared. I began thinking, *what if they kick me out of here for not having any money?* At that point, I knew I had invested a lot of time trying to get a degree, but I could lose it all for lack of money. I went to the financial aid office and told Major Fuller, "Either you all are going to kick me out of here for not having enough money, or I'm going to owe you everything I own when I graduate." His next words were music to my ears. He said, "Well, we're not going to kick you out of here, but you're going to have to work your butt off when you get out of here to pay us back!" At that point, I knew my problems were solved. I gave a big sigh of relief and promptly went back to the battalion thinking I didn't have a problem in the world.

I felt that way because owing money was nothing new to my family, so I figured it was no big deal. I think my mom felt the same way the first time she gave me all the money she had. It was actually right after I got accepted at the Citadel. They gave us a long laundry list of items to buy that we had to bring on the first day. I recall that we had to have sets of unfitted white sheets, six T-shirts, six pairs of underwear, six pairs of black socks, six pairs of white socks, handkerchiefs, shoe polish, and so on. It probably seems trivial to some people, but when you share the same size with siblings, everything is up for grabs when it comes to clothes, so having to have all this for myself was a big deal. I recall going to Rose's, which was a local Wal-Mart competitor, to go through my laundry list. I was excited about getting all of my own things. My mom went to her full-time job and received her weekly check, cashed it at the bank, and gave me every penny of it—$221.38.

I remember asking her what was she going to do for money, and she just said something to the effect that I had to have those things so that was that. She worked part-time for a lawyer in town who was a Citadel graduate. I remember thinking how nice his house and his law office were and thinking that if he went to that school and was living a good life, then I would surely be able to do the same thing. I thought his house was so huge at the time, but I hated the fact that my mom had to clean up after them just to get me the things I needed to go to school. At the time, he seemed a bit interested in the fact that I would be attending the same school he had attended. Little did I know that some twenty years later, when my parents ran into a financial situation where he was the attorney representing the collector, he would totally disown any knowledge of knowing either one of us. I went into his office to try and settle the score, and after I reminded him of who we were, he seemed so disinterested. He pretended to not even remember it was my mom who cleaned his house. I thought to myself, *you bastard! You know damn well you remember the person who cleaned up after you, your wife, and your kids. For you to sit here and not even look me in my eye over some minor financial dispute is just your way of thinking you're better than us.* Oh well, who cares about him anyway? The problem was quickly resolved, and our lives moved swiftly along.

Anthony Von Mickle

My Next Destination: Harvard University

During my years at the Citadel, I began to feel more important than the average college student. I felt like I was supposed to go out and do more than what the average graduate would do. Many times I would tell my friends who didn't go to college with me, which was all of them because no one else was up to that challenge, that I was going to Harvard. Deep down inside, I just knew I would never get accepted, but that was beside the point. They didn't understand that all I wanted to do was just go there physically so I could say I had been there. I told my geometry teacher during my junior year in high school that I was going to Harvard even if I just stopped in to use the bathroom.

While at the Citadel, I spent many days in the career services office with center director Brent Stewart carefully planning and mapping out strategies for my life after undergraduate school. One day while searching the job board, I noticed an advertisement for a summer language program at Harvard University to study Ukrainian. I thought to myself, *Wow! Now that sounds like something far from usual.* I took one of the requests for information and sent it in to get an application. Harvard responded in record time with full-color brochures, applications, and so on. I was so happy that they were nice enough to send me the information. I just felt that they had the right to tell me to get lost for whatever reason.

After I left the career services office many times shortly after that and perhaps many days before, I would walk across campus, and somehow the 1970s' hit disco song "Car Wash" by Rose Royce would come to mind. During the chorus of the song, they sing, "Heeey, get your car wash today. Fill up and you won't have to pay." For some strange reason, I would substitute the words and create the following chorus of my own: "Heeey, get your Harvard car today." That little chorus gave me so much motivation and confidence that someone really needed to accept me so I could join the program.

I wasn't going to be the magna cum laude graduate from my modern languages program, but I still felt like I should apply. One of the greatest emphases on the application was the letters of recommendation. Fortunately, Dr. Edward Tucker, a former department head of the English Department, had taken an interest in me and my future. He sent me to the Humanities Seminar at Seabrook Island, South Carolina, during the fall of my senior year, which happened to be the same week of the Million Man March on Washington.

I had never heard of Seabrook Island even though it was only twenty-five minutes away from campus.

I spent several days there in a seminar to study dispute resolution, having healthy debates with some of the area's finest. It was a prep for exceptional students going to law school, only there were two problems: I never had the intention to go to law school, and I was sure everyone else at the seminar was much smarter than I was. Regardless, I went and had the time of my life. The place was so beautiful. It was like nothing I'd ever seen. The homes were fabulous, and the entire gated community was manicured. There were dolphins that played near the shoreline at breakfast time. I could see the ships coming into port during the morning as they brought goods in from other countries. It was exciting, and I felt very important.

I performed well during the seminar and made a good impression on Dr. Tucker. The beauty of all that was he earned his PhD from Harvard many years earlier and was willing to write my recommendation. That gave me a lot of leverage in terms of competitiveness. I sent in my application and crossed my fingers. Actually, after sending it in, I talked confidently about how I was applying to Harvard, but always felt that I had a snowball's chance in you-know-where at getting in.

Two days before graduation in May, I received the letter from them saying welcome aboard. I was stunned! I couldn't believe it. After just a thought of going there to use the bathroom and confidently singing my edited version of the "Car Wash" song, I was going there for real. The greatest part was that I was even being granted some scholarship money. As generous as Harvard was for letting me come, I was being faced with the same problem I had when I came to the Citadel—no money.

I spoke with a few family members, who told me to just call them and ask if I could come later. That went over like a lead balloon. I recall calling the admissions office and explaining my dilemma. The lady on the phone basically said, "We're giving you an opportunity to come here, and you're saying, 'I'll get back to you'?" She said, "Do you know how many applications we get in a year? There's no guarantee we'll even get your next application." I promptly responded, "Prank caller!" and hung up the phone. Not sure what to do, I decided to do the best thing, which was nothing until I figured out what was next. After a few days, I decided I was going with whatever I had. I'd deal with the situation when I got there, but I was determined to go.

I had recently accepted a job with Burlington Industries in Rutherfordtown, North Carolina, with what was a high starting salary at the time of $29,500. I could have accepted the money and begun my career, but a shot at Harvard was much more appealing. Still, I had no money and had just turned down a good job. Because the program wouldn't start for a few weeks, I had to work until I left. I decided to work at Gene Reed Chevrolet in North Charleston until it was time to go to Cambridge.

One day, while I was braving the exhausting humidity of Charleston on the hot asphalt, a Jeep Cherokee pulled in. Driving it was a very nice lady who required assistance in finding a car for her mother, who had recently wrecked her current car. The lady told me her name was Mrs. Bell. Immediately, the name rang a "bell." I had heard the last name many times during my time in Charleston due to a certain medical doctor named Thaddeus Bell. He was very well-known throughout the community and even came to the Citadel many mornings to work out before starting his workday. Coincidentally, he was her husband. I was so honored! Mrs. Bell and I spent a short time on the lot searching for several vehicles that might fit her criteria. She told me she was paying in cash and she wanted a great deal. I assured her I would do everything I could.

After choosing a vehicle, she told me that she wouldn't be buying the car that day but would wait until she received the insurance money. Sadly, I told her that I wouldn't be there much longer because I was heading to Harvard. Excited, she told me to call a gentleman named Randy Kennedy when I got there as he was Dr. Bell's first cousin and a distinguished professor of law there. Mrs. Bell then told me that when I returned home to come by and have dinner with them as she wanted to introduce me to her daughter Tiffany.

It was nice to know that I would have someone to say hello to once I got there, but in the meantime, I was still faced with the money problem. Unlike my acceptance letter from the Citadel with a request for $150, Harvard needed $3000. There was just no way I was going to have that kind of money, but I never let it stop me. Actually, I sent what I had, which was $900. After that, I stopped worrying about it because there was nothing more I could do.

They extended me an invitation to stay on campus, but I don't even remember what the room and board costs were because I surely didn't have it. My saving grace was the Army National Guard. If you were a member of the National Guard, you were given the opportunity to stay at a hotel on a military base for as low as $8 a night in many cases for both room and board. I searched for nearby military installations and found that there were two. One was Hanscom Air Force Base, but they were frequently busy and there was no guarantee that I could stay there for an extended period of time. In fact, it was highly likely that I would not be able to stay there long at all. Regardless, I was not turning down the opportunity. My mom would frequently say, "If you make one step, God will make two." I was surely hoping he would make more than two for me this time.

My mom once again gave me all she had, which this time was significantly more, a whopping $300. Several weeks later, I left for Massachusetts. I had never driven that far before and was a bit nervous. I studied maps for about a week prior, trying to ensure that I wouldn't get lost along the way. Hanscom had space available there for the first two nights, but after that I was on my own. I took the deal and hoped for the best someplace else. I don't recall the reason, but I didn't want to stay at the other military installation because it seemed eerie for some reason and I had never even seen it.

From the bases I had visited in the past, I knew that the Air Force had a much better quality of living and their facilities were always exceptional. I left for school and stopped at my aunt's apartment in Yonkers, New York, for a few days to break up the drive. While I was there, my cousin Ralph congratulated me on my acceptance but told me, "Whatever you do, don't stay in South Boston because they are racist." I was very surprised because I thought all racist people lived in the Deep South in poor rural areas. I never expected that in the North.

I left the concrete jungle of New York with destination Hanscom Air Force Base. All I knew was the roads that would take me there, the fact that I had two nights room and board, and that the check-in to campus was in a few days. In fact, the first night I didn't even have a room as my reservation did not start until the next day. I just figured if I got there late enough, maybe I could just sleep in my car in the parking lot on the base or go inside and sleep on a couch in a lobby somewhere. Turns out, I chose the couch.

The next two days went swiftly by, and I fortunately ran into two other military officers in the program, who were staying at the other base. They told me perhaps I should consider coming with them because they had plenty of availability and perhaps I could stay all summer. I swiftly took them up on it and made my way to the Naval Air Station in South Weymouth, Massachusetts, my new home for the entire summer. The cost per day for staying: $8 a night. We drove thirteen miles one way to the Metro station daily and then took the subway into Harvard Square. It was a pleasing twelve miles, as the subway system was totally new for me. I felt like a well-versed, well-traveled city dweller for a while.

As I think back, my story reminds me of the famous Footprints poster where the guy reflects back on his life and asks God why during the difficult times when he needed God the most, there was only one set of footprints. God kindly replied that His love for him was great, and at his most difficult times, when he sees only one set of footprints, those were the times that God carried him. That wouldn't be the last time I had to make a major move with little money, and certainly not the last time I would be carried.

Headed North for a New Beginning

I studied at Harvard for the entire summer semester and had to leave just a few short days prior to the final exam because I was simply out of money. I will always cherish my days in the Slavic languages program, where I had a lot of fun. I spent quite a bit of time at the law school having breakfast with Randy Kennedy and engaging in intellectual conversation over ice cream some days and breakfast the others.

I returned to South Carolina and knew it was time for me to start looking for a job again. I was thinking of getting involved in information technology because that was an area of high interest and I heard it paid well. There really weren't a lot of jobs in the South Carolina area at all and certainly fewer in the field of IT. I searched far and wide, and after many weeks of nothing, I was extended an offer to come to Alexandria, Virginia, by my aunt to stay on her couch until I found my own way. She lived in a one-bedroom apartment but was on TDY much of the time with the US Army Soldier Show as the company's First Sergeant.

She told me that all I had to do was get there. That sounded like an easy enough task, but I had borrowed my parents' car to go to Harvard and given them my Toyota to drive locally because it wasn't equipped to be driven quite so far. In addition, I had a 1984 Honda Accord that I purchased with 217,000 miles on it, but it was in immaculate condition. I drove it from 1992 until 1994 while adding 100,000 miles to the odometer. It's amazing how many miles a kid puts on his first car. While I was at Harvard, the Honda sat for quite a bit because I allowed some family members to borrow it and they didn't take care of it very well.

I had given my mom's car back to her. My dad was driving my Camry, and the Honda just wasn't in shape to drive anywhere. My dad told me that he would drive me to Alexandria by one of two ways. The first was that if he got a load going through Washington, I could ride with him in the 18-wheeler. The other option was he could take me during the weekend when he was off in my mom's Ford Escort. For two weeks straight, something came up that he wasn't able to do it. At this point, I had grown terribly frustrated because I had a superb education and no job. I was really hanging my head low, and my mom had many people from our church call to give me words of encouragement that it would get better soon. That helped a lot, but still I wanted my own destiny and I wanted it now.

The next week my dad told me he would finally get the opportunity to drive me. He told me that we would leave Friday afternoon. That was fine by me, but it surely made a long, highly anticipated wait. To top it off, he had a ritual he enjoyed with his friends. Every weekend they would pick one of the friends' houses to go to and have a drink fest in the backyard. These drinking binges would last for hours. All the townspeople knew where they were, and they were very well-attended. The problem was, they would commonly have too much to drink and would forget about something of importance they had to do. In my case, it was taking me to Alexandria.

My dad came home late that Friday evening and told me he knew he was supposed to take me, but he had a bit much to drink and we would go tomorrow. A bit annoyed, I figured fair enough and looked forward to going the next day. The next morning he woke up and I was thinking we were going to leave, but he told me he needed to go back and run a few errands with his drinking buddies again but that we would leave around noon. Noon turned to six o'clock in the evening, and we never left. I was furious, but there wasn't much I could do. The next day, the same thing happened. He had to go back to work Sunday night, so that meant I would be stuck for another week. On that Sunday afternoon, I began looking much more closely at my Honda. In fact, I looked closely at it for the entire next week.

I figured if I changed the oil, which would only cost me $8 to do myself, and changed the air filter, I could get a cleaner-running engine. With a few minor adjustments here and there, I figured I could get it in good enough shape to make the trip myself. I went out to the car and proceeded to clean it up. My dad happened to be outside and could sense my anger, although I tried not to make it known. "You all right?" he asked and I responded yes, but clearly he was a lot smarter than I was. Whether you know it or not, your parents know you better than you think, and my dad knew what was going to happen very soon. He knew that at nightfall, I was about to put that car on the road with expired tags and no insurance, like a runaway slave going for his freedom.

The next Saturday and Sunday, the same thing happened. By about four o'clock Sunday afternoon, my dad came back home and emptied his wallet. He had $130 and gave me every dime of it, along with the car keys to my mom's car, and told me to go ahead. He was somber about it, I could clearly see. I asked him how they would get around with only one car. He told me, "Me and your momma will be all right. We'll figure out something."

With that, I grabbed my bags that I had packed the week before, jumped in the car, and headed for Alexandria.

Unfortunately, when I got there, my aunt had left for the long Columbus Day weekend in October. I knew there were several military bases in the area, so I just knew one of them had room and board for at least one night. I was right. I ended up spending two nights at Andrews Air Force Base, and before long, my aunt returned. With a dedicated place to stay and a lot of ambition, I was off to a new life.

Slide 68 Mind-Set: **Play the hand you're dealt to the best of your ability.**

There are always people who are worse off than you. As bad as you think your life might be, you must be willing to deal with the circumstances life throws at you, because someone is eagerly awaiting the opportunity that you are calling a disaster and he or she has the ability to win the entire house with those same cards. You don't want to trade your hand in and watch someone else prosper with it. Are you going to play the hand you were dealt, or are you going to fold? When it was time for action among my friends growing up and everyone was waiting, we'd say, "Barbeque or mildew!"

PART 2:

Define Your Dream Life and Find People Who Are Currently Doing What You Think That May Be

This Is the Time to Be Perfectly Clear about What You Want Money, Time, or Both

The people who have lots of money tend not to have lots of free time, and vice versa. It doesn't necessarily mean they work eighteen-hour days; it could just be that they ensure their time is being invested toward something other than being a couch potato. There is usually a direct tradeoff during the peak years. Still, there are some who have figured out a great balance between the two, and actually have both. While it isn't necessarily easy, it is possible. A lot of people can have everything they want if they don't want so much, but that's not really the aim of this book. I want you to have everything you want, including time, health, money, and most importantly happiness. None of this will happen until you are absolutely clear about what it is you're looking for.

At some point, you truly have to accept what it is you want out of life, even if it means that people will think you are just asking for too much. There is some guy out there who legitimately wants four new Mercedes-Benz's. He may have the most logical reason in the world, but to the rank and file of friends and associates, if they are not wealthy, they may in outrage or disgust turn their noses in the air at him at the thought of what they perceive as greed or gluttony. Do you know how long it took me to accept the fact that I could own a 14,000-square-foot home in Northern Virginia with a Lamborghini parked in the garage and a 10,000-square-foot palace in Southern Florida with a Ferrari parked in its garage, and shuttle the family between the two in my very own helicopter while owning all of it outright? I assure you that this mind-set didn't happen overnight coming out of the trailer park. That type of money may seem like a lot if you don't know anyone who lives like that, but those assets didn't cost even five million dollars. When your millions are in the single digits, it's enough to gain you the title of affluent in some circles; while in others, you'll be lucky to get a nosebleed seat at the charity ball in Naples.

Sure, you can go to the local shopping mall and spend a thousand dollars while going completely unnoticed, but measure those types of assets to wealth on a larger scale and you don't even rank. That kind of money is out there in droves, and the circle is getting bigger. Show Mother Earth your wildest desires, and she'll show you that you can't ask for enough because you don't know enough to ask for. The bigger point here is, do you believe with all your heart and soul that you want the things you want? After you start to make progress, you'll soon realize that other people are infinitely more successful because their level of acceptable success is far beyond anything you ever thought of. That three-acre parcel of land that you absolutely swore you'd never ask for anything else if it were somehow granted to you will pale in comparison to the guy who owns half a mountain range or a 50,000-acre ranch with his own private runway and two Lear jets.

The unexposed mind may very well be thinking, *where in the world is all this money supposed to come from? You must be dreaming!* Well, dreaming is clearly the point of this book, and this type of lifestyle starts with a dream, albeit a very focused dream. So if someone tells you to keep dreaming, do yourself a favor and take their advice!

> ****Slide 68 Mind-Set****
>
> **If someone tells you to keep dreaming, do yourself a favor and take their advice!**

Is it possible this is greed? Sure it is; you bet. At the same time, is there anything wrong with wanting the four new cars? I'd say not necessarily, especially if you can afford them. I've found that far too many people have dreams of achievement that are above and beyond their basic needs and even the desires of most, but absolutely refuse to accept what it is they want and choose not to aggressively pursue it. A few will silently pursue their dreams, but no one will ever hear of the details. I think that is sheer avoidance and just not accepting what you truly desire for fear of failing in the eyes of others. It would be so nice if success were a gradual ascent. Instead, the man idly perched on the mountaintop learned along the way that the wave to success was filled with troughs and crests, jagged edges and uncertain slopes. The requirements were an insatiable desire for freedom and a willingness to fall embarrassingly on one's face before enemies, friends, family, and strangers alike, knowing that you have to be willing to fail your way to the top. Wise onlookers knew he was successful long before he took his first step, but he was probably the last to know.

A large part of figuring out what it is you actually desire is determining the costs involved. The material portion of my goals had costs in real dollars, and knowing those costs was an essential component in achieving them. I find that people set very vague goals. They say things like, "I want to be comfortable" or "I want to be rich." They may say that they want millions of dollars, when they have never sat down to calculate what the costs are of the things they really want. I have also found that in many cases, it hardly costs millions, because people tend to see many items that they only think they want. When you sit down and really plan out a dream day in your dream life, you may find that there is not enough time in the week for you to entertain all the things you thought you wanted to buy.

Still, once I determined what it was I desired, figuring out what I needed to earn to get them answered a lot of questions. Simply put, if I need to earn $500k over the next two years for a garage filled with my favorite cars, investing $250 a month into a blue chip stock like Wal-Mart, which has a huge market cap and is not likely to have 200 percent growth a year for the next ten years, is probably not the best choice. Instead, perhaps a few investment properties in a great location may be a more effective choice for my time horizon and risk level.

I don't feel that I started making any real progress toward my goals until I began to accept what I really wanted out of life. So whether it's money, time, or both, at some point you have to make a choice as to what you want and be prepared to lose some friends and colleagues along the way. Why? Because some people simply are stuck on level one, and you can't expect to move a step further until you change your circle of influence.

> ****Slide 68 Mind-Set****
>
> **Do I have to write my goals down? Absolutely. When you are writing clearly, you are thinking clearly.**

There's an even more important point to all of this out-of-the-world dreaming, and that is if your mind is constrained to accept the things you truly desire, it will equally strain to find the resources to get them. What does that mean? That means if your wildest dreams require fifteen hours of total freedom every day but you only accept that you must work twenty hours a day to get what you want, then your wish will never be commanded. To put it in monetary terms, if you accept that your goals will cost you one million dollars and fully believe they are achievable, the answers and directions to getting what you want will be provided to you.

Think of it this way: if you currently earn $10 an hour but feel you need $200 an hour to live the lifestyle you've been dreaming of and can't think of any logical revenue stream that will take you there, that's perfectly okay at first. When you truly wrap your head around the fact that it really will cost you $200 an hour to achieve, you will begin to find levels of revenue that support it. How can this be? Think of all the work you had to put in to determine the figure that you needed. It didn't come easy, because you had to do tons of research to come to this figure if you thoroughly flushed it all out. As you begin talking with people who have those assets already, you'll realize what it is they do. Sometimes, knowing the title for a field or job is a substantial part of the battle. If you've been an accounting manager in small-town United States of America all your life and never witnessed top-performing financiers in major cities, figuring out the daily task of someone who earns what you need could be your missing link to set you on a path to increasing your education, career goals, and maybe a shot at a new city. At the risk of sounding like a broken record, ensure that you are clear about your goals. Don't be surprised if you edit your list thirty times in a twelve-month period. It just means that you are getting the hang of razor-sharp dream accuracy.

The $40-Million-Dollar Dream Sheet

Dale Carnegie said, "Success is getting what you want; happiness is wanting what you get." (Quoted in the book *Tough Choices* by Carl Fiorina, September 25, 2007.)

Forty million wasn't just a made-up number for me. I thought about it quite a bit. It wasn't even a limit on what I wanted to make, because it's simply not worth having one. The dream sheet is mainly a materials list, with some lifestyle items added. It purposely doesn't contain value-driven items, as I can assure you that what you do with your money speaks quite loudly about your values. So you won't see things such as time to go to the kids' football practices, because that's already built into the current lifestyle. This list assumes all the things that promote a good moral compass.

I have even heard that billionaire businessman Ted Turner said that your dreams should be so big that it takes two lifetimes to achieve them. I understand his point, but I just haven't gotten to that level of thinking yet. I felt that after obtaining forty million dollars, I would have acquired everything materially that I desired for personal use and then some, and would have earned the right to turn down virtually any business meeting that would yield me additional financial gain. Of course, the reality was that it didn't take nearly that much, but it's better to set goals that are much greater so that you don't come up short.

I won't have to put off the important family events because we'll have more than enough materially to not have to need or want for anything. My forty million was methodical. I figured the cost of everything I wanted was under $10 million, and then I doubled that for miscellaneous things I couldn't see, to get $20 million. After that, I doubled the $20 million for taxes and inflation over my life span, to arrive at $40 million. Voila, there's the $40-Million-Dollar Dream Sheet. I learned through the Project Management Institute (PMI) that goals had to be SMART, meaning specific, measureable, attainable, realistic, and timed. As much as I understand how that mind-set may work for goals where one doesn't mind or won't undergo too much heartache if they are not met, I feel that a dream sheet has to be conquered. These goals need to be so far out there that you will truly live out the popular saying, "Shoot for the moon, and even if you miss, you'll be among the stars." I think if you aim this high, you are destined for the moon or maybe even the sun.

Von's list for Slide 68 goes as follows:

1. Build my dream home, the Château D'Von (a French château with a porte cochere)—$2 million, 14,000 square feet, on three levels, with a porte cochere that I designed

2. Palais De Bellagio—$3,000,000: This gold-colored stucco home with red terra-cotta roof is a Mediterranean masterpiece. I decided to go with a designer who was more familiar with the local Palm Beach landscape than I was, and Weber Design Group out of Naples, Florida, answered the dream. The essential purpose was to provide a winter haven to hide from ice and snow, while being able to enjoy a yard filled with lush multicolored landscaping and Canary Island date palms from the covered lanai. The greatest benefit is its expansive wings, which provide family opulent living without paying for pricey hotels during weekend getaways and huge Florida events.

3. EC-120—$1,500,000: Since attending SLED (South Carolina Law Enforcement Division) Academy as a rising high school senior and riding for about two minutes in a chopper, I've forever looked at helicopters, admiring them from afar. I decided I wanted to have one for myself to use for personal and business travel.

4. The Stable—$800,000: Lamborghini Murciélago Roadster, Maserati Quattroporte, Ferrari 360 Spider, Full-Size Truck (country boy at heart), one or two other midrange luxury vehicles (you know, wife stuff, but wives aren't nearly as involved in the car game).

5. Nice Homes for Mom and Mom-in-law—$500,000: Where I'm from, people live the simple life. Ten-thousand-square-foot homes are impressive, but really not at all desired, especially when you're at active adult age. This was more than enough to build both moms nice homes with cars, with enough money to dish out to the undeserving, yet needy, relatives.

6. Charitable Contributions—$200,000 annually: Money is good for three things: spending it, investing it, and giving it away. What's the point otherwise? Money is great at solving the problems it can solve and horrible at trying to solve the problems that it can't. Let's make somebody's day at the restaurant, barbershop, fund-raiser, and grocery store on a regular basis. God doesn't need your money, but be obedient and give Him His cut anyway.

7. Quarterly Business Trips, with Downtime for Vacations—$50k per annum: There's nothing like getting away to recharge the batteries every several weeks. I really enjoy the Ivy League company of great events and issues in seminar-type environments both in the United States and abroad. The beauty is you get to take advantage of wonderful sightseeing before, during, and after the conferences. Oh, and by the way, it really increases your level of knowledge and pays dividends to your overall education.

8. Maintenance Team—$100,000 annually: Tax attorneys, CPAs, estate planners, and so on. I realized I had to have the best in the business on speed dial when absolutely necessary. A good maintenance team is the most up-to-date expert at doing what they do, which allows me to do what I do.

9. Retirement Account—$3 million: Due to my relative youth, this account was stacked with 75 percent small cap stocks and international growth funds, with the remaining 25 percent in dividend-yielding bonds, with the dividends reinvested because I didn't need the cash just yet.

10. Things I Never Thought of But Have More Than Enough Cash to Take Care of—$$$$: You just never know. As much as I love driving my exotic sports car, I drive it to $10 restaurants, with no thought of needing to be around the exotic class of people. The amount could be substantially smaller depending on your desired lifestyle.

11. Lifetime Taxes and Inflation—$20 million: As you can see, the bigger-ticketed items were just over $11 million dollars. Great tax guys help you substantially with tax avoidance, which is not to be confused with tax evasion. With the nearly 35K a year just in real estate taxes on the main house, I knew I'd pay nearly a million dollars over the next thirty years if I didn't have the right team. In any case, I added another $8 to 9 million dollars, making the total $20 million for all the things I thought I would somehow overlook price wise. What I will tell you is that you quickly adjust to whatever your lifestyle is, and with no mortgage, aircraft, or automobile payments, backed by large interest-bearing accounts, you simply tend not to spend a lot of extra money on "stuff." Therefore, I simply doubled the first $20 million ($11 million plus $9 million) and came up with $40 million. That was my rationale, to be quite honest, for arriving at that number.

Getting to $40 million was always everyone's 40-million-dollar question from me. The easiest answer for me was always to have a half-a-billion-dollar investment portfolio that provided an 8 percent return on investment before I eventually exited and went back home to think of something else constructive to do. The reality is always much different, but you have to start somewhere. Knowing that I'm an investor and not an aspiring basketball player, actor, or singer was a huge step in achieving my goal. The other major part in achieving my goal—and literally the most important part—was having one.

Ensure Your List Provides for More Than Just You.

On the surface, some of the items on my list appear awfully extravagant, selfish, greedy, or whatever word you may want to use to describe them. Not that I have to justify myself (based on my earlier comments about being true to oneself), but I'm actually a very generous person, and none of the items on my list are for me only.

For example, the Château D'Von commands a ton of space, but surely I don't need it all. I purposely added over 7,000 square feet (easily two comfortable American homes) for the use of others. The basement contains extra guest rooms for family and close friends, with a separate entry. That was created in case someone I know falls on a completely unexpected hard time and needs an opportunity to rebuild their lives without feeling like they are interrupting mine. Equally as important, and a situation I would prefer, is the same use of space for close family or friends to create a dream home of their own. Do you know how much a family can do if it doesn't have to pay housing expenses for an entire year? Think about that from all angles, in terms of lights, water, heating and air-conditioning, lawn care, and we haven't even mentioned mortgage or food costs! Commanding that kind of space puts me in a position of power to not help someone with lip service, but empower them not only with my abode but also my circle of influence and resources to help them achieve superior success.

Let's look at my other residence, the Palais De Bellagio, and all that it has to offer. This magnificent property is built in a warm climate, with a lot of open spaces and rooms that are spread apart from each other. There is a separate guest suite that connects to the main house via a bridge. There are multiple terraces, storage areas, fountains, and so on. Think about how much money is saved for family reunion costs when a 10,000-square-foot heated space yet 18,000 square feet with covered outdoor spaces has no check-in or check-out rates for family members to pay. Look at how this provides a family an opportunity to get together not just for family reunions but also holidays. Think about how a young person who desires to study in a nearby college can practically live in the guest suite without having to pay tuition. When you live in properties like these, it makes an average person at best tend to want to do better because you project a higher image and they tend to feel pressured to live up to that image.

Look at what happens when you own a four-seat helicopter. It absolutely can whisk me away to important meetings and events in little time across cities jammed with major traffic delays, but think about how empowered I am to introduce those interested into careers of flight. The son of a friend of mine is currently studying photography. Think about how he is able to see images of buildings or various landscapes when he can hover five hundred feet above them, which is an opportunity he would probably not get otherwise. Heaven forbid there is a medical emergency in the suburbs where these properties are located, but imagine what would happen if a person's life were at stake and the emergency responders couldn't get to them in time to provide the proper treatment. When you're fortunate enough to have a good neighbor who can air transport you to medical facilities within a moment's notice, it may save the life of a loved one who may have not made it otherwise.

That's My Car! As children, many of my friends and I would sit on the corner and play a game called "That's My Car," where whoever saw the coolest car first would call it as their own. We'd spend hours watching hundreds of cars go by, all wishing for the coolest set of wheels under the sun. When the sun would go down, the game didn't necessarily end. That seemingly mindless childlike game of mental images not only lasted for weeks as we'd talk about cars we saw those days and later when no one else was around, but those mental images also provided motivation. I recall taking my first exotic to my hometown and happenstance attended the funeral of Ellen Blackwell, affectionately known as "Little Bit" for her small frame. She had taken over the role of grandmother for me since my grandmother died and she was my deceased grandparent's best friend.

As we all gathered together to fellowship after the burial, I noticed a number of kids, both big and small, hovering around my car. One by one, I gave as many rides on the open road as they had desire to take. For many, that's the only time they will ever get an opportunity to be a part of an exotic experience. The parents instantly used that as a piece of motivation to tell the kids what they can obtain if they get a good education and hang around people such as myself.

The $40 million was a number I decided while ending a very uplifting conversation with billionaire Robert Johnson. Later, I was having lunch with two of my friends, Charlotte and Doug, when Doug asked me how much money I wanted. He was at a much higher number, while I insisted that $40 million was good with me. A large part of being comfortable with where I was greatly came from me doing my homework about exactly what I wanted. Of course, if you're just chasing money, it's never enough. I totally realize that you have to be a catalyst for change making a difference in the world and you'll earn more money than you can spend in two lifetimes.

I kept that number close to me and have yet to stray from it. The point is you should continue to dream, regardless of how it looks to someone else. This is your personal journey, and if it doesn't make sense to anyone else, that's fine. You never know just how much your perceived chimerical thought may have been studied and appears very logical to someone else. In my case, what I thought of as my dreams turns out to be the one percent placeholder ranking of America's elite class, according to Gene Bidell, author of *The Millionaire in the Mirror: How to Find Your Passion and Make a Fortune Doing It—Without Quitting Your Day Job*. As it turns out, the top one percent of earners make an average of $40 million dollars over a lifetime. Yours does not have to be that, or you may want ten times that. What I hope I have illustrated, among many things, is that you have to be specific. When you are specific, the over-the-top billions that many think are required for an out-of-this-world dream lifestyle is hardly what's needed. Since most people don't even want what I wanted, your ability to achieve your dreams should come a lot cheaper, but you have to be *big* about it!

If you Think Big

You Act Big.

If you Act Big

You Look Big.

If you Look Big

You Feel Big.

If you Feel Big

You ARE Big.

It costs nothing to dream and everything not to. Don't waste dream space on miniscule goals. If you're going to dream anyway, make it worthwhile. You'd be amazed at how much of it comes true if you just *believe* it will. I think that Walt Disney is one of the world's finest examples of what taking time to dream until you have the ability to dream in color can do. Walt Disney World will never stop mesmerizing people because one man had a childlike dream.

Another reason I highly recommend you create a goal or dream sheet is to help keep you from corruption. I have seen countless men fall victim to corruption for the sake of a marginal dollar. It's a shame when people who are already set for life put everything on the line for something illegal. I mean honestly, why are they doing it? I think it is because they never sit down and put together their ultimate list. Once you get the things you want or at least find yourself on a definite path to getting them, I feel that no one can come along and bribe you with some type of nonsense scheme that could cost you your reputation.

Billionaire business mogul Ted Leonsis wrote a book entitled *The Business of Happiness*. In it, he talked about how he defined a list of over one hundred goals. These were not your typical dream house and fancy car goals. He added exotic items, such as playing basketball against Michael Jordan. Ted asked for dream lists from his readers, and the ones he thought met a certain level of requirements were posted on his website. I am happy to report that the $40-Million-Dollar Dream Sheet was posted on the list, where it remained for quite some time. In addition, he also posted my praise of the book right there next to praise from sports legends such as Alex Ovechkin and LeBron James. He even linked my name and comments back to my website, which drove up my site statistics substantially. Thank you, Mr. Leonsis!

Slide 68 Mind-Set

Write the authors. I have found that when you write to authors, regardless of how successful or famous they are, they tend to respond back. Often, before I begin reading books, I will see if the author has set up a website or an e-mail address for questions or comments. I then read the book anticipating questions I might have, knowing it will provide a good chance to get feedback. There have been a few times I haven't heard back, but those were generally due to the e-mail address or website being no longer in existence.

I even decided to define not only the material goals that I wanted, but also the details of how I wanted my entire week to look after I was living the dream. I would recommend that you do the same thing if you are serious about success.

Week at a Glance

Monday

5:00 a.m. Wake up in the Chateau D'Von and grab gym bag.

5:15 Arrive at the Stable to unleash the beast, an Italian-made monster with tons of horses, and load the gym bag.

5:30 Arrive at the gym. Work out intensely for forty-five minutes to an hour, depending on what I ate the day before.

6:30 Depart to head back to the Château.

6:45 Shower and go back downstairs to have breakfast with the family before starting the workday.

8:00 Head to the office to see what's on the agenda for the day.

9:00–12 noon Check on investments. That may require phone calls and a number of short on-site meetings. If the distance is too great, set up teleconference in the home office. The home office will be in the conference center where investment forums and power meetings are held.

12:00–2:00 Lunch hour for power networking meetings, probably held at some local restaurant or private club.

2:00–4:30 Afternoon investment status meetings or listening to proposals for new business developments or speaking engagements.

4:30 Watch CNN to get the status of the market for the day.

5:00 See what the family is up to. If no homework is required, then some type of learning environment activity will be done. Perhaps a local play or outgoing excursion to learn something about something along with dinner.

8:30 Relax a bit by either watching some TV or reading the latest and greatest business success story. Perhaps write another book of my own.

11:30–12:00 Bedtime.

Tuesday

5:00 a.m. Wake up in the Château D'Von and grab gym bag.

5:15 Mostly a carbon copy of Monday, except change the car at the Stable. No need to rack up miles on the exotic, as the value just depreciates too much. Drive the family car, perhaps a top-end Lexus or Mercedes.

9:00–12 noon Check on family operating expenses. Not necessarily balance, but check the books to ensure that wifey and kids aren't overspending.

2:00 p.m.—midnight Pretty much similar events.

Wednesday and Thursday—Some variation of Monday and Tuesday.

Friday

5:00 a.m. Wake up in the Château D'Von and grab gym bag.

5:15 Arrive at the Stable to unleash the beast, an Italian-made monster with tons of horses, and load the gym bag.

5:30 Arrive at the gym. Work out intensely for forty-five minutes to an hour depending on what I ate the day before.

6:30 Depart to head back to the Château.

Slow it down a bit. Begin execution on some type of family and friends event. That may mean chopper preparation for flight or gassing up the car for a relaxing drive.

Work stops or slows down substantially in the early afternoon, probably right after lunch.

2:00 The weekend starts, and the good times roll.

Saturday

6: 30 Wake up, and the day is open.

Majorly open for some type of continuation of family or friends fun time. This is where the true benefits of hard work will pay off. Perhaps going to the Floridian palace with family or even business partners. While the family members are enjoying the environment, I will have time to look at some type of business case for at least a few hours.

The reality is when you've gotten to this level, you're wired a certain way, and you don't just play all day on the weekends. Whatever you do will involve some level of business interaction, but at this point, you have a team of expertise and a level of understanding where it doesn't take you the entire weekend away from family to get smart on some type of deal. In addition, whatever the deals are will be things that you enjoy, so once again, it won't feel like work. It may be the beaches of Miami or even the thrill of Disney, but business will be involved in some way. The family won't mind because they'll be used to it.

Sunday

6:30 Wake up and prepare for church service. If we are not at home to attend the local service, Sunday brunch is majorly important at a nice place.

Continue family fun/business operations until midday before returning back to the Château D'Von and the start of a new week.

It is worth mentioning that if you don't do this critical step of defining your goals with absolute precision, you will chase money from here to doomsday trying to figure out how your life will change with newfound riches. A lot of people will find themselves very shocked to hear that even though you have a pocket full of money, people don't just jump at your beckoning call. It is easy to assume that the rich guy goes to whatever store and can buy whatever whenever he wants. That sounds great in theory, but the reality is different. Not everyone cares about your riches, and you can find yourself on the waiting list in the most basic transactions. It is easy to accept this if you're attempting to buy a yacht from a manufacturer who only produces fifteen a year, but what about a condo in a rural area that isn't the least bit exotic? If the sales agent is slack, he is slack and won't get back to you any faster than he will get to anyone else. Just words of caution before you become fabulously wealthy and somehow get the notion that everyone wants to kiss the ground you walk on. It's not that I found out the proverbial "hard way." I was just shocked to find out.

From Millions to Just Another $30,000

A good friend of mine watched me create my dream sheet, and for whatever reason, would not create one for himself regardless of having watched me accomplish and accumulate so many great things. One day, I forced him to spend a few minutes trying it. He initially said, "Why bother? Besides, I need millions for my dreams!"

"Oh really?" I said. I told him to let's do a dream week at a glance and see what it looked like to see just how many millions were needed.

We started at the house, and he quickly told me he wanted nothing even close to the homes I've lived in and felt 10,000 square feet was simply more than anyone should ever have.

I said, "Well, going by 2001 standards, a 10,000-square-foot home cost about $1,200,000 plus the price of the land, or about $120 per square foot." With that rationale, his customized home shouldn't even be a third of that. Even more, he insisted that a home was nothing more than a place to sleep, so he had no desire to have a dream home. We then moved to transportation, and he quickly shut down any concept of owning a private aircraft, so we moved swiftly past that. There was no desire for exotics, and the car he had served him just fine, although he wanted the latest model.

At this point, I began thinking the dwelling and transportation costs were clearly the biggest items I've seen most people have; they usually ran the price up to nearly $1,000,000, so where in the world was the money he wanted going to go? We then moved to travel, which I knew he wanted to take full advantage of. So we listed all types of places; fortunately, I'd been to many of them and knew about what it cost. In short, his most ultimate dream was taking a trip to a foreign land twice a year and two domestic trips, essentially getting away quarterly, meaning twice for a long weekend and twice during the year for a week's vacation. The price we rounded up included hotels, shopping, flights, food, and so on. Our total costs for his dream life came to a whopping increase of $30,000 a year more after taxes, which a second job could probably achieve. Since he was planning to get married, I told him a sound couple's financial plan could probably be sufficient. The point is, he was like many in thinking he needed a winning lottery ticket to live the good life, which was hardly the case.

Don't Let Big Numbers Scare You: The Rich Tend to Overspend

Building the Dream Home

I recall asking a builder about the construction cost of my dream home. We referenced the French château that it was modeled after, which cost about $6 million. I had spent just under $2 million for my last estate home and I was sure the cost of my French château was going to be more, but I didn't feel it had to be substantially more.

He quoted me a very high number, but felt the number could be noticeably less to obtain the same look and feel for far less than $6 million. When I asked him why, he came up with a number of reasons that made very logical sense. He said they could have cut the price by at least $1.5 million, which is not exactly small change.

I found out the biggest reason the rich spent so much was a lack of planning and a higher perceived value on their time. Without going into the details, they simply could have planned things better and would have saved enough money to build several homes for the average American family. For me, even building an extravagant home, there are better ways to do it. As I continued to plan and realized that I had what were clearly two distinct sections of the house, I decided to build it in two phases. I could live in phase one really in the lap of luxury and build phase two down the road as the income continued to pick up. In addition, you have to think in terms of decades. Who wants to be forced to work hard to make monster-size mortgage payments while they are in their sixties? As we have seen that there is no guarantee a nine-to-five job will be there, there is also no guarantee your health will be there!

Constructing Your Dream Sheet

As a word of caution, when putting together a dream sheet or dream lifestyle, it is quite normal to have pricey items listed and a healthy dose of fear that the item is far away. That's a good thing. If it feels like something that is slightly beyond your reach, then you don't have a dream problem; you have a budget problem. Still, build your list with a time frame of when you can pay all these things off in mind. You don't want to be up to your eyeballs in debt at age sixty-five.

Stay away from those who rationalize, "If you have to ask, then you probably can't afford it." That's bad money management. Would you go into a store and buy a shirt or a pair of pants without ever checking the price tag, even if the item is in Wal-Mart? Of course you wouldn't. Always check the prices, no matter what it is, and don't believe that just because you ask a salesperson how much something costs that he or she immediately thinks you can't afford it.

The end result of my diligent efforts to obtain pricing and labor costs for a 12,000-square-foot dream home were only slightly more than the home I was living in, yet everything was upgraded and the home proved to be substantially more energy efficient. The two don't remotely compare. However, had I stopped my dream based on the senseless rationale that you can't afford it if you have to ask the price, the Château D'Von, which was the most important item on my list, would have remained a distant myth.

Preparing for the Helicopter

As I said above, ever since attending SLED (South Carolina Law Enforcement Division) Academy as a rising high school senior, I'd forever admired helicopters from afar. I would always make them a part of my family's vacation to gain those unprecedented aerial views of monuments and exhibits that just couldn't be seen from the ground.

While in Hawaii, I wanted my son to see where the eighties' sitcom *Fantasy Island* was filmed, as well as the blockbuster hit *Jurassic Park*. Each time we enjoyed helicopter flights, getting a helicopter for myself was always in the back of my mind. I would always ask the pilot about the one we were riding in, which was typically an eight-seater or some type of executive, luxury brand.

A lot of time passed before I finally accepted the fact that I didn't have to have the biggest helicopter on the market and an eight seater was simply overkill. At that very moment, the cost of the ones I'd been researching was tossed out. An entirely new model line made much more sense and, more importantly, made more financial sense. Add in that fact that I do buy vehicles new so a brand-spanking-new helicopter was totally out of the question, and again, you see that I reel these things in without going in a long-term debt frenzy for decades to come.

Admittedly, I'm a bit vain at times, but generally I analyze the total picture and do things that make sense. In the end, items I buy add the functionality I was looking for with the style that I desire. Personal aircraft, just like anything else, whether people think ownership is common or not, has a market at varying levels. I was surprised to find out just how many people have their own aircraft. Some are fancy and pretty, and some are simply functional. However, ownership means an entire new level of living, I can assure you.

Leaving the Washington DC area en route to New York City via automobile is over 250 miles. There are toll booths and lots of traffic, depending on when you leave. However, the nautical distance is substantially less, and when traveling at a conservative 90 knots, you are there in time for a lunch meeting and back to Washington before dinner. That type of flexibility in my schedule is what dream living is all about; and while it is not exactly cheap, it doesn't have to require a lottery winning either.

Big Money Not Required!

I decided to go to the local airport to get the application for my pilot training. As many times as I had been there, I never picked one up. I spent more time trying to determine chopper ownership costs than I did the fundamentals. For whatever reason, I realized that I wasn't fully taking my own advice of thorough follow-up. When I did, one of the instructors told me that there were three preliminary tests that had to be taken before fight training could begin. I was surprised by this. He told me that two of the tests could be done online for free. The other was a flight physical, and the cost was less than $100. I said to myself, "Here I am for two years checking out costs of insurance, where to buy, how to buy helicopters, and so on, and I had no idea about these requirements." In addition, after I went online to take the two preliminary tests and sign up for my medical exam, which I passed by the way, I found tons of manuals on helicopter flight. I knew these concepts were going to be tested during flight training, and many pilots probably didn't get them right away, which is expensive because you are paying by the hour. The beauty is I had a huge head start in that I was able to print out the entire book and study until I went to flight school, which isn't necessarily cheap but at $12 to 15 grand isn't exactly billionaire dollars either.

Four Exotics a Year Not Unheard of

At the service bay of a Lamborghini dealership in 2006, I was chatting with the parts manager. We talked about a few new cars that were scheduled to come in. I asked about a used Murcielago, Lamborghini's twelve-cylinder flagship model, and he mentioned having one. I asked him what year it was. He said it was a 2006. I said, "No, no, I don't buy new cars. I want a used one." He said it *was* used. I responded, "This is only April; how can it be used?"

He said, "The owner traded it in."

I said, "But the new 2007 line isn't due out for a while, so what did he trade it in on?" To my surprise, he responded, "An '06."

"So let me get this straight: he traded in a 2006 on a 2006."

"Exactly!" he said. He went on to explain to me that it is not uncommon for some guys to come in and buy two cars at a time, not for driving but for "garage ornaments." Some guys will buy three or four exotic cars a year simply because they can.

In my eyes and perhaps in yours, that may be viewed as a bit much, but if it's their dream life to do it and they aren't hurting anyone, then why not? The point is, don't let someone with seemingly infinite means scare you off from achieving your dreams just because they may toy with what you consider substantial resources. You have enough to do with working your own list, and don't be overly concerned with what richer people seem to be doing. For all you know, they could be up to their hair in debt and living a glossy nightmare instead of a dream. Dream big, but be responsible.

You Can Live a Dream Life without Creating a Pricey List

I really enjoyed reading Ted Leonsis's book *The Business of Happiness*. In it he mentioned so many wonderful stories in the very first few chapters. The most important to me helped me justify my thought process that mentioning the material items I wanted before knowing what would bring them was the order of pursuing happiness. He mentioned that if you pursue what makes you happy regardless of what that is, then you are more likely to experience business success as a result, and not vice versa. It helped the argument that money doesn't buy happiness, as he sold his first business at twenty-seven for $60 million dollars and later was still looking for happiness. It wasn't until a near date with death that he began to pursue happiness more vehemently. Still, I'm sure with $60 million dollars, his life was lived a lot easier, and he wasn't exactly unhappy.

Ted mentioned a conversation that he had during college that made a lot of sense to him in his pursuit, but like so many things, it didn't really sink in until years after the fact. "I had a roommate named Bill Macdonald, who has since gone on to be a very successful Hollywood producer. One Friday night—I think it was probably during my junior year—Bill and I had gone to the library to get some of our weekend studying out of the way. We studied hard, and afterward went off in search of campus parties, eventually getting home around midnight. I went upstairs to go straight to bed. I set the alarm clock for eight o'clock, because I had to get to my job at the shoe store on Wisconsin Avenue. That was the way my life worked at college.

"I woke up, showered, and got ready to go to my job. I walked downstairs, and there was Bill, a handsome prep school graduate, sitting on a couch with an absolutely beautiful blond girl in his lap, laughing and talking. Now this was something of a surprise to me, because the previous night, Bill and I returned to our apartment together, and somehow between when I'd gone upstairs to bed and the next morning, Bill had met up with this gorgeous girl.

"'What are you doing, man?' Bill asked.

"So I said, '*Well*, I've showered. I'm going to go get some breakfast, and then I'm going to the shoe store to work for four hours. And when I've finished my shift, I'm going to go to the library to study for a few more hours.'

"Bill looked at me and said, 'And why are you going to study some more? I thought we studied last night.'

"'We did. But I need to study more so I can get good grades.'

"So Bill goes, 'And why do you want to get good grades?'

"So I thought about it for a moment, and I said, 'So I can graduate and get a good job.'

"'And why do you want to get a good job?' Bill asked.

"I said, 'Well, Bill, I need to make a lot of money.'

"And he said, 'Why do you need to make a lot of money?'

"So I answered, 'I need to pay off my college loans, and besides, I think it will make me happy.'

"'How do you define happiness?' he asked.

"And I said, 'I guess looking at you, I'd say sleeping late and having a beautiful girl sit in my lap, and being able to laugh and giggle without a care in the world.'

"Bill said, 'Exactly the point. I'm just cutting out all of the intermediate steps.' He went on to say, 'Maybe I'm a little more of a plodder, someone for whom A leads to B, which leads to C.'

"It's clear to me from this memory that before I ever left Georgetown, I believed that achieving happiness was a methodical journey. Bill went directly to the end point, and God bless him for it.

"I'm betting that for most people, constructing your journey to happiness, just like constructing your journey to success, involves the kind of systematic approach I've learned over the years. Few are the people who have genius, charm, and luck to vault from a standing start to the sofa with a beautiful girl in their lap."

I will say that for 99 percent of the population, he is absolutely right, and certainly he was in my case until I began the road of seriously pursuing my goals at Slide 68.

I found a ton of happiness in the pursuit, but I wasn't totally happy simply because I was still gaining happiness in moments here and there. A trip to Miami one weekend or a trip to Las Vegas another was great, but I wanted to do it with more cash outlay than I had available. My guess is that in Ted's scenario, success came at him so fast that he didn't even have time to plan the money, which was the exact opposite of what I felt. Regardless, I think he is right in terms of pursuing happiness as the main priority and business success will follow.

When I'm designing my dream home or working toward the purchase of a personal helicopter, I'm just in another zone of happiness, and things tend to run a lot smoother when I've spent some time doing that. I'm sure that finally getting the floor plans for the Château, which provided a level of content, followed by not having to rush back to a job I didn't want to be a part of, is what allowed me to fully take advantage of my creative mind-set in order to pursue my goals.

Living a Dream Without Lots of Money

I read another story online (taken from *The Four Hour Work Week* by Tim Ferriss) that I think bears repeating that sheds a similar light on the concept of happiness. "An American businessman took a vacation to a small coastal Mexican village on doctor's orders. Unable to sleep after an urgent phone call from the office the first morning, he walked out to the pier to clear his head. A small boat with just one fisherman had docked, and inside the boat were several large yellowfin tuna. The American complimented the Mexican on the quality of his fish.

"How long did it take you to catch them?" the American asked.

"Only a little while," the Mexican replied in surprisingly good English.

"Why don't you stay out longer and catch more fish?" the American then asked.

"I have enough to support my family and give a few to friends," the Mexican said as he unloaded them into a basket.

"But . . . what do you do with the rest of your time?"

The Mexican looked up and smiled. "I sleep late, fish a little, play with my children, take a siesta with my wife Julia, and stroll into the village each evening, where I sip wine and play guitar with my amigos. I have a full and busy life, senor."

The American laughed and stood tall. "Sir, I'm a Harvard MBA and can help you. You should spend more time fishing, and with the proceeds, buy a bigger boat. In no time you could buy several boats with the increased haul. Eventually, you would have a fleet of fishing boats."

He continued, "Instead of selling your catch to a middleman, you would sell directly to the consumers, eventually opening your own cannery. You would control the product, processing, and distribution. You would need to leave this small coastal fishing village, of course, and move to Mexico City, then to Los Angeles, and eventually New York City, where you could run your expanding enterprise with proper management."

The Mexican fisherman asked, "But, senor, how long will all this take?"

To which the American replied, "Fifteen to twenty years, twenty-five tops."

"But what then, senor?"

The American laughed and said, "That's the best part. When the time is right, you would announce an IPO and sell your company stock to the public and become very rich. You would make millions."

"Millions, senor? Then what?"

"Then you would retire and move to a small coastal fishing village, where you would sleep late, fish a little, play with your kids, take a siesta with your wife, and stroll to the village in the evenings, where you could sip wine and play your guitar with your amigos."

For many reasons, the fisherman's current life is fine, and he wouldn't ask for anything more.

Settle on Not Settling

I'm not sure if the story is true or not. It is quite possible that it is. However, we're not sure where the fisherman was in life. For some people who have lived a healthy life over the years and have enjoyed family and friends, they may not ask for much. Perhaps they never had a Slide 68 moment. Some people can be happy their whole lives without money, although nobody I know ever professed to that. Your dream life may cost you a lot of money or it may not, and if it doesn't, that's par for the course. Just be sure you're being completely honest with yourself.

I would much rather see you be honest with yourself and figure out all the things you feel you want and desire to be happy and go after those things. Pursue them with passion and promote a healthy quest for them so that you may enjoy the ride along the way. I have found with many things that I have desired and obtained that it is so much more gratifying to track something down through a good plan of action and strategic direction gaining what you desire than to settle for something that you're just okay with. The Slide 68 mind-set says, "Settle on Not Settling!"

From "A" to CEO
to Power Broker to Billionaire:
The Enormous Power of
Informational Interviews

Corporate America has always seemed partial to a tall slim guy. Look at many of the executives in your own organization and tell me differently. I just don't think this is by chance. Some jobs simply require you to look the part. I have yet to see a rich and powerful president of anything who is five foot five and weighs three hundred pounds, not that he is any less of a person. I am six foot two and weigh 195 pounds, with an athletic build and extra-long arms. I am the not-so-classic 42 XL, meaning my suit size. Many tell me I not only look like many of the CEOs I aspired to be, but I also act the part.

Brent Stewart was the Citadel's most outstanding supporter, at least in my book. I don't know how he became such a huge fan of that school, but he was. He drove over a hundred miles a day one way from Columbia to run the career services department and teach us business management. He had a very particular style that was all his own. Every day he would come to class in what appeared to be a brand-new suit. His shirts were crisp and clean, with cuff links that complemented his outfit. His shoes were shined to inspection standards, and he would never allow a Bic pen to enter his pockets.

I talked to Mr. Stewart many times during my underclassman years on campus, but I had never taken a class with him until my senior year. I figured he would be just as sharp in the classroom as out of it, and that concerned me a bit because it probably meant a lot of work. It did. The first day of business management class, he walked in and said, "Gentlemen, if you're not here to give this class everything you've got and show the world that being from the Citadel illustrates that you've endured more and why you should have an edge, then I want you to leave. In fact, get out! As a matter of fact, get the hell out! Please. Please get the hell out, please!" We all had a slight giggle, but I knew he was serious. In fact, we all knew it, and that meant he had our attention from day one.

We studied all types of things that 1994 fall season. We talked about how the Japanese didn't talk much at the business table. We discussed what you should wear in the workplace, and even what types of cars executives were driving at the time. It was all meaningful conversation and I felt more knowledgeable than my counterparts at other neighboring institutions, but it would be what Mr. Stewart assigned us next that would begin to set me apart from the competition.

"Gentlemen," as he would often address us because of our all-male makeup at the time, "your assignment is to do a set of informational interviews." I didn't have much of an understanding of what that meant at the time, but I'd soon become very intimate with this process and absolutely nurture it for years. An informational interview was a door opener. In some cases, it was a path creator and a trailblazer. It was a way of getting in front of key people without them even seeing you coming.

---

*Slide 68 Mind-Set**

An informational interview is a tool that is a self-promoted, self-driven, and self-prescribed way to make contact with someone you need to meet in an industry you desire to gain insight into on a subject matter that you may never get simply through your own individual research. Because they are meetings that you have complete control over during the setup phase, it is encouraged that you aim as high up the ladder as possible. This can be the opportunity of a lifetime if used to its full potential.

"I don't care what field you are going into, even you folks with military contracts, but each of you will contact someone from the management level in a firm you'd like to work in." He instructed us to visit the library and look up various companies through the *Moody's Manual* and the *Standard and Poor's Opportunities Outlook Handbook*, as we didn't have the Internet at the time. That was okay by me because I felt like I was doing something important looking or something corporate. As we looked up the corporate information, it generally included a name of the president or CEO and a phone number as well as a headquarters address.

Our assignment was to contact the highest person up the management ladder we could find and cold-call them. We were to explain that we were cadets from the Citadel who were interested in working at their firm after college, but we were conducting interviews to better understand the needs of the company and what they desired in their new hires. Once they understood why we were calling, we were to set up a fifteen-minute interview to meet with them and discuss it. Because most of the class was juniors and seniors, we were to wear our Citadel blazers with tie and slacks, as opposed to the traditional military uniform, which is what the freshmen and sophomores would wear.

He said, "Write down a list of ten questions and print off two copies, one for you and one for the manager you are interviewing. Wear your blazers, ensure that your shoes are shined, and put the list of questions in a portfolio. If you don't have one, you can QM one at the Citadel gift shop." QM was our quartermaster account, which allowed us to essentially credit essential items that were needed for our day-to-day operational success. "Oh, and one last thing: take a professional-looking pen. No Bics!"

I conducted several interviews and spoke with J. R. Megginson, plant manager from Dupont, and Bill Shubert, a former CEO of Burlington Industries, two I targeted from the start. As I was instructed, I typed out the questions and met with the managers. I was quite surprised at how warmly I was received. I think some of it was because I was representing the Citadel, and some of it was because I demonstrated that I was a go-getter and not afraid of corporate management. I would later find that these guys absolutely frightened some employees.

The first interview I conducted was at 2:00 p.m. on a Saturday in Camden, South Carolina, at the home, no less, of Megginson, plant manager of Dupont's Camden location. I couldn't believe it. Mr. Megginson lived on a street I'd passed for years but never went down because no one I knew lived on that "side of the tracks" and my level of friends and associates thought it best that it stay that way. Regardless, there we were in the living room of his beautiful home having a three-hour-long conversation about life, the Citadel, Dupont, and his son, who called to chat for about twenty-five minutes during our interview. I didn't care because I still couldn't believe I was actually in a house that nice.

I dutifully asked the questions, and Mr. Megginson answered and I wrote until I could feel pains from my wrist to my knuckles; I didn't want to leave out one syllable. We had a great conversation that afternoon, and in spite of the torrential downpour outside, it might as well have been a sunny, breezy 85 degrees somewhere on the South Carolina coast. I eventually met several other key members of the Dupont staff thanks to Mr. Megginson.

My other interviews were not held in the interviewee's home, but they certainly held their own weight, especially the one with William D. Shubert. Mr. Shubert was the retired CEO of Burlington Industries out of North Carolina. He was a very pleasant and knowledgeable man. I decided to meet with him because he was a management consultant, which seemed to be a very intellectual role. I thought it was worth pursuing because it seemed that you would be able to use the skills and experience you gained over the years to share with various clients. It seemed to be a role that would allow you to be around quite a few businesses, run your own schedule, and perhaps do some travel to various cities. Because I perceived the role to be important, I just figured it paid well.

Mr. Shubert was receptive to my presence and allowed me to essentially lead the interview. Many of the questions I asked didn't really apply to him in his current consulting state, but he answered the other ones very well. We had a great chat that day, and one that I remembered for a long time; I could tell he was just as pleased to meet me as I was him. For the questions he couldn't answer, he referred me to another consultant, with whom I immediately followed up. I could never really tell what it was, but there was just a warm feeling from Mr. Shubert. Perhaps it was the view from the top. Here was a man who had risen through the ranks and I'm sure had experienced some adversity in his life, but today he was in sunny Charleston, South Carolina, working mainly when he wanted. I'm sure his financial situation was well taken care of. It was like I reminded him of a version of himself many years earlier, with passion and eagerness for success. Whatever it was, I could feel it, and it was a warm feeling.

I was glad to learn that I wasn't the only one feeling that the meeting was special, as Mr. Shubert made it known that we had met. Apparently, he was still active in VIP circles. He personally knew a man named Lieutenant General Claudius E. Watts, III, who just happened to be the Citadel's president. Bill Shubert called him Bud. How do I know this? Because he wrote General Watts a letter alerting him of what had transpired. The letter follows:

Advanced Management Concepts

Management Consulting

William D. Shubert

October 7, 1994

General Claudius E. Watts, III

THE CITADEL

Charleston, SC 29409

Dear Bud:

I'd like to tell you about a little incident that will surely bring a smile to your face.

Last week, I had a telephone call from a young man whose name is Von Mickle. He identified himself as a Citadel cadet and requested an appointment to talk to me about Management Consulting. He came to see me today and we had a delightful visit.

The purpose of this note is to let you know how beautifully he represented the Citadel. His appearance, his manner, his poise, his self assurance were very impressive. He was quite articulate, asked intelligent questions—in general, his deportment would have made you proud.

The encounter impressed me so much, I wanted to let you know about it.

Sincerely yours,

Bill

WDS/fy

Slide 68 Mind-Set

Informational interviews can render rewards that you never looked for and perks you never imagined. They can also illustrate just how small the environment of business is. Great business leaders know each other, especially the ones in the same town. Don't be surprised if the word gets around what you are looking to accomplish. At the same time, it also means do the best job you can, as you never know who may be just a conversation away.

I received more merits from that one letter that made its way to me through the chain of command than an Internet chain letter. The letter outweighed any of the good I'd done at that school for as long as I had been there.

I was absolutely hooked on these informational interviews and began to realize I had a means of attack that little of my competition knew about; only few who were in class with me even bothered to take it seriously. Mr. Stewart was pleased with my success, and I went on to earn an "A" on my project. He only asked that we complete three informational interviews, but I did several more.

After graduation, I began working as a consultant to British Telecom. I was actually employed by a company called Mindbank Consulting. Mindbank sent a few of us to British Telecom to help start a single help desk that would become the worldwide company's single point of access for troubleshooting. Our director, Robert Johnson—not the famed BET CEO, although I eventually did an informational interview with him too—was a British guy who was the brains behind the operation.

Bob wanted us to create the whole thing from scratch. We had nothing. No pens, pads, paper, computers, nothing. We didn't even have a place to sit, and that's where the magic happened. I was only there to work part-time in the evenings for a few hours, so the core staff that spent a full day there didn't pay me much attention. I was just the guy who could do the meaningless work as the sun started to go down.

After a few weeks passed, our project manager alerted me that we finally had some desk space. I was enthused and thought that was great. He said, "But there is a little situation here. We have to be extremely careful." He went on to tell me that the desk space was probably temporary and more importantly, it was the top floor of the building, directly across from the executive suite that housed Alfred T. Mockett. I still didn't see the big deal. He told me Mr. Mockett was the president and CEO of British Telecom worldwide. *Bingo!*

To me, that was great news and certainly no need to be fearful. At the Citadel, every elite team you tried out for meant you were an aspirant, so to me, I was a CEO aspirant. I figured if the "big man" was on this floor, then I'd eventually get an encounter with him. I knew it was only a matter of time before I'd get to shake his hand or have him acknowledge my presence in some way. That's when I thought back to the informational interviews. I figured there was no reason I couldn't continue to do this. I couldn't use the Citadel as an excuse, so I'd simply state exactly what I was there for, which was as a CEO aspirant.

Finding out Mockett's extension wasn't terribly difficult now that I had the directory, but I figured a cold call really wasn't necessary since we were on the same floor. I thought about whom I was contacting and decided his time was probably very limited. I decided to write a brief note and print it out so I could take it to his secretary, and so I did. I entered the executive suite through the kitchen door to keep my peers from intervening with my plans. I went directly to his secretary's desk and said, "If I have a question for Mr. Mockett, can I ask him?"

She looked surprised and said, "You do realize who he is, right?"

I said yes, and simultaneously we said, "The CEO of the entire company." I politely joined in and nodded while saying, "Yes, of British Telecom . . . worldwide. Yes, I know exactly who he is."

"I can't promise you he will answer your question, but if you perhaps write it on a piece of paper, I'll try and give it to him."

"Perfect," I said. "I'll be right back." I went back to my desk, got the paper, and promptly returned to give it to her.

She browsed it briefly and said, "I'll try and give it to him."

I thanked her for her time and walked away. About two weeks later, I received an e-mail from Mr. Mockett, and when I noticed it in my inbox, I was absolutely stunned. I didn't know if it was a note saying, "Don't ever do this again," or he was actually going to talk to me. Fortunately for me, it paid off. The note stated that he had a meeting with the CEO of Cisco on next Thursday, but the meeting was cancelled and he wanted to know if Thursday at 2:00 p.m. would work.

Are you kidding me? He could have said Sunday morning at 3:00 a.m., and I would have been right there. I even went out and bought a new suit just for the meeting. I was absolutely excited for this meeting. I decided not to tell too many of my coworkers because I realized that not everyone is particularly interested in seeing you succeed. As it turned out, I didn't have to tell anybody because the word got around.

A day before the meeting, Bob Johnson, whom I only occasionally saw, quietly made his way to my desk. In his intelligent-sounding British voice, he said, "I heard you got yourself a meeting with the big man."

I smiled and said, "You heard?" I'm not sure why it didn't dawn on me at the time that this would get back, but I was surprised nevertheless. I was also surprised because the "big man" actually wasn't big at all.

Johnson said, "I met Alfred more than once, but the rub is it was always in the john. In Amsterdam, London, Reston . . . It was always in the john. Have you ever seen him?"

"No," I said.

Bob raised his hand palm down to about chin level and said, "He's very short." I have to admit I was surprised, because I was still under the mind-set of the classic 42 long that most CEOs were supposed to be. Bob went on to tell me Mockett was clever. "You don't get that far without being clever." Bob told me to do my homework on him because he'd already done his homework on me, and wished me luck.

Thursday came, and I was patiently and eagerly awaiting twenty minutes early. Ira, the receptionist, and I got to know each other outside while I was awaiting Mr. Mockett's secretary. At 2:00 p.m. promptly, his secretary came out and got me, and for the first time I met Mr. Mockett. Just as I was told, he was a short man, with very bright blue eyes. In a very cheerful voice, he said, "Von! Welcome; come on in. You know we are business casual around here."

"Yes, sir, but this meeting is important to me." His office was huge and had the best Reston Town Center views I think I'd seen so far.

I thought for sure he would sit behind his desk and I'd sit on the other side, but we didn't. Instead, he pointed toward the yellow furniture in his sofa and lounge area. I sat on the sofa, which was on the far side of the office away from the door I entered, and he sat in the armchair opposite me. I watched his movements closely the next several seconds as I handed him the list of questions that I typed up just as Brent Stewart had told us. However, what he asked for next caught me completely off guard. "Do you have a resume?"

Drats! You've got to be kidding me! After all the business orientation I did to get my head around this moment, right when it comes, I didn't even bring my stinkin' resume! *Jesus, Mary, and Joseph*, I was thinking! I quickly said, "Yes, it is here somewhere," as I shuffled about the papers knowing full well it wasn't there. He said, "No bother," as he gave a glance to the three pages of typed, long-winded, intelligent-sounding questions, most of which came from colleagues who wanted me to ask what they were thinking. He politely threw them on the table.

So I quickly joined him and threw my copy down as well. He wanted to have a regular conversation, and I was game for that. I did, of course, bring the resume back to his secretary immediately following the meeting, however.

Slide 68 Mind-Set

There may be a lot going on in terms of excitement about who you are meeting or the logistics involved in making the meeting. None of this is an excuse for being unprepared. We can't think of everything all the time. That being said, ensure that you make a checklist of things that you may need and keep those items with you in a folder of reference or resource materials. If for some reason you do overlook an item, ensure that you follow up immediately with the item in question, even if the person you are interviewing is willing to overlook it.

I was beginning to realize that, in spite of the wits and smarts of most of these high-powered executives, they spend their days having the brightest folks kiss up to them and display all types of gee-golly presentations, and they probably don't get to see the real side of anyone except their vice staff if they have been around them long enough. I had nothing to lose at this point and found it pointless to try and impress a man who had made it all the way to the top. So we sat and enjoyed a nice conversation; we were only once interrupted by a phone call. I spent nearly an hour with Mr. Mockett that day.

The next week, I got a call completely out of the blue asking me when I wanted to start my new job. I was thinking, *is this some kind of a joke? What new job, and who is this?* I thought. The lady identified herself as a recruiter with British Telecom and said she was told to contact me regarding my new role. I thought to myself, *oh my God, what just happened? This is surely great news, but Bob is going to kill me.* After all, he had just annoyingly told our newly minted staff to stop bugging people about becoming full-time employees there. Now here I was, having not even bothered anyone about becoming a full-time employee, being positioned with a new role. I could only think of one person as the reason: Alfred T. Mockett.

I was given a role as a frame relay product manager for BT worldwide, which afforded me the opportunity to continue global travel and manage teams that were not within easy physical reach. I'm sure it was this exposure so early in my career that aided my global mind-set. I stayed in that role until the company experienced the turbulent waters of the telecom market and had to downside my department.

I used the knowledge I learned from the position in the telecom arena to start a series of workshops called "Imagine That!" In it I provided educational seminars on everything from transoceanic fiber optic cabling and geosynchronous orbits to jet propulsion and the thrust required to lift the space shuttle off the ground. I produced those seminars at schools, colleges, and large city centers for several years.

My meeting with Mr. Mockett occurred in 1998, but I did not stop using informational interviews. I found myself in a similar situation in the spring of 2006.

I had decided to pick up a book entitled *Never Eat Alone*. I generally do not read books that do not have some type of investment tips in them, but figured I needed to branch out a little more and so I did. Also, the title was catchy, as I knew I had to break my way of thinking of always trying to do it all myself. As I read the book, I thought it was good reading and an interesting story. Keith Ferrazi had gone to the Ivy Leagues and got an MBA. Like many MBA graduates, he found his way to the world of consulting. He made several key contacts along the way and worked his way up the ladder. He eventually went on to start Ferrazi Greenlight, which specialized in marketing. Ferrazi mentioned what many of us have known for years, which is who you know really does matter.

In his book, he mentioned some of the best connected people he knows or knows of. One was Vernon E. Jordan. For two pages he talked about who Jordan was and how well he was connected. I remembered Jordan from the Bill Clinton-Monica Lewinsky trial that was so famous during the Clinton administration. You would always see Jordan and Clinton together as Jordan advised Clinton but chose not to take a role in his administration. I also had the chance to hear Jordan speak at Howard University's Rankin Chapel under the leadership of Dean Bernard Richardson. Howard University is known to deliver the most powerful and motivating preachers each week to the student body and have the messages broadcast on 96.3 WHUR in Washington, DC. After I heard Mr. Jordan speak and heard so many good things about him from this book, I decided I wanted to meet him in hopes that he would share a story or two about investment returns he had witnessed.

Since I presided over a growing investment club, we were always seeking people who were eons above our status so it would give us something to shoot for. I was told by someone and never learned if it was true or not, although I certainly could believe it, that Mr. Jordan was paid ten million dollars a year just for his Rolodex, which is to say he is handsomely rewarded for his ability to pick up the phone and call people who make things happen. That was supposedly big business's way of showing their appreciation for his power-broker status. It really didn't matter to me what boards he sat on as I was more interested in the investment stories he'd come across. I was totally convinced that he could talk about people he saw or himself for that matter, who had invested some small or even large amount of money and experienced a return that was of monolithic proportions.

Dean Richardson had presented Jordan to the congregation as if he'd known him personally for years. More importantly, he struck me as an approachable man of God, and I was thinking perhaps he would be able to tell me if Mr. Jordan could be approached to entertain a request to meet him. I thought to myself that the dean, who was well respected by all guest speakers, might be a way to get me to meet Jordan, so I thought about it for a while one Sunday afternoon as I enjoyed another day of peace in a real estate market that was not generating any weekend traffic. That day was not so good for real estate sales, but it was great for me to do homework for my MBA and have peace and quiet.

Since it was Sunday afternoon, I figured that Dean Richardson would probably not be in his office that day, but perhaps I could call the Howard University Divinity School first thing Monday morning and find out what time he would be in. I figured that way I could just pop in on him and meet him face-to-face. I was confident he'd like my personality and see that I was sincere in trying to meet Jordan. But while I was hoping to meet him on Monday, a phone call to his office early that morning told me that Richardson wasn't in. I never followed up on the message other than hearing that Richardson's name was no longer listed as the dean. I even went to the school's website and found the face of someone else. I was a little disappointed. I thought maybe he had retired, but either way I was still disappointed because I was hoping to meet a good man. More thorough research later told me that the Howard University School of Divinity had many deans, and I needed to look for the dean of Andrew Rankin Memorial Chapel, not the School of Divinity. Good thing I didn't wait to talk to him to keep moving.

Since I was on the web, I decided to look up the law firm that Jordan worked for. Ferrazi had graciously put the firm's name in the book. I figured maybe I could "Google it," as Ferrazi says, and get a phone number. To my surprise, it wasn't some small local law firm; it was a major international powerhouse. They even had a website, which was candy for my eyes. As I quickly began to browse the website, I saw a company directory and figured what the heck, I'd see if I could find the name Vernon Jordan. And what do you know, it was right there. Not only did it list his name, but it also listed his phone number and e-mail address. I thought to myself, *this must be my lucky day.* So at 6:30 a.m., I decided to call Mr. Jordan and leave him a message. I knew it would have to be brief, as he must get a thousand messages a day since the number was listed as public information. I also decided to send him an e-mail to let him know what these investment forums were doing and why I wanted his insight.

As one might guess, he was not there at that hour, and that was precisely how I wanted it. That way, I could leave a message and say exactly what I wanted without any pressure to get off the phone. About 10:30, I decided to do a follow-up call to see if he received the message. I knew that chances of talking to him were slim and thought his assistant would answer. Sure enough, I ended up talking to Gayle Laughlin, Jordan's executive assistant. I said, "Good morning, ma'am, my name is Von Mickle, and I'm . . ."

She quickly interrupted and said, "You're Anthony!"

I paused briefly, feeling quite stately that this young lady knew who I was, and said, "Why, yes, I am."

She quickly deflated my thoughts of being well-known and asked, "Who are you?"

I said, "Actually I am nobody. I'm not here to sell anything or buy anything. I just want to talk to Mr. Jordan for five minutes to get his insight from the boards that he sits on at the power brokerages." I figured since he sat on these boards, then surely he must have witnessed some type of Wall Street transactions that the average guy wasn't privy to, and I only wanted the story to be able to tell at my forums.

We chatted for a bit about where I was from, where I worked, and small talk in general. We struck a chord because we were both from South Carolina. Something that was very interesting about the conversation was she continually asked me to spell things I was talking about, such as the city I was from, company name, and other small items. I was never quite sure, but it seemed as if she was writing these things down. After several minutes, she went on to say, "Well, if you want to meet Mr. Jordan—and it's Mr. Jordan, never Vernon—then you have to read his book."

I was actually beginning to research his book because I found the title *Vernon Can Read* a little weird. I told her I was planning to pick up the book today, and she quickly interjected, "You can't buy it!" I thought to myself, *why is that?* She went on to say, "However, I do happen to have a copy here at the office, and if you give me your address, I can send you a copy."

I quickly said, "Oh no. I'll come to your office and pick it up today!"

She said, "As long as you can get here before five thirty, you can get it."

That was music to my ears, and in a few hours, I was standing tall in the lobby of Akin Gump on New Hampshire Ave. She came down, and I was under the impression she was just going to give me the book and I'd be on my way. To my surprise, she asked, "Would you like to come up and see Mr. Jordan's office?"

I thought to myself, *this must be my lucky day.* "Of course," I obliged, and within minutes I was in his office. Sure enough there were the pictures of him and former presidents Clinton, Reagan, and Carter.

I ended up staying in the office for an hour talking delightfully with Mrs. Laughlin and talking about South Carolina and the Investment Forum. She told me that she would introduce me to Mr. Jordan as her "friend." Now you want to talk about completely being blown away, but that certainly did it. Twenty-four hours earlier, this was a thought in my mind, and here I was, not only thinking about Mr. Jordan but also sitting in his office talking with his secretary. I knew without doubt that this would be a monumental day in my career growth and development.

It would be three months before I would get the opportunity to meet Jordan in person. I received a call one Thursday afternoon from Mrs. Laughlin, who said, "I've been meaning to call you." She informed me that Mr. Jordan was having an event at his house the next Tuesday and Kweisi Mfume would be attending, and she wanted to know if I would like to come. "Ahh, no, I'm busy, but thanks for asking," is the way my former vice president of IT services Roger Lee jokingly put it as I retold the story. *What? Are you kidding me?* She could have said Sunday morning at 3:00 a.m. Mfume and Jordan at the same time!

I immediately asked her if I could bring my uncle John, whom I am very close with and look to for mentorship. She told me it was fine, but followed up with the fact that it was a fund-raiser for Mr. Mfume, who was running for US Senate representing Maryland. The day before the event, I asked her if I could include Doug McGee, who was a good friend of mine from work. She agreed, and Doug met John and me at Jordan's house.

We were the first guests to arrive and were eager to be in such good company. As we made our way through the immaculate abode filled with expensive décor, we were careful to not touch a thing. We were directed to the back courtyard and began to mingle among ourselves until others trickled in. Minutes later, the six-foot-five-inch dark-skinned man made his poised presence. He was so at ease. You could immediately tell that he had done this type of thing for years, and there really wasn't much you could do to impress him. Of course, none of that mattered to me because I wanted to talk to him. It wasn't long before the room was filled with guests of honor, from the president of Howard University to Representative Elijah Cummings to Mfume himself. I quickly decided that I would not mention the encounter I had at his office and would just try to blend in.

I did take the opportunity to speak with Mr. Jordan a few times but was cut short every time by bigwigs who thought they clearly had more important things to say. That was okay, though, because it only confirmed to me that I had made my way to the home of one of the most prominent men in Washington. I had one of the most fun-filled nights of any summer just seeing how the affluent class acted when given a few drinks. It was definitely my kind of crowd.

Each time I got the chance to talk to Vernon Jordan, the encounter was hastily interrupted by CEOs or politicians. You should have seen the way they clamored to get to him. They constantly said, "Excuse me just a second, young man, but, Mr. Jordan, bla-blaa-blaaaaa."

I let them have their fun because I knew this had to be the right place to be. By the end of the night, Mr. Jordan was able to identify me by face. My uncle couldn't stop talking to the VIPs when it was time to go. Jordan looked at me and said, "Can you get your uncle?" I was stunned thinking he remembered who we were. That was enough for me.

I got close to talking with Mr. Mfume, but didn't quite get the chance due to another eager man wanting to show an old picture of a ceremony where Mfume was being sworn in to Congress. I decided to let him go as I had just met a very dazzling young lady named Deborah Harrington. Deborah was apparently no stranger to this crowd, as she seemed very confident and was very astute at real estate investing. We chatted for twenty minutes or so before I realized that she had met most of these men and knew them well. She went on to invite me to a similar event at the Guptas' home in Potomac, Maryland, the following Friday, and that was where I would get my chance to meet Mr. Mfume.

Going to Potomac was very special to me because I spent hours driving through that community and gaining inspiration. Never had I seen such grand homes that I could drive past and get really good views of. I admired that community for years and was always curious as to how the owners could afford them. I just wanted to know if they were just as grand on the inside as they were on the outside. I certainly found that to be the case. I was also able to invite my uncle John and aunt Val, which was great because we all adored nice homes.

We arrived early, in fact so early that the Guptas thought we were the hired hands for the night. They quickly asked us if we could go to the basement and help move the tables and chairs around. I didn't mind and really didn't think much of it, but John reminded Mr. Gupta after a few moves that we were there as invited guests to contribute to the campaign, not as servers for the event. Soon, I got the chance to meet Mr. Mfume, and this time I didn't have as many interruptions.

He and I got the chance to talk for a good while just one on one. Shortly afterward, we were joined by another man I had heard of many times but never met named Jack Johnson. Johnson was the county executive of Prince George's County, Maryland. I had no clue exactly what that meant, but I would find out later that meant he was a very powerful man. I began to see that many of our local and national high-powered men acted very much like regular people. As I spoke to them, it reminded me of a brief encounter I had with former CIA director George Tenet. Tenet held one of our national security's most powerful positions, but I swear when I spoke with him, he was just the guy next door. I told him a few times, "For you to be such a high-ranking executive, you are quite the common man." In his thick Northern accent, he responded, "Hey, that's it, pal."

I also met Michael Siebel, Mfume's campaign finance manager. Michael was a young guy recently out of Yale, who had been given a very good opportunity early in life to see some very high places. John and I spoke at length with Mike, who knew pretty much everyone in the room. We talked about the forums, and Mike seemed to be interested. Since they were looking to raise money and my forum participants were good wage earners, Mike saw it as an opportunity for the campaign. I saw it as an opportunity to have the first VIP at my forum. I knew it would gain the attention of a lot of people who didn't really understand what I was up to and a lot of new faces would show up.

I was a bit concerned at first since it was designed as a fund-raiser because the folks who attended my forums were used to me hosting these events for free. Now they were being asked to pay $100 to $500. I knew some would see the value and gladly pay, while others would say no way. I was also completing construction of my first estate home. I knew this would be perfect because I figured if a VIP saw me living single in a an estate home at thirty-two years old, then he would figure I must be doing something right.

So I sent the note to the group as usual, and I received an overwhelming response. Over sixty-five people showed up at my door eager to see the house, attend the forum, and meet Mr. Mfume. The event was a blast. Mr. Mfume even gave me his cell phone number and asked me to keep in touch. Mrs. Laughlin and I would go on to become friends, with an occasional phone chat.

One of the most noteworthy points of interest from Mrs. Laughlin's conversation was that she told me Dwight Bush was Vernon Jordan's son-in-law. How about that for a circle of influence? Jokingly we say, "That's how the rich stay rich. Keep it in the family."

The Billionaire

Robert Johnson was the founder of BET, Black Entertainment Television. For years, I wondered how he amassed such a successful business and huge fortune. I spoke with a number of businessmen and women in the area who knew more about him than I did, trying to gain insight. I didn't get very far, but continued to watch him in admiration of his business savvy. I didn't have any plans to reach out to him until I heard that he was starting a hedge fund. At that point, I started to wonder how in the world a media mogul would know how to run a hedge fund; what would even make him want to take on such a venture?

You can think of a hedge fund kind of like a mutual fund. With mutual funds, the fund manager tends to buy assets and look for them to appreciate over time, which will provide a return to the fund. With hedge funds, the managers aren't restricted to assets that only appreciate or "go long." Instead, they can invest in assets that depreciate, or "go short." Money can be made both ways. In addition, hedge fund managers can invest in high-risk, high-reward assets that traditional mutual fund managers can't invest in.

When I saw Bob Johnson opening his own fund, I wanted to know how he did it. With the same logic as the CEO aspirant type goals, the only person to ask was Bob Johnson himself. Therefore, I put together a brief presentation and sent it to him. In the presentation, I briefly stated who I was, what I had done to date, and where I wanted to go, with a picture of my dream house toward the end. I dropped it off at his office on a Thursday just after lunch. His personal secretary called me back around three o'clock but didn't leave a message. I thought this was a very good sign. I called her back but got her voice mail.

I left the message and told her I'd wait by my phone for two hours if need be, and so I did. The only reason I had missed her call was due to the inability to take mobile phones in highly secured areas. That was clearly one drawback to highly cleared jobs in my book. Unfortunately, she did not call back while I sat eagerly waiting in the parking lot until just after five o'clock. I began to hope she wouldn't call back that afternoon at all after it got late in the workday. That way, I could just pop in on Friday and say I missed her call. This would allow me to get the opportunity to talk to her face-to-face, or so I hoped.

The next day I did return to Mr. Johnson's office, but unfortunately for me, his personal secretary did not come to work that day. No big deal for me; it just meant I would return on Monday. I think it is worth noting that his office and my home were almost fifty miles apart and I would have to pass my job by twenty miles. In addition, the Washington area is not traffic-friendly, so in order to make that happen, I would have to leave my house at the normal 4:30 a.m. time, but that would put me on his side of town hours before his office opened. In addition, I would have to find a place to hang out until the sun came up. Then I would miss my scheduled gym time just trying to make something happen. I say all that to say, don't assume things will be nice and convenient when you're trying to get somewhere.

When I arrived at his office Monday morning, she had not arrived, and I couldn't wait any longer. I went to work and hoped that she would call. She finally called me around noon that day and wasn't particularly friendly. She told me what I wanted was mentorship and Bob Johnson didn't mentor. She said he only takes business calls, and besides, she didn't understand the point of my presentation in the first place. When I asked her about the hedge fund, she told me to call the manager, gave me his number, and quickly hung up.

I took his number down and immediately called him, but he never returned the call. I wasn't particularly pleased to hear her response and was actually very disappointed in what she said. I thought, *how on earth could Bob Johnson not be willing to mentor knowing he didn't come from riches?* I didn't know where he came from, but considering the state of black America, I was pretty darn sure he came from humble beginnings. It annoyed me enough to think it out loud to a few of my colleagues. They agreed that this was totally not called for on his part if it were true.

Later that afternoon, I had to do some management training in the office and decided to call Charlotte, a beautiful young model I'd recently met. Charlotte was also an IT professional from South Carolina, who had migrated north for top billings and a bit of the good life. Charlotte was tough as nails and really had a keen ability of cutting right through BS and getting the real truth of the story.

I was never really sure how she could seemingly just look right through people and figure them out on a moment's notice, but she could. I called her because I wanted to get her opinion on what had transpired with the Johnson call. Incidentally, Charlotte had attended Rankin Chapel with me several times, and we just really enjoyed each other's company for motivation. Since she lived in Maryland, I asked her if she would have dinner with me at the Carolina Kitchen in Largo Town Center next to Magic Johnson's theaters. She politely agreed.

While on my way to meet Charlotte, I decided that at least the secretary took my call, and I'm sure a lot of people never even got that far. With that, I was hoping she'd gone for the day, as I decided to leave her a message to say thanks anyway. I called her office about seven o'clock, and to my surprise, she answered the phone. I immediately went into sincere "thanks anyway" mode to tell her I appreciated her time. She interrupted me and said she was going to try to get Mr. Johnson on the line for me. Stunned, I said, "Yes, ma'am." She asked if I had a list of questions prepared, and I assured her I did. She said, "Are you going to be at this number, as I can't guarantee you I can get you in?" I assured her I wasn't moving. She said, "Don't let the phone ring more than twice," and I said, "No problem."

Slide 68 Mind-Set

The time of day and even the day of the week can matter immensely when you are trying to contact someone. Most businesses are busiest on Monday mornings. Others are seasonally busy, while others may be dependent on a deal-by-deal basis. Knowing your audience and what they have going on can be the difference between you getting a foot in the door and totally being ignored. Ensure that you are up on the person or business's current events if at all possible to avoid bad timing.

I continued driving to the Largo Town Center. Charlotte and I met for dinner, so I explained to her what was going on. She was such a cheerleader, and that certainly made me feel good. I had Doug, who had lived in the area, join us. Right before Doug arrived, Johnson's secretary called back. I immediately answered as I headed for the door to avoid the noisy crowd. When I answered the phone, she said, "Anthony Mickle, I have Mr. Johnson on the line for you." I immediately went into thanking him for his time and went right to the point of my calling.

After I talked for just a brief minute, he said, "Well, first you have to continue to impress people like you did me."

I was thinking, *hold up, wait a minute. Did he just say impress people like you did me? You mean, I just impressed a billionaire? How could this be? Surely this guy has seen everything. What in the world could I have said or did that impressed him?* I'm not sure, but he kept talking. He went on to tell me he understood the presentation perfectly. My guess was his secretary didn't have the keen eye he had or his level of understanding, nor did she have to, I guess. He went on to explain to me the $500,000 he borrowed to start BET and the way he turned it into a three-billion-dollar enterprise before selling it. He said, "The numbers don't matter, but the point is you have to create value, much like you are doing now" (with the Investment Forum).

We chatted for a few more minutes, and I thanked him for his time and told him if there was anything I could do for him—I had no clue what that would be—to make it known and consider it done.

After the call, Charlotte, Doug, and I had a great dinner at the Carolina Kitchen and enjoyed the evening. It was at that moment Doug asked me a very profound question that I'd never thought anyone would ask. He said, "How much money do you want?"

I said, "Doug, I've already figured it out, my man. Forty million dollars."

He said, "Come on, V, you know that's not enough."

I said, "Doug, I'm telling you, bro, $40 million, and I'm good, man."

Charlotte didn't say anything. She just sat idly with that million-dollar smile and allowed us both to give our rationales. I had kind of thought about the number, but not as detailed as I would eventually get in the coming months. You have to remember that Doug was there with me at Jordan's house and was definitely starting to see my lifestyle change. We worked in the same office, but he could tell there was something more going on with me outside of work.

We continued on with our commotion for a spell, and I suppose were making a lot of noise. Before long, the waiter asked me who I was, and I wasn't quite sure how to respond. I really don't recall what I told him, but I knew things were starting to change for me. Doug left soon after, and Charlotte and I continued to enjoy the evening, exchanging opinions on what we thought created the change in Johnson's secretary. She lent a listening ear for the next several days and always had good insight to provide as feedback. It was one of those days you just never forget, and I was glad to have good people like Charlotte and Doug there to share it.

Slide 68 Mind-Set

Celebrate victories small and large with friends and family. It is good to share memories of success and failures on your way to the top. True friends will appreciate being a part of your story, and they may also add valuable insight and perspective on things you have yet to think about. It is also a way to stop and pause to give yourself a pat on the back every now and then. The reality is, if you don't do it, maybe nobody will. When you've done a good job, stop and celebrate it, no matter how big or small.

The next day, I drafted Johnson's secretary a thank-you note and I delivered some flowers, along with a $50 gift certificate at McCormick and Schmidt's next door. The note read as follows:

> I'd just like to say thank you for the $55,504.98 phone call yesterday. I calculated that a man who sits on three billion dollars and allows me to have six minutes and seventeen seconds of his time has essentially given me over $55,504.98. There is no doubt in either of our minds that if you had not entertained my phone call, then this would have never happened. From time to time, we can all use a vote of confidence by someone we admire, so it is crucial to me that I let you know how much I appreciate you taking a few minutes to talk with me.

> You could have deleted the voice mail, trashed the presentation, or just ignored me altogether, but you didn't. So I feel it is both necessary and proper to somehow show

my gratitude. I can't repay you $55,000 today, but perhaps you may need something from me. Maybe your car needs washing, grass needs cutting, or you want mentoring for a teen that you may know. Whatever the case may be, I hope this small token of my appreciation is well received, and again, thank you for being a vessel for this blessing to me. If nothing else, perhaps this will let you know that "country people 'preciate stuff.'"

God Bless,

AVM

One huge difference I did pick up on was the amount of pressure or stress in his secretary's voice between the first few calls and the last. In the first few, she seemed very hurried and impatient. On the last call, her voice was very calm and sweet. She reminded me of a sweet, older grandma talking to her grandkids. I guess with it being later in the day and most people having gone home, she didn't have to compete with a billionaire's busy 9:00 a.m. office. She was much more approachable. Regardless of what happened, divine intervention interceded and won that day.

I'm not sure if Bob Johnson mentors or not, but I did get some mentorship from him that day. After the flowers, I never heard from either one of them again. That wasn't the end of chatting with his empire, however. Once I realized that his doors could be opened, I realized he had a bank called Urban Trust, and that's what led me to Dwight Bush in the first place. Since then, Bush and I chat occasionally.

Throughout the years, I continued to use informational interviews, and they provided me with much benefit. Many of my forum attendees would try and stay abreast of who I was going to meet next and would always ask me to reexplain how I met so many powerful people. After a while, I decided I had enough of repeating myself and was going to do something about it. The last time I took such a stance, I ended up writing my first book. It was never something I set out to do, but I wanted people to have the information and was tired of answering the same questions. In the case of the book, a lot of people bought it, but I was sure they only read a small part of it. To explain the art of informational interviewing, I figured I'd do something a bit different. I didn't want to put it on audio, as there really wasn't any exciting way to explain it. I knew most people watched a lot of TV, so I figured with off-the-shelf technology, I could simply create my own DVD. That way, I could describe the entire process and show them precisely how it was done without ever having them read a single page.

I actually paused from writing this book one evening to create it. I thought that if I simply took two days or so off from writing the book, I could create a quick thirty-minute DVD and have it available for purchase on my website in no time. Boy, was I wrong big-time! Creating a concept for a DVD from scratch to record and sell on a website is a major, major task. That seemingly simple thirty-minute task took me months to complete. It was clearly one of the most daunting technical projects I ever took on, and I don't advise anyone to do it unless you are up for a serious technical challenge.

In fact, it is probably a lot cheaper to hire a camera crew and have them do it for you. At the time, I decided against that mode because I was losing too much money through a few bad real estate deals; I wasn't about to pay someone to do what I thought I could do. Let me give you a word to the wise: sometimes it is better to pay someone, to let them be the expert at what it is they do, than to try to come up to speed to compete with others who have years' more experience than you.

That's a lesson that never made much sense to me in my nine-to-five life. Many times, I would see companies pay top dollar for a smaller competitor. By doing this, they were buying companies that already had done all the legwork required to gain space in an area they were attempting to gain access to. It's far cheaper to buy a smaller company and gain access that way rather than try to learn everything yourself and compete with others who are already there. Those executives were a lot smarter than I was when it came to that, as I had to learn the hard way. However, without going through this process, I would have never totally learned the lesson. That's one of the good things about stepping out and trying things outside of work: you learn so much more about why things work successfully at work.

I decided to title the DVD *High Impact Presentation*, as I designed the presentations to have a high impact. I was creating presentations with the use of common desktop software to grab the attention of hard-to-reach executives and make them accessible. It was my technological advancement to cold calling, and it worked like a charm. I used it quite a bit to knock down the doors of powerful executives and politicians that I needed to speak with to provide me insight on things I needed to do for success. It all stemmed from that assignment at the Citadel and was a true testament to the teachings of Brent Stewart.

Slide 68 Mind-Set

As one can see, the art of perfecting an informational interview can pay off in ways that were never thought of. When making initial contact, it is important that you understand the environment and background of whom you are dealing with. To learn more about how to effectively conduct successful informational interviews of your own, go to my website at www.vonzforum.com to purchase my High Impact Presentation DVD.

As You Set Goals, Figure Out Who's Already Reached Them

When the student is ready, the teacher will come.

—Chinese Proverb

Let's say you've always had dreams of being a mechanical engineer, defense attorney, or NASCAR crew chief. You've watched them on television or read about them in the papers. From the outside looking in, the individual(s) you saw look like they're living the kind of life you'd like to live. How do you know for sure what their day is like?

Have you ever thought about what your dream day should look like? What time do you desire to get up or go to sleep? Would you like carrying a pager? These are all very real questions that many people tend not to think about until they are in the middle of these situations. If the lifestyle you desire and the job that you acquire don't match up, you may find yourself living a nightmare instead of a dream.

As I searched for people who were already living my dream, it led me to people who worked in investment banking and hotel owners and investors. I honestly have to admit that I'd worked briefly for a few hotels right out of college, but that was only until I could get a "real job." I never once considered owning a hotel. I'd read about the life of investment bankers in the gut-bustingly funny book *Monkey Business* and knew I didn't want to be a trader.

The concept of hotel ownership never fell in my lap. I built a multimillion-dollar portfolio of investments that consisted of stocks, mutual funds, and real estate—mostly real estate. In addition, many people were beginning to know my name due to several deals I was making. Fortunately, I caught the attention of some local prominent politicians and was invited to several events that helped me better formulate my next steps.

At that point, I realized something very important was happening, which was the opportunity to see people who were living my dream long before I committed time and energy to going down a path only to get disappointed much later. Don't think that can't happen to you. Unfortunately, I have seen people invest a lot of time and tuition into a field only to flush the results and start over years later.

Strongly consider finding people who are already doing what you think you want to do before you commit valuable resources to it. It's not a bad idea to find at least three people if possible, to get multiple views and see the goal from various angles.

J. W. Marriott Jr.—
The Hem of His Garment:
How I'd Like My Day to Look

A few minutes after the ribbon was cut to open the first Marriott hotel in January 1957, the phone rang in the freshly painted lobby. The caller asked young Bill Marriott if the Marriotts would like to buy the new forty-eight-room Disneyland Hotel in Anaheim, California. When consulted, Bill's dad replied, "Heavens, no! We probably won't be able to make this one work."

One day I received an e-mail from David Byrd, Deputy Chief Administrative Officer of the County Executive Prince George's County, Maryland, who kept me abreast of all the events and happenings around the county that I should be a part of. Today was the grand opening of a new 100 percent minority-owned Residence Inn by Marriott Hotel at the new National Harbor in Prince George's County. I didn't think much about a hotel grand opening before today, but I heard that County Executive Jack Johnson was going to be there so I knew this was good company to be a part of. I had time to get there early and simply blend in.

I was excited to come back to the National Harbor because Mr. Byrd made me aware of the magnitude of this project a few years earlier. I knew it was going to be something special. I even began researching the founder of the project, a developing mastermind named Milton Peterson. I didn't know who all would attend the event, but I knew Johnson's name always brought out the best and the brightest of the movers and shakers. When I arrived, I would not be disappointed.

Shortly after arriving, I met a gentleman doing an interview with James Wright, a staff reporter from the *AFRO-American*, a DC-based newspaper covering achievements of African Americans since 1892. He spoke with a lot of knowledge, so I figured he was someone important. He pointed out all types of lesser-known pieces of information in developer-speak and spoke with authority. I happened to be standing by witnessing all of this as his interview wrapped up.

I began having small talk with him and quickly found out that he was Andrew "Andy" Ingraham, CEO of NABHOOD, which was the National Association of Black Hotel Owners. He and I had a pleasant chat, and he encouraged me to look further into owning a hotel. As we talked, a colleague of his approached; I had observed him earlier as someone who "looked" important and actually turned out to be. His name was LeRoy Howard. Mr. Howard and his wife were owners of the TownePlace Suites by Marriott, located in Sterling, Virginia. I was quite familiar with the Sterling area, as I worked close by for many years. Mr. Howard and I had an extended conversation as he talked more in detail about what it took to own a hotel. It was nice that we could break up the business conversation with some boy talk, as he was also a car connoisseur, who had many older-model Chevrolets ranging from 1939 to 1970, which included one of my dad's favorites, the Chevelle.

He realized that I wasn't a hotel owner but gave me equal conversation nevertheless, pointing out the who's who of the hotel business, like the legendary J. W. Marriott himself. I had seen his face many times and had heard how tremendously wealthy he was, but had never seen him in person. Mr. Marriott was an older gentleman. He was soft-spoken, but he commanded the attention of everyone in there. As I watched him from up close and across the room, I believed even more in the American dream.

I thought, *here is a man who surely has decades more experience than I do, and his wealth puts him on the list of the richest people ever to do business.* Regardless of what it took for him to get there, I saw a human who put his pants on one leg at a time. He walked and talked just like me, which made me believe even more that my dreams are more than possible. They were miniscule to the accomplishments he achieved, which to me said my challenge, although not easy, is quite possible.

VIP Events

Mr. Marriott wasn't the only one there, however. The legendary creator of the National Harbor himself was there. Mr. Peterson graced the floor, and of all places, he stood in the back of the room. He never asked for any attention, and if you didn't know who to look for, you could have easily passed right by him. I thought to myself, *this is incredible that two of the wealthiest men in the Washington region are standing within a few feet of me.* I would not have even recognized Mr. Peterson if it hadn't been for Mr. Marriott's brief words acknowledging his presence.

Despite these gentle giants being here and so many people looking up to them, they did not represent the man of the hour, who was Kenneth Fearn, the guy who actually owned the hotel. Mr. Fearn was obviously a very astute businessman, as this was not his first hotel. He had several of them, and this was just one, although probably the best one, as was acknowledged by Mr. Marriott, but he had a string of them and was only sixty days away from closing the deal on another one.

I had the opportunity to meet him just briefly, but he talked to others in my vicinity many times. He never seemed to make a lot of noise, but you could easily tell he was the man of the hour, as he was constantly being congratulated. I saw no need to go overboard with an introduction, as I was sure he would take center stage after the program got started.

Before he even began talking, I could tell partially why he was successful, simply due to Kori Johnson, his general manager. I worked in a hotel many years earlier, and I knew the importance of having a good general manager. She had presence and personality. She interacted well with the audience, and you could still tell that she was aggressive and looking to make this new hotel a success. It seemed that just as much as she knew sales were important, she realized that a part of her job was knowing who was who in the room. This was a task she performed quite well, as she acknowledged all the movers and shakers by face, pointing them out with ease.

As I sat there among the crowd, not once did I feel out of place. I continued to experience a feeling of power and passion as I thought to myself, *I belong here! I'm supposed to be at these types of events. I belong in this environment of dignitaries and big businessmen. This is my crowd. The last place I'm supposed to be is sitting in an office trying to look interested while some guy is stuck on slide 68 with a bunch of meaningless gobbledygook!*

There was something about watching Mr. Fearn address the audience that made me feel that I belonged there. I had never thought of actually building a hotel, although I knew I wanted some part of commercial real estate, even if it was for nothing more than progress from my residential deals.

When the hotel owners all received their ceremonial scissors to cut the red ribbon, I watched very closely. I made the experience a part of me. With thumbs and index fingers spread wide while intertwined with the loops of the scissors' handles, they forced their fingers together, creating a swoosh of success, and the ribbon fell to the floor in many pieces. Their fingers held tight to the scissors like an eagle's talons hold tight to its prey. I knew that cut was a ceremonial success for them, but it was also a ceremonial step for me that proved even more that I belonged many places—but stuck behind a desk on someone's payroll wasn't one of them. Watching them hold tight to the scissors was a symbol of me holding tight to my dreams. I knew that watching the tycoons grace the stage was a rare opportunity, because tycoons, like eagles, don't flock. You find them one at a time, as is displayed so eloquently in the Successories' Essence of Leadership framed lithograph, a classic motivational piece in the Essence series from the company Successories.

Shortly afterward, the crowd applauded, and the people went many different directions across the floor. As Mr. Marriott passed me by going to shake the hands of familiar faces, I politely touched the hem of his garment. It's not that I thought of him in the ways of the old Baptist spiritual song that tells the story of a sick elderly woman who touched Jesus's garment believing it would make her whole, but it was very much a touch of respect that I wanted to confirm my success in networking with the affluent and get a step closer to my destiny.

I spent a few moments talking to reporter Wright as he wondered if I was a highly compensated athlete who was perhaps an angel investor. I hated to disappoint him on the athletic part, but I certainly was someone whether most people in the room knew me or not. I apologized for my hasty departure, but I informed him that I had to move on. It wasn't so much that I didn't want to talk to him, but ironically, I was having lunch with the Washington Wizards organization and I didn't want to be late.

Being someone who metaphorically seizes the day, I quickly scavenged a piece of the ceremonial ribbon to keep as a token of my future commercial success, and I headed for the door. As I departed, I respectfully asked the new hotel owner if I might keep the piece of red ribbon as a keepsake that I would eventually find my own way. He kindly gave me the nod of approval, and I departed for the Verizon Center, knowing that Mr. Fearn's success was the continuation of a great day for me.

A Slam Dunk

I only had a few minutes to get to the Verizon Center and was not exactly sure of the fastest streets to take, so I relied on my trusty GPS to navigate me to the city. Within a few moments, I arrived at my destination. I had been invited by Ashley Miller, who was a season ticket sales and marketing representative who had been contacting me over the last several weeks about purchasing season tickets. She sent me a last-minute e-mail about having lunch with the organization to discuss season passes and have a chance to meet with several of the Washington Bullets. I was excited about going to lunch with famed basketball stars and being a season ticket holder, but I was very annoyed at the fact that I would have to pay for parking. Growing up in a rural area, I was never one who accepted the price of city parking, which is probably why living in the city never appealed to me.

However, I knew it just came with the territory. Still, I had a bad taste of city parking in my mouth, as my business partner and I had recently visited New York on a business trip and we returned to our cars to have to surrender $70 to reclaim our keys. That just annoyed me for days. I figured that at least DC wasn't half that bad, and due to running late, I had to park underneath the Verizon Center.

When I pulled into the garage, the lot attendant asked what I was there for, and I told her I was having lunch with the team. She asked me to write my name on the ticket and pull forward and park to the left. I thought those were easy enough instructions to follow and took heed. As I drove through the gate, I thought *Wow! Look at these automobiles.* I mean, everything under the sun was in this gate, from sixty-two-inch Maybachs to the drop-top Phantom Rolls Royce. To me, it was just the law of attraction at work saying, "This is the crowd you belong with."

I was under the impression that the Maybach belonged to Wizard's famed superstar Gilbert Arenas, who had recently signed a $100+-million-dollar contract. Gil, as he's affectionately called by Washington fans, lives near and knows some friends of mine, who are luxury home builders, and they once pointed out his house to me as I was in the neighborhood visiting. I thought I saw a guy who looked just like him in a black Maybach, so when I saw the car, I thought perhaps it was his.

I went upstairs, and a look of thorough confusion awarded me a host to lead me to the luncheon, where others were already enjoying the festivities. I was given a tour of the area that I never had the privilege of seeing before, such as the posh Acela Club restaurant, with breathtaking views of the floor. Ms. Miller and I had a delightful conversation about the team's roster, the seats, and even the notorious, seemingly forbidden stories of Michael Jordan's time as a Wizard.

While touring the facility, I was interrupted by my cell phone, which had been ringing frequently as my investors needed understanding of what was going on in the current stock market. America had experienced the stock market's sixth-largest decline in history, and the presidential candidates and Wall Street tycoons struggled to find answers for the collapsing market. I fielded calls literally until midnight, explaining everything from hedge funds to derivatives trading.

This call would be delightfully different however. Several months earlier, Mr. Byrd sent out a notice that Prince George's County had an opening for a seat on one of its boards. Recognizing the opportunity, I quickly threw my name in the ring as an appointee. Today, I was receiving the call that one of the key members wanted to know more about me and needed me to fill out some information ASAP. I quickly concurred and got back to the tour of the facilities. I couldn't believe it. *Here I am closer to the stadium floor than I have ever gotten, and now I receive a call from the county executive's office to potentially sit on a board—and I just left a newly constructed hotel in the company of billionaires.* I had often told people my slogan was "From the mobile home to where moguls roam," and today was certainly a mogul-roaming day.

As the more formal part of the luncheon got underway, the host entertained the crowd and introduced the famed Bullets. We had the opportunity to enjoy an open forum with them and see their true personalities away from the court. To add a real slam dunk to the luncheon, several lucky people were randomly given the famous "Agent 0" Gilbert Arenas jersey. With the day going so well, I just knew my name had to be in the winner's circle, and after a few names were pulled, my name came up. I gladly received my jersey and felt a part of the Wizards' family. They capped the moment off by allowing me to stand between legendary stars Ledell Eackles and seven-foot-seven Gheorghe Muresan as I held the jersey to my chest like a newly drafted NBA rookie. The only thing missing was a team hat, which I replaced with my Versace shades.

I asked a few more questions of Ms. Miller, and before long was headed for the elevators to face my parking fee. As I backed my vehicle out of the gate,

I took another long glance at the luxury vehicles and slowly allowed a smile to come across my face; I knew one day those vehicles would be options, not dreams. When I went to the gate to face my parking fee, the attendant simply lifted the gate and waved me on through. As I approached the exit of the parking garage, a green light was awaiting me.

I entered the street and made my way to the interstate. The time was not even 2:00 p.m., and I'd had an action-packed day where my time away from home would allow me to miss the morning and afternoon rush hours. I knew I had time to stop by the bookstore and pick up multimillionaire Donahue Peebles's new book *The Peebles Path to Real Estate Wealth* to read tonight just in time for his celebrity book signing in Washington tomorrow. Now this was what my day was supposed to look like.

As I wrote this story, my son's mom phoned to tell me that my son had just run an eighty-yard touchdown, which was his long-awaited goal. It makes it that much harder when you're not enjoying what you do to the extent you used to or are not making the money you want to make from it. That just makes me work that much harder to create a life of freedom so that I don't have to live like this and can still enjoy a few of life's luxuries. His mom just called again. This time he ran another eighty-yard touchdown. I will award the Arenas jersey to him for a job well done. Today was almost perfect. Almost.

Quandarius Mickle pictured far right running an eighty-yard touchdown.

R. Donahue Peebles—
A Village to Raise a Child,
A Family to Raise a Titan

I met R. Donahue Peebles at the Camelot. The Prince George's County, Maryland, Economic Development office had invited him to be the guest speaker that morning for an awards banquet. I had just finished reading his first book, *The Peebles Principles*, two weeks prior. I had only heard his name twice before that. The first was on the Tom Joyner Morning Show, a radio show that targeted urban America. Tom Joyner was a pioneer who raised millions to keep minorities in college. He was called "The Fly Jock" because he flew daily between Dallas and Chicago as a DJ.

It was on his show one morning that they referred to Peebles as "the black Donald Trump." That arrested my attention. I was stunned, because as a young real estate investor, I often wondered about the pioneers in the African American community who were really successful. I had not heard of many, and for someone to call a man the likes of Donald Trump and I had never heard of him, I thought was awfully strange.

Peebles was on the show that morning promoting his first book. I immediately went online to try and find it, but a search for Peebles and real estate book didn't yield any results for whatever reason. I remember distinctively trying several times. For the life of me, I'm not sure why that was. I didn't give up, however. An investor colleague named Natasha Barrett revamped my curiosity when she told me he was featured in the business section of the *Washington Post* around that time. I bet that was the one day I didn't get a chance to read it. Still, months passed without me actually getting his book.

It wasn't until several months later that Jay and I had lunch at the Cheesecake Factory, and he asked me if I ever caught up to Peebles's book. Jay and I worked together on government contracts. We bonded after I began holding investment forums as we realized we shared a lot of the same goals. We frequently went to lunch, discussed books and bibliographies, and attended events and happenings around the city. and most importantly we realized there was more to life than the office we were in. I told him I didn't, but was going to jump back on the case. I finally found it on Amazon.com and read it cover to cover. Amazingly, preparation caught up to opportunity, and two weeks later, I was shaking Peebles's hand.

Slide 68 Mind-Set

Some define luck as preparation meeting opportunity. Whether that's the exact definition or not, being prepared in the face of opportunity can yield huge results. At the same time, if you are not prepared when opportunity comes, it's a blown chance, and you may never know where it could have taken you. The bottom line is to always be prepared.

When I met Peebles after his speech, the first thing I said to him was, "Nice going." He thanked me, and I followed up by asking him, "If I had a question about your book, could I get it to you?" In his deep voice, he replied, "Sure. Just send it to my office." I thought it was pointless to try and get a conversation with a man who had to autograph some books. I was obviously one of the few who thought that, as people were trying to stuff business cards and plans to him from every angle. I only needed an address so I could put my high-impact presentation to work.

I prepared a presentation that asked Peebles's permission to talk about him as a front-runner in the commercial real estate business in the book I was writing. I sent the presentation to his office and was contacted by Kendall Pryles, his public relations manager. Pryles forwarded the information to Peebles, and he gave me the thumbs-up. Shortly afterward, Pryles and I began working on that section of the book. After a lot of back-and-forth, we finally reached the agreed-upon words, and the manuscript was sent forward. When I received my first set of books, I ensured that Peebles was one of the first on the list of VIPs to receive a copy. I didn't see him again until that summer at the book signing of his second book.

As planned, I attended the signing of his newly released book, *The Peebles Path to Real Estate Wealth: How to Make Money in Any Market*. It was a really great party. I recognized several faces and made a number of new acquaintances; the most notable was Peebles's aunt, Mrs. Hilda McIntosh. I met her just briefly as she introduced her son Keith to an ambassador of Jamaica. As we stood in close proximity, she turned to me and said hello. We immediately agreed how great the event was and were both admirable of Peebles's success. Reluctantly, I also brought my own book; I thought it was a bit tacky to bring to his book signing, but I just wanted to ensure that he at least got a chance to see it since I mentioned his book on my list of recommended reading.

Boldly holding a copy of my book out as he turned to me, I said, "Thanks for allowing me to talk about you in my book, Mr. Peebles. Have you had a chance to see it?"

"You're welcome. My son is actually reading it now."

I also showed it to Mrs. McIntosh, and she was excited about it. Her face seemed to show a feeling of joy and excitement for both of us. I decided to give the copy to her just as a gift that she could share among her friends and family because of my admiration of her nephew. I could tell she really appreciated it, and she made it clear by giving me a warm and embracing hug.

Pulling Trump's Card

Shortly afterward, Peebles made his way to the podium. As he spoke, he reflected back on a conversation he and his wife had on the way back from California. He mentioned how she had given him the newspaper to read, and as he read an article, he burst out laughing. "What's so funny?" she said. "A book on how to get rich," he said. Peebles felt that it was easy for Trump to write a book on how to get rich when he was born with hundreds of millions of dollars.

I have to admit that I read two years earlier that Trump's father was worth four hundred million at the time he was born. At any rate, this incident was enough to convince Peebles that he should write a book, and as history shows, that's exactly what he did. I would guess he felt more credible and surely much more believable. I read Mr. Peebles's first book, and his growing up seemed about average. I never got the feeling he was short of anything major, but I certainly didn't get the feeling he was born into any type of wealth, such as Mr. Trump was.

As I listened to him, I knew he was talking about Donald Trump long before he ever mentioned his name. I don't necessarily have a problem with Trump being born with a lot of money and going on to become a billionaire, but I do see how it comes across as shocking when I tell people about his fortune at birth. He really makes it seem as if he has completely built his fortune on his own, only mentioning his father as a great role model and mentor. Regardless, I still give him credit for being a member of the coveted billionaires' list, as he could have totally blown it all. Still, I could see Peebles's point very clearly.

To my surprise, I would see Peebles again just a week later at a fund-raiser in his Washington home. I was delighted for the invite and familiar with the neighborhood, as my uncle and I had visited the home of Vernon E. Jordan some time earlier for a similar event. As we arrived at his home, we saw exactly what we expected, which was a community of wealth, affluence, and opulence. As I entered the house, outside of Peebles himself, there were no familiar faces.

That all changed once his aunt Hilda arrived. It was so great seeing her again, as she always has a look of warmth, sophistication, and loveliness. Immediately when I saw her, I had to reintroduce myself and introduce her to my uncle John. I told her how I wanted to mention both her and Donahue at the book signing as I wrote of such a great and inspiring day. She quickly one-upped me by inviting me and John to her home to talk more about the family so I could have a better perspective. I obliged, and a few days later, we sat down to discuss.

I only had intentions of writing maybe a line or two about his aunt, but after talking to her for just a few moments, I knew a line or two was not going to properly convey the message. If nothing more, there was the shocking coincidence that she was at the hotel grand opening that I attended that past Thursday. It wasn't twenty minutes after sitting down with this energetic power broker of an aunt that I saw why Peebles was worth half a billion dollars.

Early Exposure Is Priceless

She began telling me about all the success stories the family had, which spanned generation after generation. I was absolutely in awe as I heard of the entrepreneurial activity, the relentless pursuit of higher education, and the rich heritage of excellence that this family displayed. There were pictures with prominent people, including US presidents and prime ministers, news articles of countless success stories, and knowledge of higher issues that would have made me think this family was anything but black if I hadn't seen it firsthand. The more she talked, the more I thought about how I would tell the story to my friends about such a dynasty of a family.

Instantly, this had very little to do with Donahue, but substantially more to do with a legendary family that I had never heard of. For me, this was the actuality that a "*Cosby Show* family" really did exist. Many times over the years, I heard Bill Cosby get ridiculed about how the *Cosby Show* wasn't real. I never really viewed the show as real or fake, but instead as a great and funny television show that was admired across all races. Regardless, many African Americans viewed it as a fantasy. Obviously, this was not the case.

As I sat there taking this all in, I thought to myself that I might be tempted to laugh just as much at the thought of Mr. Peebles writing a book about success as he was comically relieved by the story of Donald Trump. I had no idea how much money Peebles was born with, but I was instantly certain the value his family had on his upbringing was priceless!

I believe he was richer by far than probably 99 percent of the US population from conception, just based on the magnitude of his family's core values. His success was founded on a great family upbringing, and that didn't happen overnight. Presidential hopeful Hillary Clinton said many times that it takes a village to raise a child. It had now become apparent that while it may take a village to raise a child, it takes a family to raise a titan.

Peebles was surely the biggest standout from a purely economic standpoint, but he was hardly alone. There were many people within the family who had substantial stories of their own. There was Mrs. Doris W. Carroll, Mrs. McIntosh's sister, who was the dean at Sojourner-Douglas College in Owings Mills, Maryland; and Mrs. Edith Tucci, who also has entrepreneurship interest with Prepaid Legal Services, is also a globe-trotter.

Mrs. Carroll was very sharp as well. As the campus director, she was a leader and go-getter who really made things happen. In addition to advanced education and working in a prestigious college of higher learning, she was a shrewd businesswoman. She simply knew what it takes to make business happen, and she could solicit business at will. I took the opportunity to do the book signing that she called about and was able to watch her in action at an awards banquet held by the college. She was the mistress of ceremonies and absolutely all over every detail. From logistics to speakers to food, she had it all covered.

Right on our entry into the event, she made sure that John and I were adequately introduced in the VIP suite. From the president of the college, Dr. Charles W. Simmons, and guest speaker Dr. Levi Watkins to distinguished state legislator Patricia C. Jessamy, we were placed right in the center of things.

Peebles's family sees the big picture. Simply put, they "get it." Their thoughts are always positive. John and I have talked quite candidly about families that we have witnessed, including our own, in regard to how they handle seeking careers and success. Many families can't even entertain the thought of one family member doing something remotely bigger than what everyone else is doing. They'd be called a dreamer or laughed at. There are no support people within the family who will cheer on anyone trying to excel. Since no one is willing to support that seeking individual, that probably means no one has come close to excelling. For many, that's really all it takes to kill the dream, as many a success story was born and buried right in the presence of those who are closest.

From what I have witnessed in Peebles's family, that simply isn't the case. I would think the thought of mediocrity or barely getting by would summon a royal tongue-lashing. Whether I'm right about mediocrity or not, from what I have observed, dynastic families don't just happen. Someone on the family tree decided on a life of excellence decades past, and essentially made all the other decision makers buy-in due to trust, respect, and admiration.

Somewhere along the line, it had to have been decided that the family was going to get in the business of ownership, whether it was land or business. The unpopular and relentless approach to getting everyone involved had to win out over the easy decision to go to work for somebody else. It is there that the seeds were planted for the generations to come. When the family's conversations include business, higher learning, and philanthropy and the unsuspecting children at play simply hear the noise in the background, it probably doesn't even seem to be a conversation worth listening to. I would have to imagine that at some point their ears tune in and their minds start to wander.

Mrs. McIntosh delighted in the family's success stories. She was so energetic about it. "Everyone's important! Everybody is important! Everyone is soo important!" She wasn't just talking about her family; she meant people in general. She didn't feel like just because you had a series of advanced degrees or exceptional wealth that you were any more than anyone else. However, she was going to be sure to push and expose her family to the limits. You instantly got the feeling that she wasn't going to settle for mediocrity, and why should she? There were so many examples of higher thinking and higher learning.

Her husband had passed, but he was an expert in three fields, including medicine and agriculture. She had entrepreneurial paths of her own as a prominent landowner in Jamaica, where she'd lived for more than two decades. With that, it was easy to see why she had the former prime minister of Jamaica's wife on speed dial. One minute I was hearing about the prime minister for the first time, and the next minute I was on the phone with his wife getting her address to send her my book. The next minute, I was taking down directions of an event to meet her within a few hours.

Mrs. McIntosh was a mover and a shaker. A lot of things would grow around her, but grass would never grow beneath her. She thought fast, she moved fast, and she acted on it. There would be no empty thoughts around her. Life was about execution, networking, and making things happen. It was almost exhausting just listening to her. Here I was thinking I was a person who not only grinded every day but lived my life in the grind, when Mrs. McIntosh, born in the 1930s, could run circles around me any ol' day of the week. Her energy and love of people reminded me a lot of my own grandmother, who could easily walk circles around the most active adults until she died after a few years of Alzheimer's.

As my uncle and I sat there, we gave each other brief looks of amazement at the stories she told. Her vision was superb. I began to wonder if it had something to do with her view from the twenty-third floor overlooking the city. She watched the construction, the people, and the growth of the block. She was informed, as she knew what was going out and what was coming in and who did what to whom. She was all over it!

Four months after I met Mrs. McIntosh, I felt almost like a distant cousin. I had met so many people in the Peebles's family that I surely would be no stranger at a family reunion. This was so unexpected but very welcome. In fact, Donahue himself had even accepted an invitation to be the guest speaker at the Citadel, an idea that Mrs. McIntosh had the day I visited her. I was excited about the speaking engagement, as I felt a feeling of importance that someone I knew who had a personal fortune of half a billion dollars was going to my undergraduate institution at my request. At the same time, I was planning my next investment forum, which centered on having the right mind-set in the midst of a recession to create wealth as the economy started to grow.

I wanted to discuss not only commercial real estate, but also the importance of knowing how the county government played a part in the decision-making process, which wasn't common knowledge. I also thought as a bit of real-life experience that it was important to ask Mrs. McIntosh if she cared to join the panel as an expert on what role a family has to take when one of its members shows potential and sets out for great success.

As I was formulating the panel list, Jay Pendarvis and I took a drive from Reston, Virginia, to Washington, DC, one day during lunch as I explained what I'd been up to the last few weeks. He was busily working on purchasing a million-dollar business for us to run, while I was nurturing relationships with the key players who had already achieved the success we were looking for. I told Jay I had met so many of Peebles's family members, and he just gave me his patented Jay laugh and headshake.

I went on to tell him that I thought it was extremely important to include a few of Peebles's aunts, as I thought they had an extremely large role in his success. For months I replayed the initial meeting at Mrs. McIntosh's house over and over in my head. I had met Donahue several times and knew nearly nothing about the minute details of his business dealings, but with all due respect on a purely academic level, I never thought he was any smarter than I was. In fact, I felt that it was his family that was the crown jewel that nurtured his growing up and gave him the mind-set to make it to levels nearly unattainable by most.

Don's an Outlier

As I explained this to Jay, he instantly let me know he felt the same way. He was in total agreement and excitedly responded, "Dog, you must have just read the book *Outliers*!"

"Huh?" I said.

"Ahhh, Dog, what you just described is *exactly* what this book *Outliers* talked about. I mean, you're right on point!"

At this point, my pen was already in hand as I was writing o-u-t-l-a-y-e-r-s. "Outlayers?"

"No, *Outliers*. It's the dude that wrote *Blink* and *The Tipping Point*."

"Ohhhh, right, right, yeah, I read that. I know that dude. Gladwell, yeah, Gladwell."

Jay went on to tell me about the studies of successful people based on their kid genius IQs. He mentioned how they took a host of kids who tested off the charts and divided them into three classes, A, B, and C. He then said the A's did exactly what they were expected to do by becoming doctors, engineers, scientists, business professionals, and so on. The B group did satisfactorily. The C group did miserably. Some of them never even made it out of high school. They became significantly less than their intellect could have made them. Some were jobless. The difference among the three classes was family backing. The A's were backed by people such as the Peebles family and went on to achieve the highest levels of success. The B's had families that were involved but maybe not as much as or as exposed as the A class. The C class had little to no family support, and unfortunately never made the most of their talent. I was floored as Jay explained this to me.

I was even more taken aback by the fact that my hypothesis, untold as it was at this point, had been tested and made theory and, thanks to Malcolm Gladwell, was being released to the masses in a book that was sure to become a best seller. I don't know whether Donahue Peebles was ever deemed a "Boy Wonder" or not, but I was absolutely sure that his family, especially Mrs. McIntosh, was an integral part of his success, and now experts had proven me correct.

Several years ago, I decided to create a tagline for my outgoing e-mails. It read, "From the mobile home to where moguls roam." I simply believed that to be my story, because I was raised in a mobile home. I can perhaps thank Mr. Peebles for the most notorious of invites as, just several days after leaving his Washington home, he invited me to his Florida mansion to meet President Clinton. So from the thought of what I believed my life should look like to the actuality was continuing to reign true more and more every day. I was receiving an invitation from a mogul to meet the former president of the United States. It was all happening, because that's the way I painted the picture to happen. Today is still a grind, but that doesn't mean I can't have a little fun along the way.

Anthony Von Mickle presenting Titan Raising awards to Edith Tucci (center) and Hilda McIntosh (right).

Peebles had been living a dream life for many years by the time I figured out who he was. Fortunately, I was able to meet him and help discover that the path I was taking was surely the one that I wanted.

Slide 68 Mind-Set

You have to have the courage to reach out to people who you feel are where you want to be. Don't feel discouraged if you don't know who they are immediately. That's where making your goals and dreams known to others helps you along the way. Peebles's aunt had no idea who I was, but my ability to engage in conversation without being afraid paid off handsomely.

Dwight Bush—Wall Street
Executive with Presidential Ties

Can one be happy in a nine to five job? Sure they can. Keep in mind that forty million dollars is all I was after. Forty million is what some of the new gilded age has in the garage. I know they are pocketing this and then some, because I sat in the office with Dwight Bush, then president and CEO of Urban Trust Bank as he told me how he entered a business deal with eleven million dollars and thirty months later he sold the business for fifty-two million.

That's *forty-one million dollars* in one fell swoop. So, are my goals too lofty? Well, I surely don't think so, especially if you believe you can achieve them. Besides, I bet he didn't have to front the entire eleven million in the first place.

Slide 68 Mind-Set

**"You earn within 20 percent of your closest associates,"
according to T. Harv Eker's *Secrets of the Millionaire
Mind*. On the path to success, one tends to perform along
the same ranks as those whom they most closely associate
with. That is hardly an accident. Great minds think alike,
and also one can learn valuable information from others
in an attempt to avoid mistakes, saving valuable time and
money.**

Bush was a private equity guru from Wall Street who had met billionaire Robert Johnson fifteen years earlier through some business dealings. Johnson tapped Bush to preside over a bank that he acquired. Bush might have not been on the billionaire list, but I assure you he was nothing to snicker at by a long shot. I'm not even sure why he ever agreed to be the CEO of a bank when he was contemplating buying a bank of his own. One thing is for sure: he wasn't just a CEO for anyone. Bush had just as much business and entrepreneurial savvy as Johnson and then some. He may have worked at the bank, but rest assured, he owned tens of millions of dollars of the bank's assets. He even made an unsuccessful bid to buy the Washington Nationals baseball club, but lost out to another group even though he bid more money. I'm not quite sure that it even makes sense to say the word unsuccessful anywhere in that concept.

I was made aware of Bush through Vernon Jordan's secretary, Gayle Laughlin. She told me that he was someone I should listen out for. I honestly had no plans of doing any research on him, but figured at some point we'd eventually cross paths. It wasn't long before that day came. As the Investment Forum was growing in popularity among investors, the real estate guys wanted me to lead them to a dedicated lender who understood their needs and was looking to develop a strong relationship. It was then that I reached out to Urban Trust and met Bush. I was quite surprised when I actually met him after the bio that I read on him.

I thought he would have a forceful no-nonsense hand that would make you ask very direct questions, and he'd give very direct answers and then say he'd have to go before too long. I mean, what else would I expect from a guy who orchestrated deals in the hundreds of millions of dollars and put together proposals to buy the Washington Nationals baseball franchise? Quite the opposite was true. He was actually a soft-spoken guy. He knew precisely what he was talking about and didn't spend any time backpedaling about what he thought he said. All of his words were very carefully thought out as if rehearsed and delivered very effectively. He was poised in all his actions and really quite smooth.

He made it all sound so easy as he began to explain the private equity transaction that grossed him yet another lottery-winning fortune. One of the other things I admired about Mr. Bush was he was never flashy and very even tempered. He didn't show a lot of emotion, which isn't to say he was emotionless by any means. He was always kind of one way. He certainly had the means to floss and gloss with the best of them, but he remained very businesslike each time I saw him. You could pass him on the streets of Washington and never ever think that this was a guy who not only knew the president of the United States but also vacationed with him. Now that's power and prestige in the most subtle of ways!

And do I dare even mention the story of billionaire Tim Blixseth, from one of my favorite books, entitled *Richistan,* by Robert Frank? Here is a guy near the bottom of the billionaire's list, but his lifestyle near the bottom of the list may as well be at the basement of heaven's door. He wakes up from day to day not exactly sure where he is or which of his yachts he's on, estates he's in, or Gulfstream jets he's flying. He owns land by the hundreds of thousands of acres. His personal property map probably looks like something I would view in my infantry days with grid coordinates.

The world is literally this guy's playground, and everything he touches seems to turn to gold. At one point, he was making a cool million dollars a month. He created a club, where he charged the economically elite a quarter of a million dollars just to have the privilege of saying, "I am welcome here," and that's before they sat down to actually do anything in the club. It's not like he actually needed a special resort club, because he has a nineteen-hole golf course in his backyard that's ranked as one of the top in the country.

So with Blixseth just one of many people who lives a lifestyle such as this, I needed reminders of why I was sitting in a meeting this late in the afternoon about something I couldn't really care less about even if the perception that I wanted to work here kept my lights from being turned off. Life is much too short for this.

Please Note: While many admire Blixseth's rags-to-riches lifestyle, the mega rich can find themselves in trouble. Unfortunately Tim and his wife Edra got into a nasty public divorce, and she ended up with the 30,000-square-foot mansion, but couldn't afford the 110 people it took to service the plush gardens, golf course, waterfalls, and so on. Now she was all out of cash and the mansion that once could have sold for $400 million at the height of the real estate boom went back to the market for $45 million at one point. She'd lost all the Rolls Royce and private jet privileges and was now broke after a billion-dollar lifestyle.

The point is that people can live magnificent and extraordinary lives and it's okay to strive to be like them, but you have to be able to service it and avoid the trappings of that lifestyle or you can end up in a far worse place. Yes, Gulfstream jets and yachts can all be repossessed. For more on the Blixseth story, you can read *The High-Beta Rich,* which was also written by Robert Frank.

Michael Roberts—
"Wynn"ing Big in Vegas

I went to a breakfast meeting sponsored by the WDECP (Washington DC Economic Partnership) office. They were giving a workshop that talked in detail about franchising. They put together a very diverse group of panelists to share their experience at varying angles of owning and operating franchises. The meeting was very informative and opened up an entirely new group of contacts for me. A couple great things happened during that meeting. One, they added me to their distribution list so I could stay abreast of things to come. The other was they told us about a premier plan competition, where the winner would receive $100,000 toward the enhancement of their business.

After my name was added to the list, I began receiving e-mails on all the great meetings throughout the city. I tried to take advantage whenever possible. One day in March, they sent out an e-mail on a subject of great interest to me. The message said that they were going to participate in the ICSC event in Las Vegas. For those unfamiliar with it, the ICSC (International Council of Shopping Centers) is the country's largest convention of retailers. They go to Las Vegas every third week in May to discuss the state of the retail shopping center market. Many deals are made, and virtually every major shopping center that is built or redeveloped in the world is discussed here at some point. The WDECP was a part of it for good reason, as they wanted to promote that DC was ripe and open for business.

They mentioned that their magazine would be on display for upward of 50,000 people who attended and they were selling ad space. Around this time, I watched the *Secret* DVD and was thinking back to the Chicken Soup for the Soul story. I was thinking I really needed to get my *Real Estate for Real People* book in a well-publicized targeted market space. Even though it wasn't on commercial real estate development, I figured it was closer than I had ever target-marketed anything before.

I was sure that I would get some mileage out of it. I called the office and was told that they only had a few spaces left and, more importantly, there wasn't a lot of time. At the same time, I was facing a big expense from another issue. I was torn for a bit thinking, *do I take care of this other expense later and just run the ad now?* I had to make a command decision. I decided to run the ad.

Slide 68 Mind-Set

Don't fall victim to paralysis by analysis. In order to gain some of your far-reaching goals, you will be faced with tough decisions. Sometimes they will be financial, and other times they will require other resources. In either case, you have to be prepared to make command decisions and deal with the consequences. List out the pros and cons of each, make a decision, and move forward.

As planned, the third Sunday in May, I headed to Vegas. I arrived there in 105-degree temperature. The next day I went to the conference without an agenda and thought how great it was to be on my own schedule. I went to the DC Economic Partnership booth and quickly found the ad that I had run. It was great seeing it in full color for the thousands of people to see, and it didn't take long to see an increase in my book sales.

I saw a familiar DC celebrity face, former Mayor Anthony Williams. He was busy networking with others, so I decided to spend a bit of time browsing the exhibit. As I glanced at one of the proposed developments, I looked to my right to find legendary business mogul Michael V. Roberts of St. Louis, Missouri. I recognized his face instantly from his picture on the website as the chairman of NABHOOD. He was just as dapper in person as he was in the picture, from his custom-tailored suit to his wavy hair that was silkier than the California waves at Redondo Beach.

From an ICSC standpoint, he was the first and then-only elected African American board of trustees member in the global organization's forty-nine-year history. His election was a monumental milestone because it not only gave new direction to the world's largest shopping center developers' organization, but also a voice to promote other African Americans to the board, which not coincidentally happened this very year. That speaks volumes because it not only allowed me to be a patron of the shopping centers that I frequented, but also and much more importantly, a potential owner. I have found through my travels that African Americans are not readily accepted in many circles.

126

Sometimes it just takes one organization to make the move to allow us an opportunity at higher levels to provide a level of comfort for others to do it. Mike's appointment was visible enough to make that kind of a difference.

Mike Roberts, an Industry Icon

I would do the readers of this book, especially those in the African American community who don't know, a huge disservice if I did not tell you a bit more about who Mike Roberts is. Mr. Roberts is the chairman of the Roberts Companies and an absolute legend in the greater St. Louis metropolitan area. He was born to a middle-class family, but through hard work and sheer dedication, has risen to the level of a dynamic and diversified business mogul. Roberts is one half of a dynamic duo, with his brother Steven serving as president and COO of the Roberts Companies. Both brothers are trained as lawyers professionally but have put their legal degrees to work to obtain a lot more than a career in law.

Mr. Roberts's investments are as diverse and impressive as he is. His real estate portfolio contains many noteworthy assets, with some of his most prized properties developed right in his hometown. One such property is the Roberts Orpheum theater, which provides a first-class theater and concert hall for those who want the finest in entertainment. The upcoming condo and hotel building dubbed the Roberts Tower combines luxury and smart living, is environmentally intelligent and designed to achieve LEED gold certification, and is constructed from responsible and attainable materials in the heart of the revitalized downtown St. Louis. I learned from the ICSC that the certifications are important, as they are leading the way in the future of development. I was surprised to find that Roberts owns property right in my native South Carolina backyard, with his Radisson hotel located in Spartanburg.

At a Marriott Diversity Ownership meeting, it was said that he was able to move aggressively on hotels due to his power and leverage in deal making and access to large amounts of cash. He owns a Comfort Inn in Tampa; the Roberts Mayfair Wyndham and an Indigo Hotel in St. Louis, Missouri; multiple Clarions in Jackson, Mississippi, Memphis, Tennessee, and Shreveport, Louisiana; and a Holiday Inn in Houston, as well as a Courtyard by Marriott in Dallas.

He also owns a host of elegant and environmentally friendly residential buildings. Not to be bound by coastal borders, his company owns the Roberts Isle, an upscale condo and apartment development that is the largest African-American-owned development in the Bahamas.

One of the many things I admire about him is his vision for the future and his ventures outside of hotel ownership, which help to provide platforms for other African Americans. I say this because of the footage that is aired by his broadcasting company. Again, right in my backyard, where I purchased some of my first properties in Columbia, South Carolina, is his television station, the CW47 network, which airs the best in television, with the multitalented Oscar-winning Jamie Foxx, Tyler Perry's hit series *House of Pain*, and the fabulously funny *Everybody Hates Chris*, in addition to the popular *Smallville* and *Supernatural*.

His Midwestern telecom company is doing great work and is a fierce competitor against some of the world's most-recognized names, such as AT&T, Sprint, and Verizon, which are all companies that had been around for many years, I'm sure, when he got in the business, but he never let them intimidate him. He has put a lot of his secrets to success in his critically acclaimed, best-selling book *Action Has No Season*, which has received praise from some of the industry's most elite power players. Mr. Roberts has received tons of awards, far too many to name, but you can find out more about him by visiting his website at http://www.roberts-companies.com.

As I went on about how much we praised his good works while I was at Marriott, he pulled me to the side and said, "Man, I'm a brother just like everybody else." We giggled, but then I told him what a coincidence. I mentioned that when I was at Vernon Jordan's house, he said the same thing. At that point, Roberts said, "Mohammad Ali says the same thing. He's a friend of mine." I was just done right there. I had never met anyone who knew the legendary prize fighter and historic icon personally, at least that I knew of.

We both acknowledged the disparity of wealth and resources among African Americans, but he told me, "Use it to your advantage." He suggested that I read his book, which I promptly ordered as he mentioned it would not only add to my ability to achieve wealth but also provide mentorship from someone who was more successful than I was. He was right.

He then asked me if I was going to be at the event that night. I was thinking, *what event?* He told me he was having an event at the Wynn hotel that night and the next night at six o'clock, and he asked me to come to both. His intentions were well received; his goal was to illustrate the importance of networking and engaging me in conversations that could lead to my next business deal.

Once again, I was blown away and thinking, *I can't believe what just happened.* Not only did I meet a legend, but most importantly, I met a man who in spite of all his accomplishments, did not feel so superior that he couldn't lend me some healthy and immediately usable advice. That goes such a long way when you're in a quest for something greater, as is so obvious and the very reason I'm writing this book. Also noteworthy, he gave me not only the name but also the directions and time of the event, which meant to me that he was serious about me coming.

That may sound meaningless, but when a lot of people have made it past the level of all their hearts' desires, they will tell you to go and figure it out for yourself. Here stood a man right in front of my face never even for a second suggesting anything of the sort. He was living proof that if all I wanted was the few things I jotted down as personal goals after I achieved more business success, I could do it and then some, because he was not only a living legend, but he was also paving the way.

My mind quickly thought back to my former office and how the most exciting thing anybody would be talking about right now was the rising costs of gas prices or perhaps that we were off for Memorial Day weekend. Yippeee, just break out the champagne, why don't we? Once again, I was clearly where I needed to be.

I hadn't visited the Wynn hotel before, but when I got inside, it was just as magnificent from the inside as it was from the outside. At this point, I was beginning to look at everything from a business standpoint. As I looked at the intricate details of the hotel, I was wondering how this all worked, and more specifically, how it all worked at a profit.

I wanted to know what a business plan must look like for a multibillion-dollar hotel operation. There must be tons of people on the payroll from all the services that are involved. There are groundskeepers, designers, auto dealers, restaurants, furniture, insurance, and so on. There must be layers upon layers of management. I wondered how someone kept tabs on it all. Each room had to command a certain price, each poker table needed to turn a certain profit, each flower had to stay below a certain cost, and on and on. In my simple life, everything was itemized, but owning a small city perhaps works differently.

It's not like Wynn reported to the hotel every day to sit behind a desk to ensure everyone was working. At the same time, apparently he knew what he was doing, because his Encore hotel was just as fabulous. In the meantime, I was there to have a good time just as much as I was to think strategically and make meaningful connections.

The event was politically star-studded. I didn't get a chance to talk to Mayor Williams earlier that day, but tonight would be different. In fact, not only was DC represented by former mayor Anthony Williams, but also by legendary former Mayor Marian Berry. Not to be outdone, another DC mayor, Adrian Fenty, was also there. I met him during the conference last year. The DC connection was just one of many, as there were several mayors in attendance, along with top brass from the ICSC. It was great company to be in, and I was very thankful that Mr. Roberts thought enough to invite me. I was able to share a few laughs with him on both nights.

Take Advantage of Downtime to Recharge Your Batteries

The next day of the conference, I decided to begin my day a bit late, as I had to send off some e-mails to people I met the previous day. In addition, I was relishing in the fact that I was in control of my entire schedule here. I technically didn't have to be anywhere at any time, and perhaps that was the very reason why I "worked" a thirteen-hour day. It never felt like work, and I even walked from the Hilton to the Wynn wearing a suit with new shoes on in 100-degree weather.

If I ever had to do that for an uninteresting nine-to-five job that was paying me, I would have surely complained to no end. It just goes to show that you will never work harder for someone else than you will for yourself.

I had come to realize that Las Vegas and Los Angeles were only a four-hour drive apart from each other, and I'd long thought about taking the Beverly Hills Tour of the Stars' Homes outing. I sent out a few e-mails and scheduled some meetings for later in the week and decided, Beverly Hills, here I come!

Visiting 90210

I headed to Hollywood Boulevard for a highly anticipated view of the stars' homes. That turned out to be worth every mile of the drive. The customized topless conversion van allowed the sun to warm our heads, while the cool breeze massaged our faces. I was able to get a few glimpses of the homes of some of the area's finest, such as Dr. Phil, Madonna, Snoop Dogg, Hugh Hefner's Playboy Mansion, Michael Jackson, Kenny "Babyface" Edmunds, and Paris Hilton.

I enjoyed the tour and then went to Rodeo Drive to take in the breathtaking views of the strip. The palm trees and the lovely sunny weather were almost enough to drop anchor and just live the rest of my life right there.

The beauty of an impromptu schedule is that every adventure is a new adventure and you have no expectations, so when something great happens, it's a real bonus. I am a fan of Italian luxury, not only for their cars but also their architecture and especially their clothes. As I window-shopped down Rodeo Drive, many of the clothing boutiques looked nothing more to me than a hideous way to get people to part from a lot of their money for something that could be mistaken as rags to do miscellaneous tasks around the yard.

I guess I'm just really hard on designers when they begin these highly trendy styles, because I'm generally not the least bit impressed. I always wondered who in the world wears these crazy-looking costumes at fashion shows.

The next store I came to was a real breathtaking event and validated the entire Rodeo Drive experience. As I was browsing through the windows of some of the stores you couldn't pay me to enter, I came across one that absolutely changed the game. A shirt and tie combination caught my eyes as it sat next to a very fine pair of Italian leather alligator loafers.

I walked in and was immediately greeted by a gentleman named Ray DeVeaux, and he gave me not only a lesson in the store I was standing in but he completely educated me on the history of fashion. The name of the store was Stefano Ricci, the critically acclaimed and world-famous fashion designer.

As I was given a personally guided tour of the store, he pointed out the breathtaking designs of everything from the woodwork on the walls to the ceilings to the floors. The wood actually reminded me of the wood you'd find in a luxury yacht. He told me it was actually the kind of wood you'd find in high-end luxury vehicles such as Rolls Royce or Bentley.

I thought it was interesting because I'd never seen a store with the entire wall made of such a high gloss, beautiful wood. He went on to tell me that the entire store was imported, which sort of helped me understand why I wouldn't normally see it.

He then asked where I was visiting from, and when I told him, he acted almost like a Google Earth search engine. He painted extremely vivid images of the streets and neighborhoods, although he hadn't been there in decades. He said he lived there some thirty years earlier. He told me the story of when he met Ralph Lauren long before the masses knew him when a young Lauren walked into a store in the Georgetown area of Washington DC in an attempt to sell a few neckties.

DeVeaux guided Lauren to a few other colleagues of his in the area, and a great connection was made. From there, I guess the rest is history. As he continued to educate me on the fashion industry, he pointed out the global way of thinking that the designer incorporated within his business, as no one within the store was American-born although Beverly Hills was clearly the symbol of the American dream.

DeVeaux was a highly educated, well-versed, and well-traveled man. He hailed from the high Parisian fashion streets of the Champs-Elysées. He'd successfully raised two daughters, who were doing quite well, and preparing for his retirement days, which were soon to come. His knowledge of various cultures and commanding speaking ability of multiple languages had provided well for him over the years.

He seemed to know just as much about the business as anyone and could compare and contrast many designers with infinite detail. Working in this business never seemed to be a regular nine-to-five job for him. Instead, it seemed as if the designer had chosen him for many reasons. He was very familiar with the Ricci way of thinking and could tell the story of his design method about as well as anybody.

One of the things that made this designer stand out was his ability to bring colors to life in the most unthinkable ways. He was fond of Africa, more specifically the nature of Africa. He had taken many safaris, and while many would simply take pictures and wait for the next Battle at Kruger, Ricci would capture the very essence of the color in the animals or the scenic background and create an ensemble that mimicked it in extraordinary detail. One way to look at it would be to look at some exotic colored fish in a tank and observe their unusual details.

He would take that same image and transform it into a shirt, tie, shoes, belt, and handkerchief combination that was unmatched by anyone. For those who can't quite grasp that and have any thoughts that it may look too gaudy or flamboyant, never fear, as I can assure you that if any man walked into the boardroom wearing a designer outfit from this guy, you'd immediately associate him with knowledge, prestige, and power. Perhaps it is with that reason that the store only caters to the clientele it does.

DeVeaux told me he has dressed presidents, heads of state, legislative officials, and top athletes. Their average client is among the top tenth of one percent of the food chain. It is with that type of finance that one can shell out as much as $4000 for a tie. For those of you who want to drop in and have the more nominal splurge, you can take advantage of a nice tie and handkerchief combination for under $400.

One thing I can assure you of is you won't walk into the office and find two or three others wearing the same thing. Even if the totally unexpected occurred and there was a slight hint of resemblance, the feel of the material wouldn't even come close. It wouldn't be the same league, the same ballpark, or even the same sport.

Slide 68 Mind-Set

It doesn't take a lot of effort to realize you are doing the right things while searching for your dream life. You have to understand that owning a business on perhaps one of the world's most-renowned streets doesn't happen for someone who kinda, sorta likes their work. Both Stefano Ricci and Ray DeVeaux were living dream lives. Their products and profits easily showed this. If I was waiting for my job to send me to Las Vegas with a few days of unaccounted-for downtime while looking to build a better business and a small fortune, I would still be waiting. I knew the power of taking control of my own life, and these meetings were confirmation that I was doing the right thing.

After an entertaining and inspiring day, it was time to make a return trip back to the liveliest strip in America. I wasn't quite sure how to get back to Interstate 15, so once again I allowed my trusty GPS to guide me back. I grew very annoyed at first, as it somehow got stuck on street mode and didn't get me to the Interstate as fast as I wanted. After I chilled out, I realized it gave me the opportunity to see even more suburbs of the great city.

I came across one place that I instantly loved called San Marino. The palm trees were groomed much like those in Bel-Air. The streets were manicured, and it just seemed like a place to call home. Everyone looked so relaxed and charmed. I was glad to discover a new place. I was in control of my entire day from the time I got up to the time I went to sleep. I was surely living out the lifestyle I'd been dreaming of and experiencing new things I never even thought of.

Platinum Handcuffs—
Hold Tight to Your Dreams
Regardless of the Circumstances

I was excited about the week of July 20 for a number of reasons. For one, I was just a few days shy of celebrating my thirty-sixth birthday, which I was certainly thankful for. I was also taking the week off from work to attend the NABHOOD conference in Miami, Florida. This would give me another few days to gain maximum exposure around the hotel industry's elite. Perhaps the most exciting reason was that I was going to be able to see live and in person the Chateau D'Von. I had spent the last several months revisiting John Henry's website and staking claim to what I was calling my dream house. John placed me in contact with Mike Brennon, the builder who eagerly wanted the chance to build it for me and with good reason, as the commercial real estate market was still feeling its woes. Mike agreed to meet with me to show me the house when I arrived in the Orlando area, as John was out of town that day.

I knew I was going to travel quite a few miles that week; starting it off with a trip to New York wasn't in the plans, but that didn't stop it from happening. My partner Michelle and I were made aware of a bus that departed Washington DC from the Chinatown area and took you to Manhattan and back for a measly $35. I couldn't believe it. I had driven to New York City many times, and the toll fees alone could cost more than that. I wasn't sure how they were pulling this off, but I certainly didn't ask any questions. We sat back and enjoyed the ride. Really the only thing I wanted was to experience the city like no other on foot. I wanted to take in the people and the skyscrapers and the noise and, most importantly, a gyro from off the street. Michelle was more interested in shopping, and I was her designated bag carrier for the day. I didn't mind because I was in the city just the way I liked it, which meant just a few hours and then I was going to leave that concrete jungle right where it was. Every time we went to New York City, we always said there was only one way we could live here and that would have to be in a high-rise of an exclusive residence overlooking the city with a million-dollar view. Otherwise, it just wasn't worth it. We'd share the same statement entering the city as we did leaving it. Left it we did later in the evening, and everything went fine, even including the fact that the driver got temporarily lost in Baltimore dropping a few people off.

By the time I returned home, it was past midnight, and I had to prepare for the drive to my parents' house in South Carolina. The seven-hour drive had gotten so easy to me that it was something I could do with little effort at this point. So with just about six hours' sleep, I hit the road with my son and nephew and headed south. We spent the night in Camden in preparation for a Tuesday departure en route to Orlando. I was grateful to God as my head hit the pillow that night on my mom's couch. I was thinking, *wow, tomorrow I get to see the pillar of my dreams live!* I couldn't help thinking how some people never knew what their dream house looked like, but I was certain of what I wanted after having built six houses in the past seven years.

We woke up early that morning and packed some leftover chicken that my mom had fried the night before. The beauty of the drive was that the distance was almost exactly what it took to get from my house to my mom's. Therefore I was only doing the same thing, except I was headed toward something much more exciting the farther south I got. Also, the "L" shape of the drive was almost identical. Leaving my house in Virginia, I drove for over three hundred miles on 95 South before getting on I-20 to head west to the Camden exit for just under an hour. The same thing was the case with Alamonte Springs, which was where I was headed. I came down I-95 South for over three hundred miles before turning west on I-4 and driving under an hour to Brennon's office.

En route, I received a call from one of my newly favorite people, Mrs. Edith Tucci. When I saw her name on the caller ID, I thought, *what a coincidence!* Here I was going to meet with the builder of my dream home, and after that I was going to run into Don Peebles at the Black Hotel Owner's Conference, when his aunt rang in. I shared this information with her as she kindly interrupted me to tell me that he wouldn't be there. She quickly followed with the sad news that his mom had passed, and she wanted to thank me for the special gifts that I had given her in her last days. I was just so pleased at the opportunity to share those few trinkets with Don's mom. Mrs. Tucci mentioned that the gifts brought her great joy. I was saddened to hear the news, but simultaneously pleased that I had the opportunity to be in the presence of someone who raised a titan who exceeded 99 percent of the population when it came to business success. I told Mrs. Tucci that we must do lunch soon, and she agreed.

We didn't spend a whole lot of time being saddened or grief-stricken, because Mrs. Peebles had been very weak when I saw her the first and only time; honestly, I never expected her to be around but a few more months if things didn't change. Unfortunately, I was right, but I knew she had lived a good life and fought the good fight and now was her resting time with Jesus. With that, we ended our conversation, and I said a little prayer for their family and knew that I had to keep on keeping on because hers was not a family of grievers.

I listened to my usual rap and R&B music, but because I had teenagers onboard, I knew it was important that I mix up what their young ears listened to. I was sure they wanted no part of a mixture, but it wasn't up to them. Therefore, I put them quickly to sleep by listening to my Chinese lessons in preparation for my trip to China. After getting tired of rehearsing simple phrases over and over and driving for nearly three hundred miles, I decided it was time to refuel and time for lunch. Besides, I wasn't sure how long I would be in Brennon's office, and I didn't want hunger to get in front of dream-home details. I pulled over about fifteen minutes shy of I-4 and took care of the gas and food issues. When we got back in the truck, I decided to resume taking advantage of the public library resources by listening to *Dreams of My Father*, both written and read by now president of the United States Barack Obama.

I knew the boys would be wide awake knowing we didn't have much farther, and with freshly full stomachs after finally awakening after hours of driving, their minds were ripe for listening. I popped in the second CD of the multidisc set, and we continued down I-95. It wasn't long before the boys' reaction to the CD was noticeably different this time, and mine as well. I could tell they had listened to a few lines before, but this time they were intently alert. It wasn't that the president's voice had changed much, but the complete shock to our system at what he was saying caused us all to giggle. I had to almost catch myself when I heard the president repeat a conversation he and a friend were having during his teenage years. I thought to myself, *did the president just say the words, "bitch nigga"?* Yep, that's what he said, because the boys were surely wide awake now, and if I had been sleeping, which thankfully I wasn't, I'd be fully erect as well.

It's not that he was a foul mouth, but he was just being real about a former conversation. At that moment, I was thinking I had even more respect for him than before, which was only barely possible. I'm like, *this guy was a regular kid, just like all the rest of us. He sampled a little beer, some weed, sex, and all the other things a young black teenager would be faced with, including some good ol' American racism.*

137

I guess listening to the president reminded me of quite a few things that were going on. I was always in a bit of awe and disbelief at how it seemed Obama never had a sense of urgency when it came to getting well up his career ladder to earn the top ends. It's not that everyone is supposed to be out chasing a dollar after law school, although that made perfect sense to me. The thing was, he went to Harvard Law School, and surely after putting all that effort into one of the most rigorous programs in the country, I would surely have been in the race for the dividends, but he chose a much less-traveled path. He didn't go out and make the big money; instead, he followed the path to the people. Still, with all that, he was now president of the United States, with a few million after his name, with unlimited ends surely to come after eight years in the White House. I respected his office so much that I even designed a room in my dream house that mimics his Oval Office.

All of these thoughts were running through my mind as I continued down I-95. As I rounded the corner getting on I-4 West for the final stretch, I decided to put on my good jewelry to complement my Bentley watch. I added my Citadel and North Central High alumni rings and completed my bling with a platinum bracelet that looked very similar to an individual handcuff. I bought it a few years ago because it looked different. People often said it looked like a handcuff, and they were quite right. I wasn't sure if my weight lifting was causing my wrist to get a little bigger, which maybe it was to some degree, but I felt recently it was getting a bit tighter. When I clamped it on rounding the exit ramp, it was noticeably tighter, but right at that moment I liked it. To me it was a symbol of handcuffing myself to my dreams. By making a straight line between me and my dream home, I felt I was taking an even bigger stake in my destiny and locking myself to my future. The real beauty was exposing the boys to the ability to dream and conduct business at a multimillion-dollar level without any intimidation, which was even more important toward my family legacy than any house I wanted to build.

I arrived at Brennon's office without his help thanks to the Internet and my GPS device. He knew exactly who I was, also thanks to the help of the web. When I arrived, he talked about a real love-hate, mostly hate, relationship with the Internet because the advertisement was sending him a lot of bogus inquiries on fine-home building. The web really puts the world at your fingertips, and that means people's time, even if you are serious. I think he thought differently of me because he could trace my progress. By having a book and a few articles linking me to some previously successful things, not to mention the facts that I had already constructed a forty-page report detailing what I wanted and a biography of me on my website, he knew I wasn't some bozo wasting time. Besides, traveling eight hundred miles is just not something you do when you want to waste someone else's time.

Mike and I had a delightful conversation about the home and the construction of it for nearly three hours before I began to wonder if he was ever going to show it to me. When it was time to go see it, he actually rode in the truck with me. As he guided me with a series of right and left turns, I was getting more and more eager. I knew the experience of following directions and looking for a grand estate. As the roads and traffic volume get smaller, you know you are getting closer, and after a while you can trash both the directions and curiosity because the house will eventually jump out at you. The Ravelais, which I renamed, modified the design, and placed under the new name Château D'Von, did not disappoint. He gave me my last set of instructions by saying, "Turn right up here, and the house will be right there."

I put on my signal, and my pupils probably extended another circular inch. I turned right, and it was paradise found. I took my foot off the gas, and the heavy F-150 cruised to a slow creep, as if a Crenshaw Drive-by. *Oh my God, look at that*, I thought. It was the most breathtaking home I had seen in a long, long time. It was just as magnificent as it was in the pictures. As much as I totally appreciated the appearance and what was done, I confidently and almost immediately felt that mine would one-up this one strictly from the way I designed the entry gates and would have it set farther back from the road. I didn't even feel cocky or uptight about it. As much as I appreciated what was in front of me, I felt just as strongly about my own vision. I didn't waste a lot time saying I'd change this or that; I simply took in the beauty and thought that my first priority was to have a picture taken of me in front of it looking off to the distance, with the beast of mansion in the backdrop. I gave my son the camera and told him not to be shy about pressing the shutter button.

We were only able to get a few shots in and weren't even able to go inside, as a new family had been occupying the residence for just under a year. He had called them and alerted them of my coming, but he said they were never good at making prompt return calls. So unfortunately, I never got to see one of the most important aspects of the house, which was the rear. I simply dealt the views I was given and figured that was okay because, with a few hours left at being thirty-five, I had locked in a French theme with destiny, and that was enough for now. I knew once I built my own rendition, I could take all the pictures I wanted and would probably be bombarded by others who wanted to do the same thing.

After an eight-hundred-mile journey, this leg of my trip had just received high honors. At that point, it was time to return Brennon to his office and enjoy a little R&R on Orlando's International Boulevard before returning to the swank Embassy Suites. In spite of losing another important person in what was seeming like a celebrity-death season, in the words of Ice Cube : "Today was a good day."

Yeah, Well, So Much for a Continued Stroke of Luck

When I woke up on the actual day of my birthday, I was still on a high from ending a great day the day before. We had left with thoughts of a recessionary International Boulevard in Orlando, but in spite of the loosely visited streets, the sight was still very welcoming. I also took one more trip past my dream home to end that evening with a vivid, albeit dark, image of Chateau D'Von.

I was awakened that morning by a surprise phone call from my dad wishing me happy birthday. That was cool because he was never much for words. I saved the message and went back to dreamland. Once again, I was focused on the entry foyer, the backyard, the dining room, and so on. I was painting a very vivid image once again of the place I wanted to one day call not only a masterpiece but also home. Since it was just a few miles from the hotel I was staying in, I decided just one last time to make another drive-by, as I knew once I left the area, I probably wouldn't return for some time.

I returned to the room a short while later to awaken the boys for breakfast. Before long, we were on the road en route to the last few hundred miles to Miami. My truck had been sputtering a bit lately while driving in the city, but on the open road, which largely comprised our trip, it was just fine. We drove from Orlando to Miami almost uneventfully—almost—and then life decided to throw me a birthday curveball.

As I entered the first few miles of Miami, the truck made a weird noise that made it seem as if I had a flat tire. I pulled to the right shoulder and got out to check the tires. Fortunately, the tire wasn't flat, but unfortunately, there was smoke coming from the wheel well of the passenger-side front tire. I got back in the truck, started the engine, and the tires began to squeal as if they were grinding in a metal-to-metal fashion. I was growing very concerned at the noise, but fortunately, I was near an exit. I pulled off the exit ramp and made a very slow creep to the airport Courtyard by Marriott. I was thinking what a relief that I was at a Marriott, even though it wasn't the one I was supposed to be at.

As I got out of the truck, I noticed that I had a voice mail, but I had never heard the phone ring. Once I checked into the room, I checked the message to find out the unfortunate news that the extra income that I was expecting would not come to avail. Here was a contract I had been working on getting for months, and once I was approved and set to go, I was eagerly awaiting a start date. Right when my vehicle broke down and I arrived safely at the hotel, the extra set of bad news just wasn't what I expected.

Once inside, I called to cancel my Doral Resort reservations. They obliged my request. Also to my favor, a Metro system was just across the street. I was hoping some type of transit system could keep me mobile if I needed it, but I was really more interested in a rental car. The concierge service agreed to take me across the street to the airport to try and get a rental, but warned me that the last two weeks had been completely sold out. Today would prove to be like the last two weeks. With the exception of a Corvette, all the rental agencies were completely sold out. I returned to the hotel, changed clothes, and headed to the Metro.

Just crossing the street in Miami while wearing a suit proved to be more than my skin could handle, and within minutes, my forehead was covered in sweat. I looked so sophisticatedly out of place. I asked the various transit workers for directions to the resort, and I must say they responded very well. The Miami-Dade public transportation system workers were absolutely excellent. I had been away from southern hospitality for a while, and to watch every one of these folks get up out of their seats to help me like they really gave a darn was very welcoming. So to whoever is setting the standard at the train and bus terminals, please keep it going, because it is very appreciated and not an easy find.

The changing trains and buses eventually placed me right in front of the resort in about an hour's time. Quite a few people were there at this point, but I blended right in. Aside from the fact that I told Marriott's Ray Bennett, who so favored Chris Tucker, that it was a hectic journey getting there, no one was ever the wiser. I congratulated Ray as he received an award for the longest drive on the golf course, smacking the cover off some Titleist at a Tiger Woods distance of over 300 yards!

Of course, I had to see Mike Roberts again. When I walked in the room, he was charismatically showing his leadership by pointing out to everyone why we were there. He and Andy Ingraham set the stage for everyone by not only pointing out the pioneers in the room and providing rewards to some, but also pointing out the future generation by acknowledging the students and those who had provided them scholarships.

I stayed and enjoyed the introductory session and a bit of the evening cocktails while shaking hands with familiar faces. After about two hours, I decided I'd better get back to the room. Unfortunately, getting back proved to take substantially longer, as a 7:00 p.m. departure from the event placed me back at the hotel exactly three hours later. I wasn't sure what caused the train to take so much longer getting me back, but I was just glad to know that it wasn't raining, it wasn't blistering hot, and things could be substantially worse. Because the hotel didn't have any food at that hour, I had to resort to local restaurants to get something to eat. Normally, I wouldn't have any problem with that, except that this time there wasn't anything close by. The closest hot meal was a McDonald's drive-through that was two miles away. Since I desired hot food, walking the distance it was. Fortunately, the McDonald's drive-through allowed me to walk through as the inside was closed at that hour.

At 11:00 p.m., standing in the hot exhaust of the car in front of me wasn't a lot of fun, as gas fumes on an empty stomach don't match. After leaving the drive-through with food in hand, I had no table to enjoy dinner. Therefore, I sat with my back to the side of the building and watched the cars drive by. Some were barely drivable, but that didn't matter as at least they were mobile. No one knew that I lived in a million-dollar house, had a substantial education, or enjoyed lunch with the world's elite. At that moment, I was just another guy on the corner having dinner among the elements. In what started off to be a wonderful birthday celebration, things had suddenly turned for the worse.

It just so happened that Solodad O'Brien was airing *Black in America 2* that evening, and the long train ride back to my hotel surely meant I was going to miss most of it. One thing was for sure, and that was if she wanted to video what being black in America was all about, I could give her all she wanted. Once again, I clamped my bracelet tighter to my wrist and promised myself that I wouldn't let up. In fact, I kept thinking back to Chris Gardner's *Pursuit of Happyness* story and wondering if all this was really necessary to achieve a high level of success. Whether I thought it was or not, I was getting my battle scars, but I felt that all this aggravation gave me a sense of entitlement to all the things I was working for. At this point, going back to a life of mediocrity wasn't going to happen; it was simply the standard that I had set and accepted. Watching Mike Roberts up on that stage tonight and knowing there were at least five other guys like him, who were not only financially set for life but also thoroughly enjoyed what they were doing, made the entire arduous task of getting there worthwhile. Roberts probably bought his version of Chateau D'Von years ago and was on to bigger and better things. As far as I was concerned this day, he was my version of the American dream, but he just so happened to be black. Another day in the grind . . . the saga continued.

Well, I'll Be Damned!

We had the distinct pleasure of being addressed by billionaire businesswoman Mrs. Sheila Johnson during lunch at the conference. I'd looked up to her for years for many reasons. She was not only breaking down the doors of business circles surrounded by ironclad gates, but she was also tearing those MF's off the hinges is quite frankly how I felt about it. She not only owned hotels, but she was playing with the billionaire boys' club by owning not one, not two, but three professional sports teams in three different leagues in Washington. I don't even know of any men doing that. I would say that the thing I admired most about her was, in spite of all the business success she's had over several decades, when she took the microphone, you would have thought she was just your middle-class, favorite aunt just hanging out at a family reunion. She was every bit of the title that I had given myself over the years, which was "extraordinarily extraordinary."

Of all the places I looked for motivation, there were two places in particular I revisited over and over. One was Potomac, Maryland, as this affluent community contained homes of magnificent architecture and was clearly the source of my dreams for creating the Chateau D'Von. It was there that I realized that my house shouldn't be just a home, but a masterpiece or a work of art. The other place was Middleburg, Virginia, which is located about an hour west of Washington DC and only thirty minutes from my current estate. Middleburg was a much older, affluent town that reminded me of a quaint escape from the hustle and bustle of the metro.

I'd heard for some time that the Johnsons had purchased a farm in Middleburg, and I was always a bit curious as to why. One day, I finally took the drive and realized exactly why someone of affluence would travel there—peace! The rolling hills were so serene and beautiful. With Dulles Airport being just a thirty-minute-or-so car ride away, even out-of-towners could fly in and enjoy for a bit. I suppose it is with those concepts and perhaps others unknown to me that Mrs. Johnson would begin to erect what is surely destined to be one of the most sought-after spa retreats on the East Coast. I've visited the site of her work so many times at varying hours of the day and night. Often, I would drive members of my Investment Forum out there to show them what she is doing. It is so motivating to me to see a black woman come into a predominately white southern town and erect a building that will dominate the landscape. I'm absolutely convinced that she's met more opposition than the general public will ever know, and billionaire or not, she's got her work cut out for her.

As Mrs. Johnson addressed the crowd, she warmed us up with a joke about a young boy who was pulling his wagon along and the wheel kept coming off. Each time it came off, he cried, "I'll be damned," Mrs. Johnson explained as the crowd eagerly listened in. She went on to say that the young boy was met by a preacher, who told him he should choose more godlike words, and so he did. The next time the wheel came off, he uttered some godlike words, and magically before the little boy's eyes, it all pieced itself back together, to which the preacher then cried, "Well, I'll be damned." It was humorous for the moments we were there, but when I returned to my hotel room, I found a few reasons to shout, "I'll be damned" myself, as the contract that I was awarded and then had snatched from me revealed some shocking details.

The things I do outside of my nine-to-five reek of affluence, and I like that because that is the direction I'm headed without question. Those ventures should not be counted against me. Fortunately, I have the mind-set and skill set to build and maintain my own website. Because of this, I can see each time someone visits my domain. Depending on who it is, I can see their domain name. It so happens that just before I got the call to tell me they were giving the contract to someone else, I saw that the purse-string holders had been on my site for sixteen minutes and forty seconds. I knew they had visited many times before, due to my traffic reports, but to see them on there just before they delivered the blow told me that someone took a look at my website and decided perhaps I didn't need the money, which was the furthest thing from the truth. Regardless, they yanked the contract without explanation. Instantly, I could see what had worked for me in terms of being accepted into the Private Equity and Venture Capital Program with Harvard Business School, which was sending me to China, had immediately worked against me for a contract that I really was looking forward to. The only thing I could think was, "I'll be damned!"

Alfred Lau—
The Voice of Education,
Experience, and Wealth

I wasn't really sure what to expect the first day of my commercial real estate investment class. I decided to take it after I lost my job in 2010. I was praying the night before that I'd be exposed to something good, but still had no real inkling of what to expect other than more technical details toward commercial real estate and important deal evaluation. When I arrived, I wasn't particularly thrilled about having to pay $10 to park in the city area, as in the suburbs, parking is free and open. It doesn't matter how much money I have in my pocket or how many times I go into the city, paying for parking just annoys me if it is a dime over three or four dollars. As usual, I arrived early so I could settle in and observe the environment, while I took advantage of prime real estate to gain a seat at the front of the class. I would quickly learn that the class was going to be challenging yet fulfilling as I browsed the outline for the course.

The professor's name was Alfred Lau, and he held the Certified Commercial Investment Manager (CCIM) designation for many years. A CCIM is a recognized expert in the commercial and investment real estate industry. I could immediately tell he was successful just because of his confident, yet easygoing, demeanor. He was from China, which was of interest to me as I was still thinking of my time spent in Beijing with Tsinghua University's private equity program. More importantly, he was a former information systems engineer. I wondered what made him switch into real estate, so I was very observant as he began to tell a bit about his background.

As class began, I wondered how much of a disadvantage I'd have by not purchasing the recommended calculator. I figured with the calculator I used at Georgetown to calculate all those net present value, Jensen's alpha, and irregular rates of return calculations, there was really nothing that this class would throw at me that I couldn't calculate. The problem was I hadn't performed complex calculations since my investment banking class and was a bit rusty. I figured after we went through a few, I'd be fine, and I was. Still, I was a little concerned as many of the first few keystroke commands that were issued were not readily apparent on my calculator. It's never any fun sitting in a new class and starting off a bit unsure while everyone else seems to be moving right along. In addition, Professor Lau mentioned we would have a comprehensive exam at the end of the course, which I wasn't exactly thrilled about.

After we moved into the theory of the class, things started to flow along a lot better. I realized just how valuable it was to the direction I was heading, and so following along got a lot easier. As the pages turned, I saw the relevance behind everything that was going on, and my confidence continued to grow. I was also sure that I was getting very close to figuring out if this class was going to place me solidly on the path I needed to be on. There was only one way to truly find out, and that was to explain the exact dollar amount of my material goals and let the professor know the path I was seeking to get them and get his honest feedback. As everyone else departed for lunch, I took the opportunity to pull him aside.

"I have decided that the costs of my material goals are $9 million dollars, and I have had some success with residential real estate investing and a decent-paying job over the years, but I don't think those items are going to get me where I need to be. I believe that larger investments are more likely to give me the return I need, and so I have focused on entry-level hotels with one hundred keys (rooms). I know several other people who have done extremely well, but I'd like your feedback if you don't mind."

He stood there for a moment as if to study what I was saying. It wasn't that he was in disbelief or even remotely perplexed that I'd posed such a thing, as I didn't figure he would be. It doesn't take long to know this was not your usual request. Most people would laugh you right out of their face and say, "If you find the answers, let me know." I was confident this was not out of reach for his level of investment expertise and ability. I could tell just from the things he said that these numbers didn't at all seem foreign to him, and I felt he was probably in a position to tell me exactly what I needed to do to make them a reality. Still, I watched very intently as he drew his hand to his chin and started to think.

Then he told me, "Hotels require a lot of time. I'm familiar with hotel seminars, where they tell you about ownership but they don't really tell you how to manage them. Until you reach a certain number of rooms, you have to manage them yourself, and that can mean being there twenty-four hours a day. Commercial real estate (Class A office space, in my case), on the other hand, requires less of your time. The people whom I know who have become rich have used commercial real estate to do it."

Just like that, in a flash of genius, I knew without question he had the insight I needed. He went on to explain how hotels gave strong returns not so much based on their daily operating income, but from the land that they sat on after the sale. He mentioned that perhaps if you owned a three-acre lot in a prime location and you paid perhaps a few million for the hotel, then in a few years' time, the land could appreciate greatly and you could sell it for many times the price, which would provide a large cash profit. I continued to nod in agreement while he spoke, all the while thinking about how much sense the things he said made.

I always appreciate the thought process of the Asians that I meet in the United States. They are always very methodical. I recall my first days at the Citadel and talking with a few guys I met from the far East. They all studied strong sciences, such as mathematics or engineering. When I asked why, they said there was only one answer, whereas with so many other majors, the answers could vary greatly. It's not that real estate had only one way of making a deal happen, but Lau's thought process was very intense, and because he was formerly an engineer, I could see the methodical thought process hard at work.

Things got infinitely better as I decided to head to lunch. I wasn't quite sure of the area at first, so I walked in the general direction of where he told us to go, hoping to find something that would catch my eye. To my surprise, after a few moments of walking, I looked to my left, and there he was, inquiring about what I'd be having for lunch. It was very comforting to see him again, as I surely wanted to hear more about his theories and successes but didn't want to keep him from his lunch hour. To my surprise, he mentioned that perhaps we could go to lunch together and he could tell me more about the very theories I was curious about. In sheer delight at this point, I allowed him to lead the way, as whatever restaurant he chose was going to be just fine with me. As we crossed the street, everything began to look so familiar, and I remembered the area very well as we were in downtown Silver Spring, Maryland. We ended up going to a Chinese restaurant.

As we sat, he inquired more about the things I'd been up to, and he seemed genuinely impressed. After I told him I too was an information systems engineer, he mentioned that he thought they made good real estate professionals due to their thought process. He went on to tell me more about why he decided to change professions. "As an engineer, it's not like being a doctor or lawyer. After doctors and lawyers have been in the field for twenty-five or thirty years, they are well-respected, and they build on their experience. When engineers have been in the field that long, they become obsolete." I knew he was right and had heard a similar thought process before, but the way he put it drove it home. In addition, he talked about the cap that was placed on the engineer's salary, which I had been facing in the last few years, but he found a whole new wealth with his real estate career because there was no cap placed on you. When you work by the hour, there is only so much you can make, but when your money is making money for you, your potential is limitless.

He told me that I should also look at international investment opportunities, as the United States was more stable and the laws kept things pretty stable, but internationally it was still the Wild West. I believe he meant that substantial deals not made in the United States could still be made outside the borders. He reassured me that my timing for coming to the class was perfect, as the market was about to change dramatically and this was a good time to get in. I told him how I had spoken to several other people who had done well for themselves, but they were very unresponsive to multiple requests. I explained that I never wanted much from them, as I knew they were busy. I only wanted to send an e-mail every now and then to ask a question or two or perhaps get a short conversation, but more importantly, consistently so I could continue to build on the foundation.

He not only understood my predicament, but he also gave me his card and told me to keep in touch with him. He said he felt I was going to be very successful and that he wanted to track my progress! I'm sure he had no remote idea how good that made me feel. When someone who has achieved as much as he has provides me a bit of validation that I could do the same and more importantly is willing to provide guidance to ensure that it would come to pass—well, he can't hardly know the impact that makes. I think a lot of people don't realize that it doesn't take much to mentor someone who's already driven. Fortunately for me, Professor Lau was willing and able to make himself available, and I certainly didn't want to take that for granted. He mentioned that he retired or at least semiretired several years earlier and mentioned something about age fifty-five. I lost track of the exact comment for a moment as I didn't think he was actually fifty-five. He told me he wasn't fifty-five, but sixty-three instead. I was then even more blown away at his youthful look. He said that his investments more than took care of his living expenses, and his wife told him to do something to give back after he complained of being bored. Thankfully for my class, he chose to teach. He topped the lunch off by even paying for the meal. "Your success will be my payback." How's that for giving back?

After lunch, the class got even more enjoyable, and we dove into quite a few calculations. I could see frustration brewing on some of the other students' faces, but it was at that moment when I realized all the complex financial calculations I'd done previously made things a lot easier for me. With my extra time after a few keystrokes, I was able to help out a few fellow classmates at my table. That felt really good.

You have to understand what had just happened here. I spent the last nineteen months searching far and wide, leaving no stone unturned, looking not for any riches, but the source, the very source or path of what would lead me to prominence. I'd traveled from New York to Los Angeles, Miami to Kentucky, Beijing to Reno. I never wanted a handout from anyone. Here I was having had lunch with a man who was very capable of helping me reach my goals, and it was like a huge burden being lifted. It's not that I had to abandon any of my other investments or newfound knowledge. Surely they were valuable assets to still shoot for, but the fact was that this man was here in the flesh, fully in charge of his day, his week, his month, his life, and willing to help me. It simply doesn't get any better than that. None of this suggests that things are going to be easy, as nothing in life comes easy, as this can be a tough business, but it is one I'm interested in and I have a fairly decent level of aptitude and understanding for it.

Once again, I have found that the Chinese are very intelligent people in terms of their beliefs. I was out of a job, and most people would define that in this economy as a crisis, but the Chinese define crisis as danger and opportunity. There is no way I could have been there if I was working, especially considering I would have just taken three days off to go to Reno to present my High Impact Presentation DVD at the conference. You can't keep taking off to pursue your outside passions, or eventually they will tell you to just stay away. That's just it, though: you can't pursue your passion for one thing by being someplace else. By definition, that proves that you will never have success until you release outside interests to pursue your passion. Whether people hate it or not, once again, guys like Trump are not only right, they are absolutely flawless in their understanding. Until you pursue what you're passionate about, you may never find success. The other thing is to never give up, which is a quality I hope I've displayed over these last nineteen months. This was surely going to be a class I wouldn't soon forget, but more importantly I had met a professor from whom I hoped to gain more insight in the future.

After class on the next and final day, I decided to log into Leonsis's website to see if he had made any updates as I was reading his book during the evening. I was really thankful that he not only shared his list of goals and dreams, but he also asked that his reading audience share theirs as well. I figured that was easy, as I already had my $40-Million-Dollar Dream Sheet handy on a separate page of the Investment Forum's website. It was a simple copy and paste for me, which is precisely what I did. In addition, Leonsis also asked for comments on his "praise" section. Many very prominent figures had left wonderful comments about not only the book but also Ted. Guys like Ken Chenault, CEO of American Express, LeBron James, Cleveland Cavaliers' All-Star, Maria Shriver, First Lady of California, and others were among those who had commented. Right beneath all of their names and comments was mine. I couldn't believe it. Here was a guy who was clearly at the top of his game and owned all of Washington's professional sports teams, and he'd placed my name and comments on his website.

As I read his book, I noticed that he mentioned Sheila Johnson as one of the members of his investment team, which helped me understand how she too was a partial owner of all the local teams. It is so interesting how things come together when you continue to read the stories of the great ones ahead of you. They are all only two degrees from each other. They have similar goals and interests, and it makes sense that they all know each other. Speaking of goals, I decided to check his lists of those who had submitted their sheets to see what he had decided to do with them. Once again, I was blown away, as right there, number four from the top of the list, was my $40-Million-Dollar Dream Sheet. He even went on to link my name right back to my website, which essentially linked his website to mine or mine to his, however you want to look at it. Superficial or not, it instantly meant to me that I was only one degree of separation away from a man who dominated not only the IT world but also the sports' ownership world and had infinitely more than what I ever desired to have. I equated that to being on the right path in so many ways. I wasn't sure what the next set of progressive steps was going to hold for me, but I knew I was finally advancing from Slide 68 for sure.

To really top the day off, by the time I got home, I'd received the updated floor plans for the Chateau D'Von from John Henry. They were such a beauty. He had it all there. From the circular driveway to the massive roofline, from the two-story library and dining room to the porte cochere that led to the helicopter storage and conference meeting area, from the elevators to the groin vault gallery in the main hallway to the boudoir in the presidential suite, he had nailed it. What a day, what a week, what a life!

PART 3:

Stock Your Tool Kit with Education, Contacts, and Relevant Events

Don't Focus on the Crops; Just Keep Planting Seeds

I was having an annoying day at work. I wasn't annoyed because anyone was doing anything to upset me. I was annoyed simply because you can't control the time. Things happen in due season. I was just annoyed that I was even more sure that I didn't belong there and wasn't financially suited to leave. I have seen many people get fed up and leave to *start* a venture. *Start* is the operative word here. I don't think you should leave to start a venture if you haven't already begun a revenue stream for it or sealed the deal on a new contract unless you have a long-term financial plan. With a huge pay cut still lurking and the economy officially in recession starting the New Year, I simply wasn't set to leave.

What I perpetually did, however, as somewhat demonstrated in other chapters, is plant seeds. Some of the stories talk about what happened from beginning to end, while others never made the cut. Sometimes I planted seeds in very fertile soil, while other times it seems that I planted them in dried mud. When I returned to my hometown at the beginning of the year to do the interview for my last book, *Real Estate for Real People*, I was impressed with the interviewer. Her name was Jade Anderson, and she served as the LocalLife editor. I was under the impression that Jade would ask a few superficial questions about the book, followed by questions on where interested consumers could get it, take a picture of me, and that would sum it up. Fortunately, I was wrong.

Jade had a ton of very in-depth questions, and she seemed legitimately interested in the things I had going on. She asked why I wrote the book, how the process started, who my target audience was, and why I felt I was qualified to write it. She then asked, "So what else do you have going on?" I told her about my DVD, and once again, she dug deep to ask questions about it. As she scribbled in shorthand, she completed page after page after page of notes. Her inquisitive look made me continue to talk more, yet slowly, so she didn't have to remind me she was writing. She covered my education, upcoming books, book signings, where I lived, and the Investment Forum. What could have easily been a three-minute interview quickly grew to at least twenty. She took several pictures of me as staff members busily walked by, wrapped up her questions, and escorted me out. "It should be out in about two weeks" were her final words as we said our good-byes.

As I rounded the final corner before leaving the building, I noticed two of the women in the office enjoying ice cream. I thought it looked like a cool afternoon treat and a nice way to break up the afternoon monotony. As I got in my truck and began driving away, I left quite impressed and very pleased. I replayed the scene of them eating the ice cream and then thought to myself—lunch. Repay the staff at the *Camden Chronicle Independent* by providing lunch. I figured pizza was always a winner, so I visited the local Pizza Hut and had a chat with my longtime friend Lakeia Kinard, who was recently certified as a professional food service manager, and she knew precisely what to do. A quick ten minutes was all it took for me to pay for and place the order. Since it was Friday afternoon, I figured having the pizza delivered on Monday would be a great way to start off the workweek. With the seed planted, I was off to other things.

The following Monday morning came and went so fast that I totally forgot about the lunch treat. When I got in my vehicle to head off to lunch, I noticed a few missed calls. Honestly, I figured it was just someone I was not interested in talking to. As I drove away, it dawned on me that it was just after noon, and perhaps they had received the pizza surprise. I was right.

"Hey, Mr. Anthony Von Mickle, this is Jade Anderson [surprised voices began to provide background noise] with the *Camden Chronicle Independent* in Camden, South Carolina, and I'm just calling to thank you because you have *thrilled* my entire office [beginning to laugh]. As you can hear, they are sorting out pizza and pasta and breadsticks and chicken wings and Pepsi and everything. So, umm, there was a little bit of confusion—we were kind of at a loss at first—but thank you very, very much!" Hearing the joy in Jade's voice and the laughter in the air absolutely brought a smile to my face. I instantly forgot all about the drab of work life, and their acceptance of my gesture was more pleasing than anything I heard all day.

Slide 68 Mind-Set

You simply never know when the crops will come in on a seed you've planted. The only way to find out is to keep planting seeds that you think will bear the fruit that you desire.

We've heard a million times that we live in a microwave society. You simply have to understand that some things just take more time than others to materialize. Sometimes the elements of success are out of your control, and you can only do so much. That doesn't mean don't do anything. Always look to make the most out of every day, regardless of whether you think it will be the greatest day of your life or not. The trouble with not living every day like it's your last is that one day you may wake up *dead* wrong!

Several weeks passed, and the article was published. To my surprise, they ran the story in such a way that it made me look like a star to my friends and family. My brother's friends were buzzing about it. My older brother Trent called and told me how much all the people we grew up with enjoyed seeing me in the spotlight. My family, friends, and local church all heard about it, and it was really the talk of the town for a few weeks.

Perhaps one of the most unexpected and best gifts of all was a new family connection that was forged. Mickle, which has Irish origins, means great or many and is not terribly common in any circles I've ever traveled in. So when I hear the name, I tend to pause and gather as much additional information about the person that I can. I found out that I wasn't the only Mickle who felt this way. As it turns out, there was another, more senior fellow named Andrew "Daddy Mick" Mickle who lived in Camden years ago but had moved to Gainesville, Florida, many years earlier. He left Camden for better opportunities and started his family there. A local real estate tycoon, by local standards, he owned nearly one hundred acres of land. To keep tabs on the local area, he was a longtime subscriber of the *Camden Chronicle Independent*.

When the article came out, he asked his granddaughter Stephanie to contact me. Stephanie reached out to me via LinkedIn about a year later, as she had just moved to Washington. We exchanged phone numbers and decided to meet in Washington for dinner. We hit it off instantly and decided with so many wonderful stories that we shared with each other, we were officially cousins, regardless of whether the bloodstream crossed or not. It just so happened that Stephanie was an honor student and received a full-ride scholarship to Harvard to study law and was there just a year before I got there.

She was just the tip of the iceberg, as there were other great stories to be told from her. Her father, Stephan Mickle, was also an author, but more importantly a federally appointed judge sworn in by President Clinton. Both he and his wife, Evelyn, were trailblazers at the University of Florida in Gainesville, as he was the first African American to graduate from the law school and Evelyn was the first to graduate from the nursing school. Stephan and Evelyn had three kids. Stephanie was an attorney working in Senator Clarence Nelson's Office. Ironically, I worked on a project to upgrade the information technology infrastructure for all the senators a few years earlier. Her younger sister, Amy, lived and worked in Gainesville, and their brother Stephan Jr. was also an IT professional in the oil industry in Texas.

It turned out that Stephan Sr. was a chip off the old block when it came to trailblazing, as Daddy Mick was a legendary pool instructor in Gainesville. Our families loved the new bonding so much that the Gainesville Mickle clan, led by Daddy Mick, drove all the way to Camden in March 2010 to make a formal introduction, and we've been united as one ever since.

"Andrew 'Daddy Mick' Mickle serves the first piece of cake in celebration of his 90th birthday, which was earlier this year, during the summer opening last

Friday of Mickle Pool at the T. B. McPherson Center in southeast Gainesville. For more than 50 years, Mickle has taught countless children and adults to swim in Gainesville."

Jenny Wilkinson/Special to the Guardian

Gainesville Guardian June 2, 2011

Education:
An Advantage, Not a Guarantee

Currently the richest man in the world has declared that having certain attributes certainly had something to do with his success. I read a *New York Times* article on July 15, 2007, entitled "The Richest of the Rich, Proud of a New Gilded Age." In the article, Warren Buffett, a gentleman for whom I have the utmost respect, said something that actually made me reread his statement about five times, wondering if I had really read what I thought I did. The article stated, "Like them, Mr. Buffett, 78, sees himself as lucky, having had the good fortune, as he put it, to have been born in America, white and male, and "wired for asset allocation" just when all four really paid off. He dwelt on his good fortune in a recent appearance at a fund-raiser for Hillary Rodham Clinton, who is vying for Mr. Buffett's support of her presidential candidacy."

I can check the male "box," but not the "white" box. Mr. Buffett is forty-four years older than I am and many billion dollars wiser, but he acknowledged that his skin color certainly had something to do with it. He never said that if he wasn't white or male, he wouldn't have made it, but the fact is that he acknowledges it means something. I'm not about to waste my time petitioning Capitol Hill for slavery reparations nor am I even remotely concerned about looking for a handout, but I am saying that I face barriers that I can't do a darn thing about.

The American public school system has its share of ups and downs. Although I've never done any formal research on it, I have seen probably some of the best and some of the worst. I grew up in a rural area for the most part, and I actually thought I wasn't a bad student academically. I never thought of myself as the best, in spite of the fact that some of my friends looked at me as being smart, but I certainly was not the worst either. I figured schoolteachers presented what some highly regulated school superintendent's office pushed down, meaning they taught what they were instructed to teach. I knew nothing about administration or office politics, and as a student, I just figured we did whatever teachers asked, and that was about it.

I relied on the teachers and the school system to educate me on a number of things like career and personal finances. Not that I even had an inkling of what financial guidance was, but I just figured when I needed to know it, they would teach me. As I went through the high school curriculum, I figured we wouldn't get any financial insight there, but perhaps when I got to college and took some business classes, I'd learn the sophisticated talk that would increase my knowledge of the various financial markets and guide me substantially closer to financial success. That wasn't the case in college either, despite gaining a degree in business administration.

When I got to college, I found out that there was a great disparity between what was gained by the average high school student in a public school system and those who were fortunate enough to attend private schools. Their grades were better, and they just seemed to have an overall better understanding about what was going on in life, regardless of any parental guidance. I recall attending a Citadel function several years after graduation and talking with Mike Rodgers, a career federal FBI agent and distinguished Citadel alumnus. Mike's wife and I had a very casual academic discussion about the difficulties I probably faced when I got to the Citadel after she realized where I was from.

As I assured her how right she was, she smiled lightly and said, "You didn't even realize you were behind, did you?" She could not have been more right. There was a world of difference between what was introduced to not only private school students but students in much more diverse and affluent communities. This is not to say that these students would automatically gain financial understanding and have a much better shot at being wealthy, but they seemed to be better prepared for curveballs, as the exposure gained from their local community teachers and curriculum had prepared them on what to watch out for.

Dr. Dolf de Roos, a real estate mogul who never held a job, yet earned a PhD in Electrical Engineering, discovered something early that was in front of the faces of many, but they never thought about it. When he graduated from high school many years ago, he had the same talk with his parents that many students have with their parents today. They told him to get a good education and that would get him a job, so he could make good money and live a good life. For whatever reason, he decided to question the status quo.

He believed that by their rationale, education should equate to money. If that was in fact the case, then college professors should be the wealthiest people on earth, but we all know that's not the case. In fact, for many years, the world's richest man was a shining example of someone who never finished college, as is the case with many people who join him on the world's richest list.

After I graduated and started working, I simply or perhaps naively believed that you would remain employed forever if you had a college degree. I knew that people were subject to layoffs and downsizing, but I really thought this was more for people who didn't have advanced education, in spite of the fact that we talked briefly about this in a few business classes.

To be perfectly honest, I didn't spend a lot of time asking questions or wondering about employability or downsizing, because I just figured if I focused on school while in school, I could focus on work when I started working. I won't necessarily say this was a mistake, and I'm not even sure if professors or teachers talked in detail that students would be terribly concerned. However, there is a lot that can be learned and many seeds that can be planted with the ups and downs of what really happens after you start life in the workforce.

Sure, I understood whether public school system-educated or not, that one should live within their means, but in no way did I think I'd have to take a 50K pay cut after I had risen to a respectable level of management in my career and spent twenty months in a layoff situation. One might think that if I was laid off for eighteen months, then I should have been prepared for a 100 percent pay cut at any time, and while that may have some truth to it, I was laid off following the attacks of September 11, 2001, which made any work in the Washington DC metro area extremely rare if you didn't have a top secret clearance, which signifies that the government has thoroughly researched your background and given employers the okay that you are worthy to work there. Such clearance seemingly meant years of progressive gainful employment, but I would find out different. Even being cleared guaranteed nothing, I later learned.

I began thinking, *why in the world are we not discussing these very real scenarios in business school? I mean, is it really that difficult to incorporate what is likely to happen in the job life?* We spent countless hours talking about so many other aspects that may or may not affect you, whereas a pay cut or a layoff hits center mass more directly than the planes that crashed into our nation's buildings on September 11 ever could.

Raiding Your Retirement Accounts 101

I spent an entire year at Georgetown learning financial planning inside and out. One of my favorite portions of the class was calculating investment returns, regardless if they were for college, retirement planning, buying a new home, or whatever. Long before studying in that program, I was fascinated by compound interest, or as Albert Einstein calls it, "the eighth wonder of the world." When I began my professional career, I would frequently go to online calculators and play with the numbers to see just how rich I'd be by 2038, the year I'd decided I would retire based on conventional wisdom.

The number would fall in a range from three and a half million to four million dollars. I just knew I'd be the richest old man around. I watched others perform the same calculations thinking that they'd retire as millionaires several times over. There is a problem with those calculators, however. The story that simply goes untold is the assumptions they make. These calculators, or the financial planners behind them, that make you feel good when you're socking away at least the company match on the offered qualified retirement plans assume that you'll be employed from the day you start contributing. They assume that you will also have a short-term emergency fund so as to not touch your retirement or college planning accounts.

Those are great planning assumptions, but life doesn't come to you textbook style. Life can hit both you and your spouse with unemployment at the same time, even if you have a year of short-term savings. There is no guarantee that you will be back to work in a year, even if you have advanced degrees with magna cum laude status.

I've seen people have to take those unfortunate deductions from IRAs and 401(k)s to the point of draining them dry. When you start over, the new calculated numbers aren't even remotely close to the original ones. When I went through that scenario, I began talking to people who were already retired. Some of their stories surprised me.

My suggestion at this point is to really try and think about the lifestyle you want when you walk away from work, and begin putting together those pieces now while you're working. Working actively toward a specified goal now is better than socking money away into an account that you hope will swell to those beautifully calculated numbers later.

It is easy to assume that advanced education will result in more wages, which hopefully will make life's finances a little easier. While studies have been done to illustrate that those with a college degree will earn over a million dollars more over their career than someone with a high school diploma, you have to understand that a college degree does not guarantee success. In addition, it is best to proceed with caution even if you are looking to gain a master's degree or PhD. Advanced education is a wonderful asset to your life skills, but it usually comes at a high premium. The cost of an education is expensive, and the price is getting steeper every year. You cannot assume that if you earn an MBA, it automatically means a huge pay raise. It simply means that you will be introduced to the skills to make better business decisions. It could certainly mean that you may be entitled to higher wages, but you have to do your homework before you enroll.

Seek out company HR departments and talk candidly with them before you pay the costs for the degree. A bit of research may show that the new salary you hope to acquire may not come immediately, while the amount due from loans acquired to earn the degree may be due upon graduation. Even if a raise is gained, what is the break-even point before you are cash-flow positive from the investment? You may find that it could take ten years or more before you break even and that the earnings beyond the ten-year mark are moderate at best above the money required for the degree. No school and no degree is bigger than a recession, and while education certainly gives you the advantage, it is imperative that you understand it doesn't necessarily mean newfound riches.

We all know that education is expensive, but I'll pay for it before I pay for ignorance any day. Education provides you a critical way to think through problems with a level of confidence that perhaps someone without an education may not have. It is an advantage without question, but it is not a guarantee. It never has been, and it never will be. There will always be Bill Gateses (Microsoft) and Mark Zuckerburgs (Facebook) out there, but I wouldn't bet that those rare jewels have the advantage.

Lexus LS 400: My Motivation for Higher Education

Sitting at the stoplight in Camden, South Carolina, during the spring of 1990, I recall my older brother and I in the right-hand lane waiting for the stoplight to turn green. Just after we came to a halt on the yellow light, we glanced to our right and noticed this hot, new, unrecognized four-door sedan. We were both car buffs, so not being able to identify a luxury car meant this had to be new to the market. We were sure it wasn't a Mercedes, Volvo, or Cadillac, as those were the main luxury vehicles of that time, but we weren't quite sure what it was.

Fortunately for us, the car stopped just after we did, which gave us a full stoplight cycle to check it out. In the span of thirty seconds, we drooled over this black beauty with gazes that left our mouths hanging wide-open. Unfortunately for us, the driver and his son didn't feel particularly safe at the thought of two young black guys eye-piercing their new wheels. Apparently, they thought we were going to carjack them. In the split second when we finally stopped looking at the car long enough to make eye contact with them, the light turned green. In that millisecond, all eight cylinders opened up, the rear went down, the front went up, and the luxury beast vanished as quickly as it had appeared. I knew right then, I had to have that car.

Several weeks passed before I discovered what the car was. I had to go to the chiropractor's office for treatment following my first fender bender. While sitting in the office browsing through a magazine, I saw the exact same car, color and all. I murmured to myself all types of silly pronunciations of the Japanese word, but for the life of me didn't know how to say it. It didn't matter, though, as I knew I had to have that car at some point in the future. Growing up in a trailer park, my mind often wondered about a better life. I knew it was out there, but I wasn't particularly sure what to do to get it. I'd often heard teachers and community leaders talk about higher education being the key, and while I figured that all sounded good, I still could never quite put the whole puzzle together. That wasn't particularly surprising, I suppose, considering no one else in my family had gone to college so I saw no direct benefit.

In a search for more motivation to go to college other than being a decent student, I decided to use the Lexus. Why not? Even at that time, I knew that there was more to life than having a nice car, but I also knew that I wanted a Lexus lifestyle. That meant I wanted to drive the car, but if that meant parking it in front of a trailer, then my quest was superficial at best. It was that simple logic that caused my thoughts for higher education to become much more focused and more direct.

There were tons of college choices out there, and I wasn't sure which one made the most sense. The only thing I thought was the harder the college, the better my chances for making enough money to drive the car. Quickly becoming a standout within the JROTC ranks, I figured going to West Point or the Citadel would be the most obvious choice. Since I knew nothing about New York and didn't want to go that far away from home, the Citadel became the target. I applied and was accepted in the late spring of 1991.

Slide 68 Mind-Set

Use your natural abilities to your advantage. I could have chosen many schools to go to, but I chose a military academy due to the skills I gained while rapidly advancing through JROTC. This was a course that I enjoyed and naturally excelled in due to leadership qualities that I learned from my family. It was a much more efficient use of my time to build from what I had already started in hopes of gaining a better advantage.

The word quickly spread around our trailer park about where I was headed. No one knew anything about the school. All we could gather was that its graduates seemed to live economically better lifestyles. When you're on the bottom, the only way to go is up, and I felt going there would put me way up. Anytime I mentioned the institution, people always tried to link it to someone they knew, no matter how far they had to stretch. It wasn't uncommon for someone to say something to the tune of, "My cousin had a best friend whose brother went to the Citadel."

All summer I was excited about my college decision and talked about it a lot. Many people gave me a pat on the back for stepping up big and making it happen. I was proud of the accomplishment. To help put together the lifestyle I wanted, I began driving to Columbia, South Carolina, through Wildwood, which was an upscale golf course community. Many of the homes were sprawled out on a lake, and a lot of them had a Lexus parked out front. I would commonly ride through, closely observing each house and the nice cars they had. My brother thought it was a bad idea to be on that side of town riding through those neighborhoods, but I ignored him, knowing I wasn't doing anything wrong but simply using what I could to gain motivation for a better lifestyle.

The night before I reported to the Citadel, my ex-girlfriend Denise and I went out to celebrate by going skating and bowling, two things we'd never done before. I came home really late and snuck into the house to get a few hours' rest before our 4:30 a.m. departure for Charleston, South Carolina, which was about a two-and-a-half hour ride. It seemed as if my head hit the pillow for no more than twenty minutes before my mom was coming in my room to wake me up. So there I was, exhausted from a great night of skating, bowling, and having fun, but also with only $5 to take with me to college. It just never dawned on me that I would need anything more if I would simply show up. And so it was that I reported to the Citadel with my trusty friend Abraham Lincoln.

I returned home four years later with dual bachelor's degrees. One was Modern Languages, French, and the other was Business Administration. I have to thank the generous people that gave me scholarship money every year, including the Daniel Fund, Cadet Store, and Gift Shop Scholarship. I even gave Lexus a shout-out as a statement under my senior yearbook picture. It read, "Lexus LS 400, I'm on the way!"

Slide 68 Mind-Set

You have to find motivation to do things wherever you can find it. For some, the thought of leaving home and going on late-night drinking binges with newfound friends may be your motivation, although I wouldn't recommend the heavy drinking under any circumstances. For others, it may be the opportunity to see a new city. Regardless of whatever it is, you have to use it. Not everyone is built the same way or motivated by the same things.

Private Equity with Tsinghua University and Harvard Business School: A Class in Persistence

"So let me get this straight for the third time. You've run out of money because your deal hasn't paid off, you haven't paid for tuition yet, so you're not officially in the class, you have no more leave on your job, Harvard is patiently waiting while sending you friendly e-mail reminders, and yet you're still going to China, as in the other side of the world, thinking that you might just benefit from this deal-making program somehow? So what are you going to tell them if the deal doesn't pan out by the time registration starts?

"Ohh, I know, why don't you say, 'What? Haven't received my money? Oh, heads are going to roll. Somebody's about to be fired! Let me call my secretary and get back to you!' Meanwhile, you've bought your ticket, booked your hotel room, which was supposed to be included with tuition, and you're going to China? Unbelievable! At this point, you don't have to do anything else to impress me. I can honestly say I don't know anyone—*anyone*—who would go all the way to China on a hope and a prayer. Dude, that is like the most."

"Well, B, that's exactly the situation," I said. "You know you're going to have to video this, right, because this footage has to be a part of the documentary? B, if nothing changes between now and then, that's exactly the plan. Now granted, I certainly hope that something comes along that I don't have to roll this way, but if nothing changes, that's the plan so far. I've even mentally drafted a hot commercial to put on my website advertising the Slide 68 movement."

This was the conversation that Michelle and I had several times, but she continued to be baffled by my willingness to go around the world just to chase a dream. I suppose she had a good point, but at that stage of the game, I didn't have much else. In all actuality, I did have one other option in terms of the extra money to pay for the program, but it was going to come from the

Investment Forum's credit card, and I simply couldn't afford to pay it back in the time allotted. I kept stalling, looking for other options other than my side business, but nothing else was making itself known. It all reminded me of the first time I went to Harvard and was short on money. It was very frustrating because I just never thought I'd be short on cash again—ever. You tend to have those silly thoughts when you're young and inexperienced. When you've had enough, though, you've just had enough.

I still had a larger-than-average salary, so my life would have gone on, just not to the degree I wanted it to. I chalked it up to the good and bad of business. I've learned it is better to fail now rather than later, as you have to fail your way up. I've also learned that success is a lousy teacher. When I was doing well and didn't have a lot of opposition, I thought I really had a better understanding of business and investments than I actually did. Like many, I'd mistaken a bull market for investment expertise. When the markets are good, everyone is winning, and many think it comes from their uncanny wisdom or due diligence, which is possible but not probable for the masses. A rising tide raises all ships.

Going to China to take a class with Harvard Business School sounded sophisticated, intelligent, expensive, and all those things, and in many ways it was, but to me it was more a test of faith. I believed in my heart of hearts that it was going to help give me the tools to create the resources I needed to live out my dream life. I just accepted it as one of God's little tests for me to see if I would take a leap of faith.

My money really did get very tight, but once again, out of nowhere came an account balance that I swore was not enough to buy a plane ticket but it suddenly showed a sufficient amount. I even had to scrape that week to get my passport renewed. On top of all this, I received the money for the ticket and the hotel at the exact same time that I received the passport. There are coincidences in life, but this wasn't one of them. I just felt that there were too many opportunities and signs coming at me for me to back out of this. Sure, I thought of perhaps putting it off and maybe waiting until things got better, but then I'd think back to the first time I went to Harvard and how it all worked out. To be perfectly honest, it was not that I thought a class that lasted only a few days would teach me enough to come back and become a deal-making guru. It was more about moving, trusting, believing, and stepping out toward something better.

I reference upscale homes a lot, because that is my American dream. Even when I look at my current home, I think of how it never just came to me. It never fell in my lap. People have things because they want them and they went after them. The introductory page to my dream house design shows a very unique picture, which I have included below:

At the top of the page, I have inscribed the following words: "Move to the Beat of Your Own Drum." The picture shows seven birds perched on a tree limb. Six of the birds are looking one direction, but the bird on the right end, which happens to look exactly like all the other birds, is looking in the total opposite direction. Below the picture, it states, "Follow Your Dream. If a person does not keep pace with their companions, perhaps it is because they hear a different drummer. Let them step up to the music they hear, however measured or far away. Henry David Thoreau." I added a few other words that I thought made the statement that I wanted to make: "I had the *ambition* to dream of it, the *audacity* to hope for it, the *confidence* to make it known, and the unshakable *faith*, one-one hundredth the size of a mustard seed, to *believe* it would come to pass. I *saw* it vividly, I *wanted* it, and I *went* after it."

I recalled the picture from many years earlier when I first saw it and thought it was a great way to introduce my dream house to whoever wanted to see it on paper. As it turns out, a lot of people wanted to see it. Although the words were meant for me, anyone can apply them to anything they want in life.

When I was out of work in 2001 and 2002, I recalled seeing tons of homes when I was out scouting real estate properties. Two of them became my absolute favorites. One was a gold, stucco-colored house called the Hallard model. I thought it was the serious bachelor pad, and based on style, it was number one. Then there was the Georgian Hampton model by Toll Brothers, because it was an all-brick estate home with movie theater, ridiculous-sized owner's closet, sunroom, morning room, and so on. In a very short time, not only did I end up getting one of them, I ended up getting them both and owning them at the same time. In addition, I was able to buy four more houses to go with them, plus an exotic sports car and world travels.

When I saw all this, I was about as broke as I had ever been, but I never let it stop me from dreaming. It all occurred to me while listening to a song by the Sounds of Blackness called "Everything Is Going to Be All Right." There was a verse that said, "What you see is what you're going to get." I said, "Ohhhhhh, that's it! Yes, what *you see* is what *you get!*" It took several years before that finally dawned on me.

Slide 68 Mind-Set

What you see is what you're going to get. Some people say, "I'll believe it when I see it," but that's exactly backward. You won't see a thing until you believe it and believe it with all your heart and soul and can paint a picture of it with intricate detail. It is only then that your dreams will start to become a reality.

Preparing the Table

When I was very young, I used to love staying with my grandparents in the country. Even though their house was all of eight hundred square feet, with no running water and no bathroom, there was no other place I'd rather have been most of the time. There weren't many other kids around, and a lot of the time it was just me and them, but I just loved being in their company.

Before dawn every morning, I'd awake to the sound of the rooster crowing. That was my signal to get up, as I knew both my grandparents would already be up and at it. Their assignments were regimented, and they moved in concert every day to the beat of the same drum. My grandmother would go in the kitchen and get some lighter wood from a small box. Then she'd get some other small, dry wood from the bottom of a bigger box, which was used to store small logs. She'd place the small starter wood into the bottom of the potbellied stove, and she'd place some old lit newspaper under the small wood. Within a few seconds, a small fire would be burning, at which point she'd place the larger wood on top of it. We'd then go outside from the side door to a well that was located just a few feet from the back door. She would place an old metal pail underneath the spout and begin pumping for fresh water. After taking the water inside, the fire would be near the temperature she needed to start preparing breakfast. At that point, my granddad and I would then go outside through the front door to the chicken coop. There we'd find fresh eggs right underneath the hen's bottom. We would take the eggs in the house and go out the back door to the garden to pick fresh vegetables.

After returning from the garden, I'd find my grandmother in the kitchen kneading dough for fresh biscuits every morning. She'd then go into the icebox and slice off a chunk of butter to put in a plate and pour warm syrup over the top of it. While finishing breakfast, she'd allow me to dip the biscuits in the warm buttered syrup and watch as she prepared the table. That was the start of their day every morning before the clock even thought of striking 6:00 a.m. In fact, it is no wonder why I find myself writing this chapter at the 6:00 a.m. hour outside of the gym, where I find myself every workday morning, parking in or near the same place and beginning my workout regimen with the same set routine. The alarm sound on my clock is a rooster's crowing, by the way.

I feel strongly about my goals because of synergy, which I learned a lot about by going to the gym. Several years ago, I set a goal of bench-pressing 315 pounds. It's a rack of six forty-five-pound plates plus the forty-five-pound bar that separates the men from the boys. A personal trainer told me I'd never get there because my arms were too small. I never gave much thought to his words and proceeded anyway. The one thing he did tell me was that I would have to increase the dumbbell weight that I was pressing with each individual arm. Normally, I would use dumbbells ranging from sixty to seventy-five pounds. That always kept me strong enough to bench-press 250 pounds without too much strain. I then focused solely on dumbbell pressing until I was able to safely use 105-pound dumbbells in each hand.

After that, I felt I was strong enough to at least attempt 295 pounds. Fortunately for me, I was off by about ten pounds, because I was able to lift ten pounds more than I expected. When I went back several weeks later to attempt the 295 goal, I did it with ease and went on to 305 that day. With just a few more weeks of training, I was able to obtain my goal pretty easily. In fact, the morning before I attempted the weight, I had to drive to Charleston, South Carolina, from DC so I actually drove all night and was exhausted. However, because I was at the Citadel's gym, I was pumped and psyched up to be back on campus. So I dove right in and hit my goal.

In the process, I learned a lot about synergy. With each arm pushing one hundred pounds, the most I would have thought I could have bench-pressed before getting into weight lifting was two hundred pounds. It made no logical sense to me that just because each arm was doing one hundred pounds individually, that together with my chest secretly getting stronger, I could achieve 50 percent more than that. In actuality, what happened was by combining the arm strength with the chest strength, the results were so much more. I went on to bench-press a good deal more and decided, with my ultimate goal met, I could back down off heavy weights. I haven't had any interest in going back to levels that high. I knew I wouldn't stop until I got what I desired, but learning about synergy was a huge extra bonus.

I see my other goals in the same way. Just because some come at a monetary price means it's just another form of currency. I had to pay the price of discipline and weight training for my weight-lifting goals, and I pay the price for my other goals in the same fashion but with other forms of currency like patience, diligence, education, strategy, and so on.

By going to China, I was simply preparing the table. I knew the training I'd receive would help my deal-making strategy to the level I needed it to be in order to make bigger deals. With deal making, you have to show a track record. When you show success of smaller deals, it makes banks and other partners feel more comfortable that you can handle bigger deals. They don't just show up at your door. Sometimes you have to literally go a world away to find the opportunity of a lifetime.

The Harvard Situation

Five days before I was set to fly out, I received an e-mail from the executive offices at Harvard Business School to say that they still had yet to receive my payment and they needed to hear from me right away. Well, no surprise there. I figured fair enough and sent them an e-mail. Essentially, I told them that I wasn't going to be able to fund the program and would gladly return their precourse study material to the registration desk once I got there, as I had all intentions of going to Beijing. They said that I could hold on to the study material and let me know that I was subject to the entire program tuition because of the last-minute notice. They also mentioned that they could defer me for up to one year for the next program, but the date for the next one wasn't until the fall a few years later. That was just music to my ears, as the first time I went to Harvard, I was under pressure to move at that moment. This time things played out more favorably to my time and resources.

To me, that meant we were in this for the long term. I had no problems owing the world's top business school, because to me it meant I had access to the world's top business education. Now that everything was safely out of the bag, meaning they knew my intentions and I knew theirs, I was prepared to let fate decide what would happen. Meanwhile, I was still thinking that somehow, somewhere, something was going to happen so that this would all make sense. I felt that even if I never saw anything that remotely resembled the class, I would learn something that would bear fruit, which said this was more than worth my time and effort of going so far. I was going to operate with my eyes wide-open, just looking for anything to capitalize on.

In the meantime, I simply continued Plan A, which was to go right back to studying my case studies in preparation for discussion. Plan A was to get on the plane and head east. There was no plan B. I'd figure out my days when I got there.

When I arrived at JFK, my patience had to take a backseat because the plane left a bit late and I only had about forty-five minutes to get to the gate. Unfortunately for me, I'd never flown to JFK before, so to find out at the last minute that I had to leave one terminal, get on a train, and get to another one wasn't a good time to find out. As luck would have it, I got on the train going the wrong direction. I had to get off and try that again, as the clock kept ticking away. When I finally arrived in the right terminal, I couldn't find Asiana Airlines any better than I found them at Washington Dulles.

After asking a few of the employees, they pointed me to the counter, but there was no one there. One lady said, "They just left and are right around the corner, so you'd better run." Fortunately, she was right; I caught up to them just as they were about to push the elevator button to head toward the gate. If I had missed them, I would have been totally screwed. They looked over my ticket, and we walked back to the gate to get me checked in. Because my flight from Dulles was late and they rerouted me, it wasn't exactly easy, as they explained they would have trouble getting me from Seoul to Beijing. I said, "Just get me to Korea, and I'll figure out the rest from there."

This Part of My Life Is Called Running

They got me checked in and pointed me to the gate. If only things had gotten easier there, but they didn't. Since I was in a new terminal, I had to check back into the airport, meaning take off my shoes, remove my laptop from the bag, lose the jewelry, and so on. I completed all that as the clock said I had about five minutes to get to the gate. As I grabbed my things and took off running, I thought that I was too light. Something was definitely missing. I realized that the cordial check-in officer who wanted to have a conversation that I wasn't interested in at the moment had taken my mind off what I was doing just momentarily. That was enough for me to realize that I left my lifeline on the X-ray counter. As I got back to it, there was the bowl with my jewelry, my wallet, and my cell phone. Talk about being royally screwed if I had left without those items. So once again, I took off in a dead sprint toward the gate and thought momentarily to Will Smith in *Pursuit of Happyness* again when he said, "This part of my life is called running." I arrived at the gate in New York City to board the plane third from last and headed for Korea.

When I arrived in Korea, the hours slowly passed by, and I even received a few phone calls, which was surprising because I never expected my phone to be able to work, but it did. (I wasn't too excited about it when the bill came.) The bulk of the people on my flight showed up about twenty minutes before departure. I was finally able to talk with a representative to get squared away for my flight with ease. Just before everyone started to board, one of the representatives approached me. Because she badly mispronounced my name, I thought she had the wrong person, but when she pointed to my passport and showed me what she was saying, she proved that she was right. It didn't take a genius to figure out who I was, as being the only non-Asian on the plane and being six foot two, which is not excessively tall by American standards, but apparently very tall by Asian standards, made her guesswork easy. She delivered a shocking blow when she told me that my luggage was at LAX. I thought, *boy, this just keeps getting better.*

This was a real issue because the Tsingua program wanted to take a group picture and have a formal welcome reception at 5:00 p.m. and had asked us to wear a suit. If the needed money became available, I would have to have something better to wear for the group photo. Although my Jordan warm-ups were quite expensive and a bit too dressy for the court, I didn't see them making the cut. Furthermore, my razor was with my luggage, so even if I had more clothes, I was going to feel dirty with an unshaved face. Once again, I just laughed to myself and said, "Oh well."

It was sort of a relief to be honest, because whether I wanted to make a drastic credit card transaction or not, I didn't have any clothes and had been wearing the same ones for two days by the time I got to Beijing. It wasn't smart money management to force the transaction because my entire budget would have been blown to bits, which was the last thing I wanted. Furthermore, I had really been through the ringer with leveraging money from my past few transactions, and this would not have been good fiscal responsibility.

On my way to the lobby, I passed the registration desk for the school program, and they looked right at me because I had the study materials still in hand. Great, now what? I knew my name was probably not on the roster any longer, and sure enough, it wasn't. B was my saving grace, as she called me right as I was checking in. That allowed me to momentarily avoid the whole tuition issue, as I was able to walk away and take her call briefly before returning to the registration table.

I explained that the e-mail I received pulled me from the list. I told them that we had some confusion, but I was going to check into the hotel and deal with it later. We chatted and giggled a bit about me losing my luggage. They asked if I wanted to go ahead and pay for the program. I told them I wasn't sure and especially now that I didn't have any luggage. They pointed right down the hall and said, "There are some wonderful men's stores in this hotel, and they can fix you right up." I wasn't particularly interested in buying a new suit of clothes.

As I told them I would think about it, I pointed toward the check-in counter and told them I just needed to get settled. They once again asked me if I thought I'd be joining the program by tomorrow morning. I told them I didn't keep a high balance on my business debit card, and the transaction might trigger a default if I tried to pay the balance due. They said, "We just need to know that you plan to pay. Our offices are closed right now anyway.

We don't like using credit cards by e-mail, but maybe we can get you to fax your credit card number to the Boston office."

I said perhaps I would do that. As much as I considered what they said, I knew that would put me on the hook for a high balance pronto. At the same time, I figured maybe I should just do it. I mean, here I was all the way in Beijing, so there was no need to start self-defeating. As I was about to walk away, they said, "Here, take these additional cases, as we need you to study these tonight for class in the morning." I walked away thinking, *great, just great*. I took a deep breath and headed for the check-in counter, calmly trying to figure out my next step.

43XL Saved the Day

After checking in, I sat and thought about it for a bit and then figured I'd at least go downstairs and browse the men's clothing store, as you just never know. It didn't take long for me to realize my common sense was a bit slow that day. I was clearly the tallest guy on the plane to Seoul, the tallest person on the plane to Beijing, and taller than most of the people I'd seen all day. What in the world made me think that they'd have anything in my size, knowing how next-to-impossible it is to find a 43 XL on an American rack? So the trip downstairs pretty much gave me my answer.

After returning to my room, I figured I'd at least go back down at 5:30 and attend the kickoff opening, even though I'd be ridiculously out of place. The program officials recommended it and said they really didn't mind. I considered the facts: for one, I was again the tallest person in the room, and two, I'd be wearing two-day-old clothes that were better suited for the basketball game than a formal welcome into a distinguished international program. I considered all that and went anyway. When I got there, I met the majority of the thirty-three people who were accepted and exchanged business cards. We had delightful conversations on what brought us there. I felt proud that my introduction was in both English and Chinese and was well understood in both languages so my tapes really paid off.

As I listened to the other guys in the room, I knew for certain this was the right place. Anyone working a nine-to-five should understand that creating a business concept, executing it successfully enough to make a living from it, and eventually selling the business is very, very difficult. Imagine doing that three times with very well-known names and successful businesses, and then deciding to change when you've been your own boss for twenty years. Even better, imagine being in the top of your class for over thirty years, assuming you started kindergarten at age five, never stopping attending school, and successfully becoming a brain surgeon after you've given up so much of your social life for extremely complex subject matter, and then one day saying, "I'm going to turn this all in." Can you imagine the price tag behind that decision? In both cases, let's say the men who made these decisions then decided to apply to a top business school and once accepted, flew to the other side of the world and paid the hefty price to attend a program that forced you to also stay at one of Beijing's most expensive hotels. I mean, really, what would make you do all that? Reaching for a dream life was all I could consider.

After the introductory reception, I spoke at length with one of the staff members about what I was going to do in terms of the money. She really put me at ease because she said there were other programs that I might be interested in checking out. She went on to mention a few of the ones at the Boston campus and highly recommended that I look at a real estate course in India that they were doing. She remembered from my application that I had written a book on real estate and a lot of my investment success had come from it. We delighted in the rich culture of HBS.

I was in Beijing, well-rested, and there wasn't a cloud in the sky. I booked a trip to go see the Great Wall, which I would not have had time for otherwise. At this point, the partygoers and those content with life are probably thinking, *I'm sure you have a problem, and you should redefine it. However, while you jump on that, we'll be back after midnight local time, exhausted and eagerly waiting to hear all about it.* The next few days were great. I've never been accused so many times of being an NBA basketball player. If I could just switch salaries with them, maybe we could talk. I also learned that sushi means seasoned rice. The dish was started when the Japanese used rice and salt to preserve fish.

The Numbers 6 and 8 Mean What?

I felt good about my decision to go to China and believed that my efforts weren't in vain. I decided to take a trip to the Great Wall completely out of the blue. Johnny (our female tour guide) said, "By the way, in China the number 6 means everything will go your way, and the number 8 means wealth." *Huh? What? Hold up, what the heck did she just say?* She said the numbers 6 and 8, in that order, without any reference to any other numbers at all. I asked her to repeat it, and she delightfully said it again. No one else asked her anything about numbers. No one even said anything at all. We were just quietly listening and watching. At that point, all I could do was sit back and smile. What a moment of peace that was.

There I was writing a book called *Slide 68* encouraging you to take advantage of your life and live out your dreams, when I found out that the numbers meant precisely that in Chinese. Talk about your karma! I knew right at that moment that, class or not, going to Beijing was absolutely necessary and essential to my continued success.

Fortunately not all was lost. I attended the opening ceremony and met fellow students from all over the world. We were instructed that we had a very formal introduction to look forward to, and I was ready. Because I studied various languages in other programs, I knew one of the most important steps for me to take was to learn the phrase, "How do you say the word 'blank' in Chinese?" I knew that other cultures appreciate it when you attempt to speak their language.

I had not formally studied Mandarin before going, but after being accepted, I purchased a language CD and learned quite a few basic and some advanced phrases over the months leading up to the trip. That helped me make a very respectful introduction when it was my turn. I was able to exchange business cards with a number of people, even one gentleman who was in IT, from Atlanta, Georgia.

I learned a lot in the ensuing hours among the male-dominated group. Regardless of where they were from, everyone seemed to be looking for a big payday. They were all sharp and well traveled and had some level of success in their current fields. I believed we were all reading similar headlines to the Wall Street guys who were taking home bonuses every year that were equal to or greater than our salaries and investments combined. We didn't discuss it because no one was talking about it at the time; none of had figured out that those record-breaking earnings and many of the headlines were the result of cheap credit and one of the big reasons why I ended up losing so much. I even found out that some of the most successful bankers in the Washington, DC, region had spent some time at Tsinghua University along the way. That made it feel even more like a good move to make. It was great to be a part of the crowd and share similar ideas. I'm looking forward to making a return trip to Beijing—and next time, I will make a detour in Macau to observe some of Roger Thomas's and Steve Wynn's Chinese digs.

Fried Macaroni and Cheese: Great Food for Business Meetings

I decided to take more heed of Keith Ferazzi's advice and began to spend more time dining with others. Honestly, it was not like I intended to do it, but with a few successes and curious other people wanting to know my next move, I was dining with others a lot. The beauty was that most of the lunches were paid for by the people whom I was dining with, as they wanted to pick my brain. Some wanted the audience of Investment Forum members that I had created, while others thought I was a great source of inspiration, and yet others thought I was an investment guru even before I wrote *Real Estate for Real People*.

Either way, I was doing a lot of dining with others, and my favorite meeting place was generally accepted like an accounting or finance standard. I would ask if they could meet me at the Cheesecake Factory in Tyson's Corner, Virginia. The Cheesecake Factory is a nice restaurant. It is not too expensive, the food is good, with hefty portions, and the prices really aren't bad. I hear the cheesecake is pretty good, but I never have any room left to eat it after the meal, and taking it home just isn't the same.

Ever since I was a kid, my favorite dish was fried chicken with macaroni and cheese. I'd eaten macaroni and cheese in what I thought was every conceivable fashion, and I have to give a hearty honorable mention to Michael Jordan's Steak House in Grand Central Station, as they prepare macaroni with some ingredients I don't readily remember, but it was very good. Some genius figured out a way to fry macaroni and cheese in some type of ball with a fried outer shell and baked inside. I haven't a clue how they did it, but it was an instant hit with me. I wish they'd serve it as a side dish and not an appetizer because I'm generally not interested in sharing it with my lunch guests. Regardless, they allow me to have my fair share, and we get down to business.

The guy I tend to meet most regularly is Jay Pendarvis. Jay is a well-informed, highly intelligent guy and very motivated. For the life of me, I thought he was a kid when I saw him, as he isn't very tall, but that's not it. He must have figured out whatever Stacy Dash was doing, because my man didn't age much. As time would eventually tell, he was actually older than I was, but it certainly didn't show. Jay and I were in similar places in life. I think Jay was a bit more in tune to the skills that it took to succeed before I was, and he left the big company's decent wages to create a much higher income for himself by bidding on the same government contracts he was used to working on; instead of working for a big company, he could do it for himself. That way his new M5 BMW could still be enjoyed, but it was now part of his business expense. I never would have thought that one could drive such a luxury car and write off the monthly payments as part of a business expense. That was the beauty of meeting with people who were a few notches ahead of you in some areas.

Jay was also further ahead of the game because he had been exposed by great parents. His dad was a lawyer and grew up during the civil rights era, so he and Jay's mom had him reading profusely ever since he was much younger. I didn't really get involved in becoming a serious reader until after business school. I really have to give credit to Donald Trump, as I read his book *How to Think Like a Billionaire,* in which he said that if you want to achieve great wealth and success, then you absolutely have to read the best-selling guys who write about how they did it. It was then that I began to discover that you can spend hours with billionaires, but the deal is you have to read their book. Jay had long ago figured this out and was not only reading business books; his library was quite varied. He even taught me about keeping a book in the queue to read after I finish reading the current one. He agreed with Trump in terms of reading at least one book a month.

Slide 68 Mind-Set

Meeting regularly with like-minded people helps build your knowledge base and your contacts and keeps you up on the latest events. You don't need a lot of people in this circle; a few dedicated teams or individuals can be all you need to advance your success.

Jay and I would have power lunches pretty regularly, and we shared ideas and passions about how we'd make it and how passionate we were about "getting up out the game," meaning we were so sick of the BS nine-to-fives where we had to sit and look interested even when our tasks were done but we were five hours short of quitting time. Jay also read the business section of the *Washington Post* regularly, and we got sick of seeing the stories of how others were making multimillion-dollar private equity or investment banking deals while we were trying to figure out how to get to our big payday.

Jay reached the acquisition theory much earlier than I did. I was continuing to think that if we just kept working organically, we would one day be where we wanted. There is nothing inherently wrong with that, except it may take a lot of time or at least more than you want. We both understood M & A (mergers and acquisitions), but he had really gotten his head around the concept that you just buy your competitors instead of spending so much time trying to beat them. That's how the big boys were doing it, and he understood it and believed in it. I was slower to the table, but after a few more of those boring meetings at the big organizations, which had me on the semimonthly leash, I began to feel the urge to look into this much more.

One of my most coveted Cheesecake Factory guests came by total surprise. I was awaiting my good friend and colleague Lois Houston one day, as she wanted a copy of my real estate book and agreed to meet me there to have lunch while we discussed the current state of affairs on a number of topics.

I went ahead and sat down, ordered my fried macaroni and cheese, and continued browsing my messages. Shortly afterward, the waitress brought a young lady to me and asked, "Is this her?" I looked up as the waitress was asking the young lady if I was him. We gave each other a look and simultaneously agreed that we were not the people that we were waiting for. Apparently, she was waiting for a tall slim guy named Anthony, who was pretty much my build and certainly my name; ironically he also was known to order fried macaroni and cheese.

As the waitress seated her near me, she came up to me and said, "I just have to shake your hand because of Barack." I said, "Screw that; give me a hug!" She said her name was Michelle, so that was easy to remember considering it's the First Lady's first name. There was a lot of secret handshaking and black people giving each other secret grins to celebrate the first black president of the United States. In fact, I recall listening to the radio when famed talk show host Donnie Simpson was interviewing Jamie Foxx. He mentioned that he was checking into a hotel, and the bag assistant was the only black guy around and was assigned to help him out. As he described it, it seemed as if the two of them were hoping that they would be assigned each other. On the way to the room, down the corridors and on the elevator, they remained calm, but knew in the back of their minds they were thinking the same thing. Once they arrived in the room behind closed doors, they both exploded with excitement as they simultaneously screamed, "Barack!"

For the life of me, I couldn't understand why so many famed and successful black people kept saying they never thought they'd live to see a black president. I totally disagreed, and not just because I was younger. We had first black everything else, so why not the president? I was a bit more open with my enthusiasm and really didn't care who heard me, as I never thought or said anything that should have been considered offensive.

At any rate, Michelle was seated just out of my peripheral vision, slightly behind me. We struck up a conversation and just had a great time chatting as we waited for Lois and Anthony, our respective guests. Michelle mentioned that she was from California, and we talked a lot about the much nicer weather and life in Cali in general. She told me that she ran an organization called Celebrate Life Foundation, as it was her personal testimony to being a cancer survivor and her quest to educate the masses on life with cervical cancer. I told her about the Investment Forum, and she felt that we could hook up and perhaps have an event because we had very similar drive and motivation.

While we were waiting for our respective guests, our appetizers came out simultaneously, and to our surprise, it turns out we both ordered fried macaroni and cheese. As we enjoyed our lunch, I realized we had a lot in common. She was tenacious at business and life. We hit it off instantly, and what we were calling the "wrong" person actually ended up being so right.

We could feel an instant vibe and agreed to come back the very next day and have lunch there again. We returned at high noon the next day and ended up staying there for hours, just talking about our respective business ventures. Michelle was so sure we'd do business and start a great friendship that she told me we were going to be in each other's lives for the rest of our lives. It was a bold statement and surely a leap of faith, but I have to say I believed her. We just had so much in common. We wasted no time collaborating, and she hosted my next investment forum in a swank DC hotel. It was a great event and the start to a long-lasting relationship.

I began to ponder what it was about a dish that I never heard or saw advertised that was such a hit among the business community. As I began to talk to more people who dined there during lunch, I realized many high-caliber people were making the order. I believe that fried macaroni and cheese, especially in the South, is a dish that makes people feel good. It is a dish that relaxes us, and we look forward to it. From the business perspective, it is a meal that can be enjoyed during the workday without sitting too heavily on the stomach and tiring us out as we go into the home stretch to finish out our day.

I went on to meet many more people and sign several business deals there. Who says we had to meet at the golf course? I believe in what Ferazzi was saying in that there is so much you can learn by dining with others. Whether it is insight gained on a book that you both read or a meeting you both attended, the knowledge and insight you walk away with are immeasurable. Even more important is the fact that you simply can't go it alone. Whether you work in an office with people you don't like or not, you simply don't have all the answers; sharing some of your insight with others is a great way to advance your cause, whatever it might be. In the meantime, you get to know some great dishes at some great restaurants. Also, I had to occasionally remind myself that even after having ten meetings and it seeming that I hadn't gained any significant insight, that I was probably gaining more than I realized. Oftentimes it is the pie effect. You are gradually expanding and not seeing a lot of ground coverage, but when you look back after a year or so, you realize that not only were you gaining ground in one direction, but you were also avoiding having to go down useless paths in other directions.

Finding a Platinum Mine
with the Donald's Wharton Club

Slide 68 Mind-Set

As you chart your path to success, you will find that frequent meetings during the lunch hour are common places to get things done. Whatever restaurant or eatery you choose, ensure that it is something that doesn't distract from your mission. A heavy meal, such as barbecue ribs, while it is very good, requires a lot of hand cleansing. You can't follow any discussion that includes presentations or agendas without having to constantly wipe your hands. That can become very distracting for the people you are meeting with if they have to continuously slow down or stop what they are doing while you clean yourself up in an attempt to follow along.

My years at the Citadel had served me well. In comparison to my friends, I was clearly a few notches ahead and was looking to go farther. I think a lot of that had to do with my time and exposure there. In a very honest fashion, it had taught me to not be afraid of or intimidated by white men who looked wealthy. As I watched my colleagues who were there, most of them—white men—had a supreme level of confidence in the face of authority. Where I would surely have backed down, they were just not afraid, and in some cases not even impressed.

I think a lot of it had to do with the fact that a number of them were already middle class; their parents or family members were in middle—to upper middle-class jobs and were well-educated. I thought for years the middle class were actually the rich. I had no idea what it was like or the life you could live if two people worked together with a combined income of $170K for a few years.

After I began working professionally, I saw this in much more common fashion. Also, because I was new to the DC metro, I decided to take advantage of the DC-area Citadel alumni club. I thought for years that I'd find many men who had soared through the ranks in corporate America making a few hundred thousand dollars a year. I thought there would be tons of insight on how to really get out there and make it happen. Instead, what I found was a super-thick chain of camaraderie and pretty much average middle—to upper middle-class guys in support of their alma mater.

There were surely some highly successful people scattered about, but it wasn't the norm. Most of these guys were either currently serving as officers of the military or recently retired and now working on government contracts. I'm sure their median household incomes in many cases were $150 to $175,000+ under the two working spouses' rule. That was without question the middle class, whom I was thinking were rich when I was in college. There was nothing wrong with what these good men and now women had. They were red-blooded, taxpaying Americans, and that was what many people aspired to be. We owe many of them a great deal of thanks for their military service careers, which allowed us to have the freedom to pursue our goals and wildest dreams.

It took me eleven years to finally get the big picture and realize the network of people that I aspired to be around was probably not going to be found within the typical meeting of my alumni network. I was going to clearly have to find them some other way. Also, around this time, I was spending much more time paying attention to the *Washington Post* business section to see where all the events and happenings for the week were.

Out of years of curiosity, I was made aware of the top floor of a building in Tyson's Corner, Virginia, that skied above all the other buildings in the area. One day, I simply went into the building and went to the top floor. When I got there, I found the Tower Club. The Tower Club was a private "C"-level club that was the lounge for a number of executives and high-ranking government officials. I arranged for an appointment and realized that I really should explore having a membership there. Because my operating income was down so much, I knew it was senseless to try and add it into my budget. Instead, I continuously asked about it. Surprised, I found that some of my colleagues were already members but rarely used it. I was shocked, thinking *why in the world would you pay a monthly fee for a nice club and never use it?*

One day as I was browsing the face—time section of the *Washington Post*, I noticed there was a breakfast meeting on professional selling in the Tower Club, and the cost was only $30. I thought that these were surely my kind of prices for the moment. I attended the meeting to find out that it was being hosted by the Wharton Club. I knew the benefits of Wharton because Donald Trump always hailed it as the best business school in America. I was willing to argue slightly, but knew without question that this was surely at the top of the pile. Wharton was hailed as the best in terms of finance careers, for sure.

After I arrived, I observed the ambiance and the people who were there and felt quite comfortable. We had a great meeting, and toward the end, Alan Schlaifer, the club president, encouraged us to come out to the many events that Wharton sponsored throughout the year. I really liked Schlaifer because of his intellect and his knowledge of presence. He could be thrown on the spot and come up with very intelligent things to say that acknowledged virtually everyone in the room. He was aware of his surroundings, and his intelligence gained from past experiences was at his beckoning call. He could combine it all and make an impactful statement as if it were well-rehearsed. That was a trait I respected because I was known to do it in similar fashion from time to time, but I could tell he was much more versed, a lot smarter, and well-traveled. As soon as I realized that I could take advantage of attending meetings with the organization, I took full advantage.

I began to realize that great institutions like the Citadel had students who were just as smart as Harvard's and Wharton's, but a lot of the success to be gained after leaving school had to do with alumni exposure. The Citadel was known for placing young men in the military and in government jobs, while Wharton was placing many men and women in the top echelons of the corporate world. A Wharton degree was never a guarantee that you would make it to the top, but the odds were surely better than for graduates of many other schools.

I instantly took advantage of luncheons that I would have never had access to with the Citadel's network. I attended lunch with Vice President Dick Cheney, lunch with Bob Griefeld, CEO of the NASDAQ, dinner with the Ambassador king of Morocco, Aziz Mekouar, and so on. Every event that they hosted was like this. There was lunch with Richard Branson of Virgin Atlantic, Dolly Parton, Mary Tyler Moore, DC Mayor Adrian Fenty, and the list went on and on with people at the top of their game. I realized that this was the circle I had to spend more time in, and it wasn't free. Each event could easily run $30, although some of them were free. The point was that as long as I stayed around the middle-class mind-set, I was only going to get middle-class results; until I stepped one foot outside of that box, not much was going to change. I remembered that insanity was defined as doing the same thing over and over but expecting different results.

I really must drive home the point that just because this caliber of people are at these events and you are allowed the ability to interact with them doesn't mean an instant connection to residual millions. What it provides is perspective on things. Personally, I was given the opportunity to bounce ideas and theories of things I'd thought of and read about to the people who were much further along than I was. I found in a large degree that throughout my many readings, I was able to put together some very intelligent fact-based questions. When I saw that these people never gave me an awkward look, as if I were saying something that didn't make sense, I felt justified that I could continue plowing down the road I was on. These were the opportunities for those smarter than me to correct my field of vision if I were heading down the wrong path. In addition, I commonly asked for their address to send them follow-up information on concepts I was working on. These were the platinum opportunities that I just wasn't getting in many of the other group meetings I was attending; I found more expert events in Wharton's club in a month than I could process in years in other places.

During a Harvard Business School alumni meeting, I was able to present a business plan, and the judges liked it so well that they asked me to entertain the idea of chairing an investment club for the DC chapter. The jury is still out on exactly how they want to move forward, but it's certainly a golden opportunity should it come to fruition.

Slide 68 Mind-Set

Some meetings one may attend will help immensely in defining who you want to be or what you want to do. If you think automobile dealer ownership businesses will provide you the income to live your dream life, you may find out that you are really more interested in the service aspect as opposed to the sales, and perhaps you want to build an empire on servicing the cars as opposed to running the dealership.

PART 4:

Putting It All Together

So This Is What I've Been Called to Do!

Remember the *Real Estate for Real People* newspaper article?

It turned out that many of the people in my hometown had not forgotten who I was and they still read the local paper. When the article came out, my family was phoned by several people, who apparently read about me and sent congratulations. In addition, North Central High, my local high school, had also read it. One morning, I received a call from the principal's office. I was thinking that perhaps my son had gotten into some trouble, something he wasn't known for doing. Mr. Worth Thomasson, the principal, assured me that my son was fine, and he wished he could clone him. He went on to say that the school was trying something new and wanted to know if I would like to be a part of it. He said that they decided to change the format of the commencement address and wanted to invite back the most successful alumni they had to give the speech. He said that I was the unanimous favorite and he would be honored if I accepted the invitation. I was absolutely honored to receive his call and gladly accepted.

Several months later, I gave what I was told was one of the best addresses the packed stadium had heard in years. It just so happened to be my twenty-year class reunion, and I couldn't have dreamed of a better way to celebrate it. I couldn't help entitling the speech "Outlasting Success's Fleeting Nature." I recited the name of every teacher I had in the Kershaw County school system from kindergarten to high school and ensured that the crowd gave them all a thundering round of applause. I'm not sure if they were impressed with the act or that I was able to recall every teacher I had from K-12. Either way, I had always dreamed of holding a special ceremony for all my K-12 educators and had never really gotten around to doing it. That gave me the chance to do it in grand style so that neither they nor the community would forget it for a long time to come.

My parents were there front and center, right along with Toni, my aunts, cousins, brothers, and other extended family. I think they thought I'd be nervous or a little tense. Normally, I am a bit jittery before speeches, but that entire morning I was as calm as an ocean breeze. I could see my mom's bright smile from the podium; I knew she was so proud to see me up there. My mom and dad looked on with intensity. When the valedictorian introduced me, the biography she gave was so impressive that I had to wonder if it was even me she was talking about. All those nose-to-the-grindstone moments had paid off; the sound of victory coming from her lips and echoing off the stadium seats as she introduced me was one of the best moments I could have never imagined. I gave a heartfelt, yet commanding, speech about my days of success and failure. I gave them straight talk about personal appearance and the tatted-up generation to the importance of higher education. I was very forward in letting them know that even the most advanced education was no guarantee for success. I provided snapshots of my dealings with the business and political elite and dared them to soar to higher grounds than I ever dreamed of.

After the ceremony, I knew I would take lots of pictures, shake lots of hands, and see tons of old friends. What I didn't expect was my parents running up to me ahead of the crowd to congratulate me. My mom's first words were, "You sounded like Martin Luther King!" My dad interrupted and said, "No, Barrack Obama!" It was clearly one of my parents' proudest moments. I never asked the school for a dime in terms of compensation, and I can assure you whether they gave me $10 or $40 million, none of it would have equaled the feeling I got from being back in my community as a celebrated success story. Bathed in sweat from the sun's rays that had finally come out, I indulged in the moment. At the same time, I felt a bit bad for my son because a lot of his friends knew me based on what they would hear about his exotic vacations or my exotic cars, but everyone who didn't surely would know that he was my son now.

After the ceremony, we threw my dad a surprise birthday party, and at midnight I hit the road to Miami. I had one of the best trips that we ever had, enjoying everything—gorgeous mansions, fattening foods, great music, and just a great time in life. It was one of the richest weekends I'd had in a long time. It became clear to me that my mission was helping the common man live an affluent life regardless of where his finances were in the past. Investing my six-figure earnings was simply the vehicle that provided me affluent experiences! It took me years to really get my head around the concept, even overlooking it while designing the Arc De Triompe, a $400,000, three-thousand-square-foot conference center in my French château, as a vehicle to do it. Talk about overlooking the obvious!

When did it finally hit me? After reflecting on the question "What am I passionate about doing?" so many times from reading so many books, I'd finally pondered the question enough to write the answer while reading *The Presentation Secrets of Steve Jobs* by Carmine Gallo while sitting in a bookstore, Books-A–Million, in Potomac Mills mall. Nearly three and a half years after I starting writing this book, the answer finally revealed itself. On page 30, I read Chris Gardner's story about "find something you love to do so much, you can't wait for the sun to rise to do it all over again." I had read Gardner's comments many times before, but sometimes it just takes the right environment for them to sink in.

Slide 69: From the Poorhouse to the White House

Ironically I had just, in a very unexcited yet appreciative fashion, received a job offer for 150K a year in salary, which was probably going to yield another 30K in bonus before I began to invest it. It was going to take several months before I could get a start date for the job, and to be perfectly honest, it was just going to be more of the same type of environment. I knew I could maximize 401(k) contributions with just 11 percent of my income from one income source, and likely far less than that after bonuses. The money was going to be a great start, but mentally, I was going to be about as moved as where I was when my journey started.

Around this time, I received an e-mail from an office at the White House, where I had applied to do some work right after I gave the commencement address. The opportunity was forwarded to me by my aunt Pumpkin, who was mentoring a good friend who was in the army but also stationed there. When I got the message, I thought to myself, *that would be very neat if it happened. I mean, after all, how many people get to work there doing anything?* The application was laborious to many because it contained so many thought-provoking essays, but that wasn't a problem for me due to all the newsletters I wrote to my Investment Forum followers and the fact that I was in a doctoral program where all we did was write.

When I opened the message, I was under the impression that it would be another rejection letter that I would soon discard; however, this time things would be different. They wanted to schedule a phone interview for me to talk more about the role I'd be doing. I immediately responded and eagerly began background research on the new office I'd be potentially working in. I would not be caught off guard by anything they would ask regarding anything business—or policy-related. I was so confident at that point that I edited a newsletter that I had written to my group and announced my new venture as I was so confident it was meant specifically for me. Sure enough, they called me a few days later, and I had a successful interview. They told me that they would give me a decision within a week's time, but the affirmation actually came within a matter of hours.

I took the role very seriously. I knew while some might look at it as a great opportunity, I looked at it as a time in the nation when diligence and trust had to be restored. Washington reputations were taking poundings as the American people had lost confidence by leaps and bounds that our elected officials were serving us. I felt that by working that closely near the president, I would find opportunities that I never dreamed existed. I felt I could gain understanding and pass those nuggets of wisdom onto people who could benefit from them. I was very excited about where I could go, but I immediately put the interests of others ahead of mine. While my French castle and helicopter were important, this was my chance to do something important for an entire nation, and I wasn't going to let that opportunity pass just to cross off the items on my material wish list. Make no mistake about it, however: I'd done enough reading about those who went on to enjoy great success—some of them even talked about in this book—whose success started out on Capitol Hill. I knew right at that point my next venture was huge, much more than I probably could even imagine, and this would be the opportunity not only for me to live a dream life but to find the answers that many others needed to help them do the same.

At that point, I knew the transition was complete, and I was finally ready to move on from Slide 68. I had no concept that I would end up in the White House, though it may be easy to see for someone who is reading my story; but I assure you it was the result of me taking every day for what it was, and this was a new opportunity, one in which no stone was left unturned.

I wrote this story as it unfolded, assuring myself that I would find something very special in the end. It was my self-test that would ultimately prove to me, and especially others, that when you set your sights on a better life, with the mind-set that you won't give up regardless of what happens, success cannot escape you forever. I was sure that I would have found some great opportunity within twelve months after setting out on this journey, but it would be forty months before a great opportunity to change my life came my way. I stress this to all, to let you know that some things are out of your control; as much as we'd like to artificially place a time line on when we will have the results we desire, it's not always up to us. Hang in there, fight the good fight anyway, and you are sure to find the path that leads you to the lifestyle you've been dreaming of.

You've Made Key Contacts— Now What? Marriott Introduces a Piece of the Pie, While Steve Wynn and Roger Thomas Shed "Light" on Things

J. W. Marriott

Earlier, I talked about one of the best days I ever had. I mentioned all the great people I met, like J. W. Marriott Jr. Normally, when I go to events where there are VIPs, I don't have an agenda. It's just nice to be around the movers and shakers, because they think at a higher level and discuss ideas instead of people. That being said, I don't avoid agendas either. What I've found is everyone is busy trying to get face time with the most successful people in the room, whereas I tend to hold back unless I just happen to be face-to-face with the person and the conversation lends itself to that. I prefer to send a follow-up letter and mention that we met at whatever event and follow up that way. In addition, I don't follow up with people just for follow-up's sake. If I have a legitimate reason to follow up with someone, I will.

In this case, I decided to write to Mr. Marriott several days later to legitimately thank him for his time spent. I truly did appreciate his humility regarding the astronomical success he's had. When I wrote to him, I wanted to get his permission to write about the memorable day I had when I saw him. Amazingly, he wrote me back. What was even more amazing was he handwrote the response. He could have gotten one of his staff members to either send me an e-mail or call me to give me a thumbs-up or thumbs-down, but he did it himself.

Several days later, I received another handwritten letter. This time it was from a lady named Kathleen Matthews. When I saw the name, I kept thinking I knew that name from somewhere. Several days passed before I finally decided to look it up; when I did, I was pleasantly surprised. Kathleen was the former anchorwoman on Washington's ABC News Channel 7. Also worth mentioning, she is married to Chris Matthews of *Hardball with Chris Matthews* on MSNBC. She had stepped down from her role and started working with Mr. Marriott as his Executive VP of Human Affairs. She wrote to let me know that she totally concurred with what I saw in Mr. Marriott. Her gesture was surely the uplift for the week, as I was riding pretty high with his handwritten letter also.

Several months passed before I reached back out to Mr. Marriott. I wasn't sure he would continue to respond, but I thought it was a legitimate enough request so I thought I'd give it one more try. On February 25, 2009, I attended a meeting in Washington DC at the Economic Partnership office. The office was very similar to the economic development offices I visited in Prince George's County. The meeting that day focused on franchising. They had a group of panelists talk about the ins and outs of franchising different businesses. At the end of the meeting, the center director mentioned that the office was giving a $100,000 prize to the winner of the best business plan. I figured there was no way I was passing this opportunity up without at least taking a chance. I really didn't know what type of plan to put together, even though the rules mentioned the plan should be for a continuation of your current business.

I knew I could extend the plan for my investment forums, but I figured if they were giving that much money, perhaps I should look for something more sophisticated. So I decided to put together a business plan for a franchise. I really didn't know which business to do, and then I thought back to Mr. Marriott. I figured that hotels are franchised, and what would be a better decision than writing a business plan around building a Marriott in Washington? I knew that I wanted to get further into a commercial real estate development, and a hotel would be as good a start as any I figured. Besides, after meeting several black hotel owners, I figured I could do it if they could. Even more, I figured if I asked Mr. Marriott to simply appoint one of his staff members to answer a few questions for me as I put together the business plan, I would hit a few birds with one stone. I would gain more contacts within the field that I would eventually need. I would extend my name within the Marriott organization, which couldn't be a bad thing. I would have a resident expert to help me look at the plan, which would increase my chances of winning. If I won the contest, that would be great seed money to show potential investors that I at least had a start. I figured even if I lost, the only thing I risked was the opportunity to fail, and that was a great failing opportunity if there was one. There was no way to lose on this deal.

Being obedient to the spirit of my mind and heart, I wrote to Mr. Marriott again. This is exactly what I said:

Mr. Bill Marriott:

When I saw you at the National Harbor back in September as Kenneth Fern opened his Residence Inn hotel, I just felt that I belonged in the company of great people such as yourself. I wasn't going to sit around and dream my way there, so I started working toward and executing a plan. Since then I have done the following:

ICSC—International Council of Shopping Centers

- Become an active registered member of the ICSC

- Registered for the Strategic Leadership Summit on Capitol Hill in March

- Registered for the upcoming Global Retail Convention in Las Vegas

- Volunteered for ICSC Alliance Committee for the Washington DC region

NABHOOD—National Association of Black Hotel Owners, Operators, & Developers

- Met and spoke with Andrew Ingraham, CEO of NABHOOD

- Registered for their July conference

- Working on getting one of NABHOOD's premier speakers an honorary degree and confirmed him a speaking engagement at the Citadel in South Carolina

Washington DC Economic Partnership

- Registered for several of their economic development events

- Registered for their $100,000 business plan competition

Real Estate for Real People

- Began an aggressive marketing campaign for my real estate investment guide

- Moved up to #38 on publisher's best-selling list

- Increased online book sales in Europe

  The reason I'm writing is because I have all intentions of giving my best effort to win the DC Economic Partnership business plan competition. I decided why not put the effort of the plan behind doing a feasibility study/business plan around franchising a Marriott-managed hotel? As I am aware that it takes substantially more to own and operate a star-quality hotel, $100,000 is a start in the right direction. In addition, I have increased membership in my investment club by 10 percent, some of whom are corporate real estate investors and fund managers who may be able to help gain funding for a location.

  Is it possible to work with someone from your Owner and Franchise Services to get some pertinent questions answered as I prepare this business plan?

  Thanks tremendously once again for your time, and I assure you that it is substantially appreciated! I just can't get over the fact that legendary business leaders such as yourself and Mr. Warren Buffett are willing to pause from what you are doing to entertain brief questions from people aspiring for success like me. I couldn't think of a thing you would ever need from me, but should there be something, please don't hesitate to make it known, and I won't hesitate to make it happen.

  Sincerely,

  Anthony Von Mickle

  The Investment Forum, *presiding*

Again, he had an answer. He forwarded my note to Ray Bennett, Senior Vice President North America Lodging and Development. Ray called me a few days later and asked me about the letter. I explained it to him, and he was willing to help. As it turns out, my timing was perfect. Marriott had a two-day symposium coming up where they were going to entertain the idea of minority hotel ownership within the organization, and Ray invited me to the conference. In addition, Andy Ingraham, who was the president of NABHOOD, was going to be speaking. Incidentally, Ingraham and I had spoken since the day we met for about forty-five minutes. He mentioned that he was heading to Don Peebles's house that weekend for an event. He really schooled me on terminology regarding the industry. As we ended the conversation, he told me I should come to his conference in July for their annual symposium to discuss the state of hospitality for minorities.

I didn't know Ingraham was going to be speaking that week. I called his office to get further information on the dates of his symposium and register as a new member. It was only because I had some information on my application that they needed to verify that he called me. It just so happened that the Marriott two-day conference was going on at the same time. When I received Ingraham's call, I reminded him of who I was, and we had a pleasant conversation. It was near the end of the call that I told him what I had in the works, and he told me he was going to be one of the keynote speakers.

Marriott Putting Its Money Where Its Mouth Is

I can't let this moment go without spreading the good word about Marriott's diversity hotel ownership program led by Ray. It was hard to believe Ray was newly appointed to this executive position, as he absolutely flowed right through it. He was a great pick for this job. I knew who he was long before he ever extended his hand to me. He was poised, confident, and looked the part. His stature was easily backed when he began to speak. A lot of companies talked a lot about how much they cared about diversity, but Marriott was not playing any games. They actually carved out time, which in their business is big money, to introduce to some and manifest to others how they wanted minorities to get a piece of the pie. Ray understood this and was making it abundantly clear in his message.

I watched other hotels talk about diversity. I listened to their executives dance around the question of what they were doing when asked by African American potential investors. However, when someone asked Ray what Marriott was doing, it was as if he was just waiting to explode with answers. There was just no competition, and he made everyone understand that they didn't just give lip service. Ray's answers were polished and backed by concrete evidence, with dates, names, places, and literature to answer every question imaginable. You could tell he wasn't some token pick from Marriott to look good for investors, but instead, the choice of a grueling selection process in something on which the Marriott reputation was riding. I would invite any successful business team reading this who is seriously interested in hotel ownership to look them up. It is time well spent for the opportunity of a lifetime.

Steve Wynn and Roger Thomas—The Dynamic Duo

I was eager to get to Vegas so I could have a slightly more detailed look at the Bellagio hotel. I knew I'd find things there that I wanted to incorporate into the Château. I spent some much desired time in the Bellagio studying the moldings and ceilings. They did a spectacular job with the impressive display. One of the areas I enjoyed the most just happened to be right next to a chocolate fountain that seemed to be a part of the store called Jean Phillipe Patisserie. They created the most delicious and crafty desserts I'd ever seen. I couldn't resist, and I am sure I ate more this time in Vegas than ever. I wanted to see their presidential suite, but the elevators were guarded to keep people out who were not hotel guests.

Next I went to the Wynn, and it was here that I found the chandeliers that I had to have. I'd been to the Wynn the year prior, but there are so many things going on in this hotel, both inside and out, that you can't possibly catch them all the first two and maybe even three dozen times. Every square inch had been meticulously thought out.

Coming to Las Vegas, I had to remember that we were in the middle of the desert. Someone had a vision that turned a gambling hole into a world-class vacation resort, and he did all this within one building, several times over. I had to ponder what was really going on here. To me, it was a man's thinking that he would bring man, woman, and child unto him in a desolate land and they would spend with him all their money and be willing to do it over and over, making him wealthy the world over. It taught me the beauty of living in an area where there is nothing. That meant I could create a palace so beautiful that people would drive down my street just to catch a glimpse of it.

There was so much to see that you simply could not move in a hurry. Everything was effectively placed, so that way one thing wouldn't impede the others. Wynn had famed designer Roger Thomas create an upside-down, three-tiered parasol chandelier that was like nothing I'd ever seen. It was one of the most magnificent pieces of lighting ever created. I spent so much time gazing at the ceiling observing all the chandelier concepts that I'd never fathomed and tracing the large moldings. The moldings reminded me of a thick layer of icing that was drawn on a tasty pastry. The dark colors in the background and the thick, rich, white moldings in the foreground almost made the ceilings appear scrumptious and ready to eat, if you could do such a thing. Who would ever think of a ceiling as tasty?

For the life of me, I wondered how in the world someone would think of something like that, which is probably why Wynn chose Thomas in the first place. Whatever the case, I kept thinking that lack of money in their personal financial situations could not have been in the picture. I simply believe you create your best when you don't have to worry about the light bill. I do realize that some people use arts and crafts to escape whatever life's problems are, but still at some point, when the crafts go away, reality will set back in.

I had no idea that Thomas even existed until I began a search for these chandeliers. It didn't take me long before I found a lot of opposition in figuring out where I might be able to obtain a few for myself. Most custom makers would not even respond to my request, while others tried to push products they'd already made. While some of the products were very nice, nothing quite made the parasol statement. We are so fortunate to have the world at our fingertips with Internet access. I was able to find interviews of both Wynn and Thomas and see their actions and reactions to different questions.

From there, I learned enough about Thomas to feel that he was approachable and decided I would contact him. I explained to him that I was building a magnificent French château and how the chandeliers would be absolute showstoppers in my two-story foyer, much like they were in the hotel. To my surprise, just a short while later, he called me back. He caught me totally off guard. I was leaving the White House after a long day of listening to people put the Obama administration on the spot for small business ideas and was really looking forward to changing the subject. As I was leaving the gate, I noticed the 702 area code and figured it was probably his admin, but to my surprise it was him. He and I had a delightful chat talking about global interior design and architecture, as well as some of his recent projects. He granted me permission to purchase the chandeliers for my new home on the basis that I wouldn't put them in a hotel. I assured him I wouldn't, and he gave me the manufacturer information and we began working together on color design. It was such a rush to think a world-famous designer would consider allowing me to use the chandeliers in a hotel that's deemed one of the finest under the sun in my own personal residence.

Again, it just goes to show that capital connections pay off when you put something behind them. Anyone could have met Thomas in a number of places, but if you never follow up and provide people the opportunity to help you go further, then you're simply a social butterfly. If that's what you want, that's fine, but I think you can gain more mileage for your time and money.

PART 5:

Dealing with Success—
The Good, the Bad,
and the Ugly

"Just a Man I Met in the Bathroom": Your Reputation May Precede You

In the movie *Coming to America*, Eddie Murphy played the role of a prince named Hakeem from an imaginary country in Africa called Zumunda who has come to America to find his bride. He was out of place and out of touch with the local society, as he was used to being catered to from his meals to his royal bath. He decided to leave Zumunda to have fate decide who he would marry on his twenty-first birthday, instead of the traditional handpicked bride. He wanted to blend in and be known as a commoner to keep people from being attracted to his rich and powerful family.

As he began his new search in Queens, New York, he found himself in love with a young lady named Lisa, who was the daughter of a fast-food restaurant owner of upper middle-class means. Unfortunately the young lady was already involved with someone, who was not exactly handpicked but highly favored, but she did think Murphy was a good catch for her sister. Lisa invited him to join herself, her sister, and her boyfriend for a St. John's basketball game. Because Hakeem was a king in a faraway land, most people didn't recognize him, and he was able to blend into the crowds—at least until he found himself in the bathroom. As kingship would have it, a janitor recognized him and began to bow gracefully before his presence.

He tried to give a slight level of acknowledgement to the citizen of Zumunda and keep things moving. A short while later, the man returned with yet another citizen of Zumunda and pleaded for Hakeem's attention as he was headed to his seat. The second gentleman was pulled in to take a picture of the excited citizen and the prince. Just after the picture was taken, the two men bowed repeatedly and excitedly before his presence. As rotten luck would have it, the bowing took place just as Hakeem's party was walking up. Naturally, the friends gave him the most unusual look as he exited the bathroom to witness two men bowing repeatedly to a fast-food worker With a strange look, Lisa asked him, "Who was that?" He responded, "Oh, just a man I met in the bathroom."

I live a very regimented lifestyle. Each day I wake up at 4:30 a.m., put on my sweats, and head out the door, with a direct route to the gym. I've worked at many different government buildings throughout the last five years or so, and luckily most of them have a gym somewhere in the basement. I assume that the government has come to understand that a healthy employee is a more productive employee. Regardless, I take full advantage of the facilities, as gym memberships can be very costly. I've made acquaintance with many guys over the years as we've shared a dumbbell, weight bench, or squat rack or two.

My previous job location also had a gym on the ground floor, and each morning I found myself there bright and early with the same people, who also had regimented schedules. For the most part, I didn't have a lot to say. Actually, none of us did, unless there was some story on TV that just commanded our response. We weren't looking to make a lot of conversation because we wanted to keep our schedules moving so we could get upstairs and get to work so we could continue on with our day and our life.

One July morning, I entered the gym to find a new face. The young man was on the treadmill grinding away as I entered. I had never seen him before. He looked up briefly, and we gave each other the friendly nod and both continued our direction. I spent my usual twenty minutes or so in the gym and headed for the showers.

This gentleman also finished up his workout about the same time. Because my mind was probably already a million miles away and running by that point, I didn't really notice his presence. Before long, he initiated some small talk, and somehow we ended up talking about investments, which happens to be my favorite subject. From there the conversation just took off. We talked about all types of investments and books. I recall that we spent a large portion of the conversation talking about a book that was written by Donald Trump and Robert Kiyosaki called *Why We Want You to Be Rich*. Thomas, as I would later learn was his name, had already read the book and was giving his take on it. By this time, I was already in the showers and yelling over the water flow as Thomas continued his shower prep. We began talking about local movers and shakers, and I responded with whether I knew them or not. Thomas then asked me something that caught me totally off guard. In a sort of excitement. he asked, "Have you ever heard of a guy named Anthony Mickle?"

I paused, thinking, *is this some kind of a joke? I mean, surely we'd introduced ourselves.* But then I had to rethink the issue. Actually, we did not introduce ourselves.

We were just doing what I commonly do when I meet someone, which is just keep talking until I find some point of interest that makes me say, "I want to continue this conversation further." At that point, I will generally exchange names if it hasn't happened already.

So there I was in the shower washing and yelling over the gym curtain, leaning toward the sound of the voice while trying not to touch filthy, nasty, plastic by-product, wondering, *did this guy just ask me have I met the very guy he is talking to? Does he legitimately not know it's me that he is talking to?* Realizing I had been momentarily silent, I grabbed the shower curtain and pulled away just enough to allow my head to show without exciting the guys and exposing my rippling muscles. I shouted, "Are you serious?"

As I posed the question to Thomas, the look on his face reminded me of the little Big Wheel-riding kid in the hit cartoon movie *The Incredibles*, where Mr. Incredible picked up his car and was about to slam it down after the door wouldn't shut. It was his way of venting his frustration after a long, dry day at the nine-to-five he hated. While Mr. Incredible was about to make mincemeat out of his vehicle, the neighborhood kid was just idly sitting by, watching the whole act unfold. Just as the car was about to be smashed to bits, the muscle-bound, frustrated man happenstance looked over and saw the kid witnessing all this in wonderment. The look on the kid's face was one of simultaneous innocence and amazement, yet it was also one that was awaiting an explanation. Thomas's face expressed a very similar look. Hopefully in what seemed a split second, I realized that Thomas wasn't kidding, and he was asking me a legitimate question.

Coming back to my senses, I said, "Who?"

He said it again, "Anthony Mickle."

I said, "I am Anthony Mickle!"

He said, "No way. Are you serious?"

"Yes," I responded.

He said, "Wow, my wife has been talking about you for years."

I said, "Who is your wife?"

"Her name is Mary Harrelson."

"Get out!" I screamed. Mary had been my State Farm insurance agent ever since I bought my first town car in Lake Ridge in 1998. The thing I would always remember about Mary is her laughter and positive vibe. She was always in the greatest of moods. It might have been 85 sunny degrees in the most torrential downpour or a snowy blizzard because you would never know otherwise while talking to her. Right at that moment, I could see where it was nurtured. Thomas was a great guy, I could tell, and not because we had met in that way. I could just tell that he and I would enjoy each other's company and feed off each other's motivation.

As our conversation continued, we were both blown away at what had just transpired. I'm sure I'd win the prize for the most excited or blown away. I mean, here I was just trying to make it through a tough time, and to have someone whom you never met before ask you if you have ever heard of yourself, as if you were discussing Donald Trump or Robert Kiyosaki, is a pretty extravagant thing. That was enough to lift my spirits for the entire month easily.

As Thomas and I continued talking, I told him more about the Investment Forum and my dealings throughout the area, and he shared his as well. I have to thank Thomas for not only supporting my first book signing; he also invited me to one of his monthly investment events, chartered by a great investor whom we affectionately call Mr. Daniels. Mr. Daniels invited me to be the guest speaker at his event to promote my new book, and his group purchased every copy I had available that evening.

Because Thomas was capable of having access to a bit more of my personal information than most, it placed me in a sort of pressured and awkward situation. We had a lot of respect for each other and constantly gave motivation to each other in daily conversation. Still, the fact remained that Thomas's wife had access to my insurance records for my real estate, jewelry, and art collection. I'm just grateful that they always displayed the utmost level of integrity and never allowed her insight to affect any of his opinions about me.

Slide 68 Mind-Set

You simply never know who is watching or who is listening. When you are conducting business, many people will tell you that if you like their product or service, please mention it to a friend. There is no recommendation better than that which comes from a trusted source. If people like what you do, they will tell others. If they hate what you do, they will do the same. Bad news tends to travel at a higher velocity than good news. Also, people tend to remember the details of bad news more than they do those of good news. As you continue your journey, never forget that this is a small world, and this is the information age. In literally seconds, someone can spread a word, be it good or bad, about you or what you are attempting to do. That can be spread through social media with the addition of pictures and video, making a great thing hard to erase but simultaneously a bad thing nearly impossible to forget.

Haterade—Is It in You?
The Drink of Choice for the
Jealous Population

I also had to contend with the looming problems of jealous colleagues who were not exactly thrilled to see me share the same office space while living a more extravagant lifestyle. In the first few years, it wasn't a big deal, but as my level of success increased, the jealousy took on an entirely new level. My jobsite was located in the Washington DC suburbs, and fortunately it was very close to the Lamborghini/Ferrari dealership. These were not cars that any of my colleagues drove or even mentioned in conversation, but I simply figured they either couldn't afford them or they didn't make practical sense for their family needs. Still, I decided it was probably better to not drive those types of vehicles to my jobsite because of the extra added attention they might bring.

One particularly busy week, my exotic needed an oil change, and due to a thirty-mile commute one way, I figured it was senseless to go back home afterward just to come all the way back and drop it off. I decided to drive it in, but to cut down on the visibility, I parked the car at one of the spaces farthest away from the building. When I went to leave the building for the day, I noticed another vehicle awfully close to it. I thought perhaps it was someone just trying to get a closer look on their way out of the parking lot. In actuality, it turned out that the car was actually parked so close to mine that I had to get in on the passenger side. To make matters a bit more interesting, the individual left his name in plain sight, so as to let me know exactly who did the deed.

This Time It's the House

I had multiple job offers during the time I held that job. It was just what I wanted—an MBA, a six-figure job, and now my opportunity to purchase a dream house. I decided to work for a consulting firm that I thought was going places; I liked the growth potential of the people I met with. We seemed to have a mutual respect for each other, and I felt that was great for the new relationship.

They gave me the assignment of what I'd be doing and asked me to meet with the client to ensure we had a good match. The client's representative was a strikingly attractive young lady, whose good looks were matched by her wit, charm, and education. We hit it off really well during the interview process, and she delightfully told my new firm that she'd love to have me join the team on the client's site.

Just before I started the new assignment, my firm gave me a pep talk and told me to "tear the walls down with your smarts and expertise." That was exactly what I was determined to do. I wasted no time letting them know I was there to get the job done. Every day, I ensured I was dressed for success, as I wanted to make a good impression. I quickly established great working relationships with many of the office staff, and I was hearing that many of them were impressed right from the start.

One day during lunch, I had to make a few interior selections for my new home, and I decided to bring my brochures into the office. My intent was to browse them after a late afternoon meeting. Unfortunately, I got a bit wrapped up with what I was doing and accidentally left the brochures out on my desk before I went home for the day. I figured it was no big deal and that I would get them on Monday when we returned from the weekend. When I returned the next week, the brochures seemed to be there right where I left them. I saw no reason to think that anything was wrong with what happened or was out of place.

Happenstance, my mom called me over that weekend and asked me how the new job was going, as well as construction on the new house. I told her everything was fine in both cases, and I think she could hear the excitement in my voice about both. She told me to be sure that I not mention anything about the new house. While she hadn't seen any of the blueprints, she was keenly aware of what my dream house looked like. She knew that not everyone would be as eager about my success as I was. I honestly chalked it up to her being from a different generation. I mean, what was the big deal about me building a nice place?

Moms Still Know Best

On Tuesday morning, now in my second week on the new job, I got a call from the firm. They asked me how things were going. I told them I thought they were going well. They told me that they were already hearing good things but wanted me to stop by the headquarters office on the way home from work that day. I said sure and was looking forward to the visit.

Later that afternoon, about thirty minutes before I left, they called again to remind me to stop by the office. I assured them I hadn't forgotten and that I'd be leaving in just a bit. While en route to their office, I received yet another call from the division vice president, who asked me where I was. I was delighted to hear from him as well and thought he was just calling to happenstance check on my progress. I was wrong. He told me to drop whatever I was doing and report to the office immediately. I agreed and continued en route.

When I got to the office, the secretary instantly picked up the phone and said, "He's here!" as if it were some type of television drama scene. She told me to go to the boardroom. When I got in there, the entire executive staff was sitting there waiting. At that point, I was thinking, *WTF is going on here?* They explained to me that I was doing a great job and how in just a week and a half, all the reports were as positive as they'd seen in a long time. I was thinking, *okay, great, but if I'm doing such a good job, what is all this about* because there was no indication any of this was about to be good.

They began giving me some roundabout conversation about the young lady whom I initially met with and how much she thought I was a great fit for the team. They went on and on and on. At that point, I told myself to listen very carefully and watch the nonverbal communication, because their current words weren't helping me out.

Over the next several moments, I kept hearing them say words like *house, affluent, upscale living,* but no one would come out and sum up what they were talking about. The next thing I knew, they were asking for my badge and placing me on indefinite leave without pay. It still hadn't hit me at that moment what was going on. As the executive staff began filing out of the room, I told them to just give me a second.

I thought back to other offers I'd turned down, and figured based on my credentials, I could easily call the other firms back and take them up since I was there less than two weeks. I figured at least two of the positions were sure bets, as the recruiting staff told me should I reconsider, they'd love to have me on the team.

On the way home, I called my parents and explained to them what had just happened. They were very upset at the news and asked me to think hard about my interaction with the new team. I told them I barely had time to get to know anyone at all since I was only there seven days.

My mom then asked, "Did you tell anyone about the house?" I told her I didn't but that I did leave the floor plans on my desk over the weekend. "Ahhaaaaaa! Didn't I tell you not to let anybody know about that house? I knew it! I knew it! I knew it! I knew something didn't sound right about this story. How many times do I have to tell you that people don't want to see you prosper? You are going to have to realize that, as much as you don't think they care or as much as they say they are proud of you, everybody ain't proud. These people who are smiling in your face are not your friends. Get rid of those floor plans and don't take them back to work!"

After we got off the phone, I just didn't want to believe what was happening. I tried to think who would have even come to my office during the first week. There was only one person I could think of, and that was the very person who made me feel so welcome. I thought *surely, she couldn't have been behind this*. To me, she seemed to be doing fine. She seemed happy. What could she possibly want that I had that she couldn't get?

The next few days, I looked through the office directory and thought about whom I could remotely trust to give me some inside information. I called a guy whom I went to lunch with a few times and gave him just a glimpse of the story. Within moments, he filled in the blanks, and the arrows pointed right back to the very person who I never thought would have had any jealousy whatsoever. It was her. To my surprise, I found out she wasn't acting alone. There were several people who had decided to join forces to get rid of me. Their rationale was that I was not about to outlive them when they'd been there for years.

I hate to admit it, but I didn't want to believe what had happened for several months, but eventually I came around. My parents had lived through too much to be making these things up. They could see changes within their colleagues just based on my success. I'd given a Lexus to my mom, and when she drove it to work, her supervisor began to treat her very negatively and told her she would never get another raise. Had we been talking about a lot of money, I would have thought twice about it, but she made less than $20,000 a year. She then told my dad to drive it. He was very hesitant to take her up on the offer. He is a long-distance truck driver, and they aren't exactly known to drive flagship Lexus vehicles. He was instantly met with opposition as the supervisor asked him if it was his car after he saw it in the parking lot. He told him it was his wife's car, to which the supervisor replied, "Don't ever drive that thing here again!"

So badly do I want to say this is all a crock of merde, but you can live in the land of make-believe or you can deal with reality. Some people do not want to see you prosper.

The Slide 68 Itch:
Listen to Your Soul,
or Pay the Price

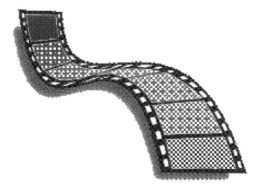

2004 went down on record as my best year to date. It was just wonderful from start to finish. I had turned thirty years old and was driving my dream car, built my dream house, earned a magnificent income while recording extraordinary returns on my investments, and engaged and contributed to my family and community. My son was happy and the envy of all his young classmates. It was just great. I was quite proud of myself.

Right after I moved into the new home, my mom decided to come up with my son and nephew to stay with me for the summer. I'll never forget my mom's reaction when she walked in the door. She was silent and simply looked around very slowly. The first thing she asked me was if I had a broom. She then followed up by asking if I had a mop and then cleaning rags and detergents. I was completely lost, because the house was brand-spanking-new and not so much as a speck of dirt anywhere was to be found. I obliged her requests, however, and gathered the things she asked for. After that, I went back to unpacking the truck and bringing their things inside.

A bit later, I went back to check on her, and she was cleaning as if the place had been filthy. Then she created a list of all the things she needed for upkeep and maintenance of the house. Once again, I simply obliged, and later we went to Bed, Bath, and Beyond, which became one of my favorite stores. Because I had a pretty comfortable cash cushion, I simply allowed her to roam free, getting any and everything she desired. When we got to the register, the bill was over $800. She and I both were a bit surprised, but it really felt great to allow her to do that and not be the least bit affected by the amount.

When we returned home, she called everyone she thought was home and told them all about the place. She described every square inch and was so proud to see the day that she knew I'd dreamed of for many years. I'm sure she felt a bit out of place with the community since it was mostly upper middle class, but she never let that stop her from blending in. Once she saw that we fit in just fine despite never being able to live a life like that twenty years earlier, I think she began to realize that the community wasn't filled with stuck-up rich people. Whatever she thought of the community, she had just become a part of it.

Seeing me live that lifestyle and living in that house meant so much to her for so many reasons. It meant a lot to me as well. I recall after being accepted to the Citadel, I needed so many things for my first week that she had to take a part-time job cleaning the homes of people in the middle class just to make things work, as she and my dad simply didn't have the money we needed. My dad took on a part-time job at Wal-Mart. I remember going to visit her at the home of a lawyer. I was proud that he was doing well and thought that one day I might have an opportunity to live like he did. He seemed to be a nice man at the time and even chatted with me on occasion.

I think the fact that I was now living in a house almost twice the size of a home she used to have to clean for others to earn the extra money for me to start college and now she was able to stay here without having to leave was just a real testimony for her. She was quick to tell everyone she knew all about it. I simply let her have her moment.

A few weeks later, my fiancée and I took our sons on a vacation to California. I used my Hilton timeshare to do an RCI exchange so we could stay in Escondido and have the opportunity to visit many parts of Southern California. We landed in San Diego and immediately headed for the San Diego Zoo. We got lost temporarily and stopped several times to ask for directions. It was mind-boggling to me how many people worked not even three miles from the San Diego Zoo and had no concept of where it was. We eventually stumbled on it and had a great afternoon before leaving to check into the Lawrence Welk Resort.

The next day we decided to go to Mexico to buy some souvenirs and see what life was like across the border. We quickly realized that we were so fortunate to live the lives we had, and I was quick to point it out to the kids. We spent the later part of the day joyriding through La Jolla. In an accidental turn on the wrong street, I found an exotic car dealership, so the family was at my mercy for about a half hour or so, but they didn't seem to mind. As we left the dealership and headed back to the resort, I recall driving over a hill and seeing the most breathtaking views I'd ever seen. The gorgeous luxury homes were perched high up on the mountain and overlooked the Pacific Ocean. I just remember thinking, *wow, I've clearly made a lot of progress, but there is still room to grow.*

The next day we decided to go to LA so we could spend the day in Hollywood and Beverly Hills. It was just a wonderful experience hanging out in the tourist area and allowing the kids to take pictures with all the imitated movie stars like Jason and Freddy Krueger. We spent the entire day out there just enjoying the wonderful weather and participating in the excitement. When we drove through Beverly Hills, I had to second-guess the price of S-Class Mercedes, as they seemed to be a dime a dozen. There were literally three or four at every stoplight. I was thinking maybe they were cheaper out there or something. Later that day, I stopped in a Bank of America on Rodeo Drive to get some cash. I asked the teller if the difference between this bank and the ones back in Washington was just that the account holders had a lot more money. He leaned in and whispered that the accounts were staggering. I asked if they were movie stars, and he said no. He then said one lady came in every Wednesday to withdraw $10,000 to go shopping on Rodeo Drive. I asked why she didn't just charge it. He said she just didn't want to. When you've got it like that, I suppose you can do whatever you want.

The next day we decided to just enjoy the resort by relaxing and taking in the mountain views. We got to chat with the other vacationers and allow the kids to enjoy the water park. In a conversation with one gentleman, we got on the subject of Las Vegas, which was a place I had never visited at the time but wanted to. When I told him I'd have to make a trip back to the West Coast to visit, he told me it was only four hours away. I was totally surprised and told the family tomorrow we were headed to Vegas!

As planned, the next day we went to Vegas. We decided to leave later in the afternoon so we could see it come to life at night. On the way, I noticed the heat of the desert and wondered how in the world anyone had found this place. I answered all kinds of questions for the kids and really made it an adventure. We stayed in Vegas for hours. I recall getting a bit tired and told my fiancée we needed to split the drive back. She was quick to agree until we got in the car. It wasn't thirty minutes before she was dozing at the wheel. I had to reach way down to my innermost night-driving strength to get us back safely.

The next day, we went to another San Diego Zoo ; I didn't know there were two. Fortunately, it was in Escondido, so we didn't have to drive far. It wasn't quite as thrilling as the main one, but certainly worth the time and the money. That day we just relaxed and chilled out. We didn't go far because we had to deal with some unfortunate racial issues at the resort that just aren't worth talking about. I'd certainly hope that the matter was resolved, and no one else has to deal with them.

I don't recall much of what we did the next day, but I do recall the day before we left. We had been out and about that day, and I told my son and nephew that when we got back to the room to go ahead and pack their things up. They looked at me with the most wide-eyed and surprised look I'd ever seen and said, "We have to go home?" I said, "Of course we have to go home. We can't stay here forever." They were totally caught off guard. I guess I can't blame them after a week like that. If it was great for me, it had to be out of this world for them. It was far more than they could have imagined coming out of small-town South Carolina where none of their friends had even seen an airport, let alone flown on an airplane.

All throughout that week, I was able to buy many items for the house and mail them back home. Pretty much wherever we went, I paid for everything. It wasn't the least bit of a strain. I didn't usually spend a lot of money, so to really enjoy the vacation and go through $8000 in a week was the most enjoyable week of the year. It was family, it was fun, it was entertainment, great weather, California excitement, and so on. It was a time I'll never forget. I was just so relaxed, so at ease, and so happy with life. It was euphoria!

When we returned to Washington and faced the reality of the daily grind, something very unusual happened to me within the next few days back at work. One morning at my desk, I felt my arm itching and naturally scratched it. After I scratched it, I noticed a few moments later that exactly where I scratched it, it seemed as if Freddy Krueger himself had clawed me. The trail of the marks was inflamed, and it was a horrifying experience. At first, I thought it was because I was using a new gym that wasn't being cleaned very well, and maybe somehow it was connected to there. I asked my colleagues who were also using the gym if they'd had any reactions. They agreed that the gym could have been cleaner, but they'd had no reactions.

Over the next few days, I noticed that the same thing was happening, except the reactions were jumping from one part of my body to the next without any rhyme or reason. I went to the drugstore and began explaining the issue to the pharmacist. I tried every cream known to man, but nothing worked. Some days I would have the issue and others I wouldn't, but the problem simply wouldn't go away. I finally went to the emergency room late one night as I began itching so bad that I couldn't control it.

Sitting there at 4:00 a.m., I felt like an absolute crack phene badly in need of drugs who had been attacked by Freddy Krueger. My stomach, arms, chest, and back were all red and swollen. As I looked at each section of my body, I could clearly see the claw marks. If it wasn't Krueger, it must have been a bear or jungle cat to say the least. I was itching uncontrollably and had no answers for what had happened. If I didn't know better, I would have thought I blacked out and someone did this to me, but I knew I had been alone for hours

They told me it looked like hives, but they couldn't give me any reason why this was happening. They sent me to a specialist the next day, who prescribed some medication. The pills I took made the hives disappear, but the problem was if I didn't take the pills, they returned. After about a month of this, I asked the doctor how long I would have to do this. He told me this was now my new daily medication. I said, "What?" I refused to believe that I would have to take a pill for the rest of my life over something that had come completely out of the blue and no one could give an answer for. He told me this was common. I said common or not common, I was not about to be a part of it. One day, I simply told my body that was it. I was not taking another pill another day, and just like that I stopped. I felt that this was going to have to be one of those times where my body would create its own defense. My body accepted it, and the problem disappeared just as it came.

After several months, I still often wondered what in the world had made the issue happen. Nothing I pointed to made any sense. After thinking and researching and more thinking and more researching, there simply weren't any answers. I decided one day to replay the entire vacation week in my mind, which was something I did many times just because it was life's best experience. I came up with something that I'm still convinced to this day is the answer. I believe that my mind was allowed during that week to be free of any and all pressures. I had no financial, medical, work-related, family, or other strains whatsoever. I had achieved things that I had only dreamed of. My parents were happy and proud, my fiancée was happy, our kids were ecstatic, and life was like a dream just for that time.

When I returned to the nine-to-five status of life, I believe my body came out of euphoria and was forced back into what I was accustomed to, and the chemical imbalance was so much that my body responded the way it did. I'm not a medical doctor, and I have no research to prove it. However, all the medical doctors I talked to couldn't give me any better explanation. In fact, they couldn't give me any explanation whatsoever. Therefore, I remain convinced that when you obtain things that you only dreamed of, it puts you in a place where you've never been before, and the feeling is so gratifying, so free, that any other place is a shock to your system. Perhaps it's your body's way of telling you that there is a better life destined for you, but you have to first see what it is and then you have to go and get it. With that, I permanently accepted living the lifestyle I was dreaming of, and I never saw another hive.

Protect Your Dream

The mere possession of a vision is not the same as living it, nor can we encourage others with it if we do not, ourselves, understand and follow its truths . . . . To be blessed with visions is not enough . . . we must live them!

—High Eagle

PART 6:

Time for Some Action

Don't Make Your Dream a Nightmare: En"list" Many Avenues

Many of life's failures are people who did not realize how close they were to success when they gave up.

—Thomas Edison

This chapter is here to provide you with some action items that will put you in the right frame of mind before you set off to achieve your goals. Some of the items may be things you are already familiar with, and others perhaps not so much. Over the years, I have found that many of the people I have helped have had aha moments in areas they least expected. These items are all important, but you need not start at the top and work your way to the bottom. Go first to whichever one makes the most sense to you.

Make a List—If you don't start with a list of things you want, you're going to reach forever but never find success or happiness. I know people with more money than they can ever spend, but they are too busy to enjoy it. That's just nucking futs. Why else are you making it if you aren't going to enjoy it? Figure out what you want, and then research every item as if you had the money to buy it today. No matter how far away it seems, you'll be surprised at how close you actually are once you start a plan of acquisition. This also keeps you away from corruption, as people may come along and try to get you involved with something that will bring fast money. Without a list and a plan, you may fall for it and ultimately ruin everything you've worked for.

Don't Expect Things to Happen Overnight—When I first created my dream sheet, I was sure that by gaining a razor-sharp focus, within a year, I'd be well on my way since I was already starting at elevated ground. Two years passed before I could even blink, but that's the beauty. Time passes by quickly, so counting it doesn't speed it up at all. There is nothing wrong with having time lines and goals to stay specific and measurable, but you can only control so much. Control the things you can, and the rest will take care of themselves. These aren't exactly motivating words, but it is a lesson you will have to deal with.

Family First—No meeting with anyone is more important than your family. That doesn't mean sometimes you can't miss a family event; just know it's not more important. If someone great is going to be at an event and you can't make it, relax; they will be back or somebody else knows what they know. Don't get too upset if a family member causes you to miss someone who you swear is so important to whatever. Nine times out of ten, they won't put you before their family.

Business Basics (Looking the Part)—Whether you are in a nine-to-five job and want entrepreneurial activity or have already started the venture that you hope will make you millions, don't forget the basics in business and business communication. You don't need to wear a Bentley watch, but do look the part of a business professional. Ensure that you have a few pieces of decent business attire. It doesn't have to be the most expensive and really nobody cares if you're wearing a $1000 suit, but you do need to look the part. Ensure that you have business cards, an e-mail address, and a website. Business is online these days, and either you're online or you're losing business. Keep up with your appointments, so have a day planner or use the one in your mobile phone; they all have them now.

The costs for looking the part should not cause you to spend tons of money or charge money you don't have. I spend about $1000 a year for my business infrastructure, which includes my website and e-mail addresses, Constant Contact e-mail for my newsletters, business cards, dry cleaning, and so on. Meeting fees will vary on the type of events. Don't waste a lot of money by always attending the most expensive meetings. Most of my meetings never exceed $30. The bigger conferences are much more expensive and are generally out of state or country, but they are rare. I use out-of-town business trips for multiple purposes. You will find that millionaires don't take vacations; they take business trips, with a little downtime after meetings. It's much more tax efficient and enjoyable.

Financial Planning Basics—I would be remiss in not mentioning that you should keep your fundamental financials in place while you tackle the world. As boring as it is when you want a world of monetary excitement, you still need ten to sixteen times your salary for life insurance, and most of you are underinsured. You have to have an emergency savings account, and as you have seen with my story, six months isn't even enough, especially when you're out there networking. You wouldn't want to get the call to go to China and not be able to pay the light bill. You still need to contribute the minimum amount your company will match to your 401(k); otherwise, you're leaving free money on the table. If you have kids, they still need to go to college. If you have a mortgage, ensure that it fits your short-term direction. In other words, don't sink a ton of money in an investment deal knowing your adjustable mortgage could rise sharply in the midst of the deal and you wind up in a horrible situation.

Be sure to use financial instruments to help you achieve your goals. For goals you want to achieve in between one to two years, you don't want to put your money in risky investments, but you do want some level of return so look to money market accounts. For goals in the two—to four-year range, consider short-term bonds, as they will generally have a slightly higher return than money market accounts and still protect your principal. For goals four to ten years out, I'd consider an index fund. I've used the Vanguard S&P 500 index fund personally, as it is a diversified portfolio of five hundred of the most widely held US stocks and returns historically between 12 to 14 percent, although past performance is no guarantee of future results. Goals ten-plus years out may require a more sophisticated look at your overall portfolio. Be sure to contact a local financial planner to help you.

There are lots of financial planners out there, but the best way to find one that fits your needs is to get a referral from someone you know. If you don't have any friends or colleagues who use financial planners, you can do a search online. Interview a few until you find one that feels right. Some of them will be eliminated via your portfolio size, meaning some of them have an asset minimum requirement before they accept new clients. I've been told by many that they were afraid to talk with planners because of the disarray of their financial situations. If you are in this situation, you are the candidate most likely to need one, so don't feel bad as they have seen and heard everything.

Chamber of Commerce, Maybe Not a Local Visit—Many of the meetings that I've attended were mentioned in this book. Some of the most advantageous ones came by way of the US Chamber of Commerce out of Washington DC. I don't live in Washington, but I do live within a thirty-mile radius. I attend the meetings of the DC chapter because they tend to include much more powerful businesspeople and lawmakers. Their thoughts typically go beyond the borders of the continental United States. I am not limited to the Chamber events of DC either. I routinely check chamber events in the larger cities in the United States. I have even attended events sponsored by the greater Los Angeles chapter. I would also advise getting a passport, because they are good for ten years and you never know if some event or happening mentioned in a meeting that you want to be a part of will be outside of the United States. In order for big things to happen, sometimes you have to attend big things, and they may not happen on local soil.

Stop Falling for Hairbrained Schemes—There is no get-rich-quick scheme out there that's going to deliver you to the promised land in two years. Some people promise you pie-in-the-sky dreams and it is an easy sell when your emotions are appealed to, but you have to be brutally honest with that little voice in your head to know when something is a load of crap or not. Christians need to be aware of people pulling the Jesus card. When people pitch investment deals and there is a lot of talk of God in the presenter's voice, be wary. There is nothing wrong with thanking God for your blessings, but too much emphasis on God over technical detail means somebody is hiding behind Him for lack of detail.

Luck—People say luck is when preparation meets opportunity. There are a lot of people out there preparing who don't seem to be lucky enough to ever get to the opportunity. At this point, I say there is such a thing as luck, but I think it is more about staying diligent until your break comes. You have to be willing to work for an unspecified amount of time while some guy seems to lazily come right behind you and find his payday in no time. The key point is it's *his* payday, not yours. Everybody is on a different time line, and you can't be concerned about what the other guy is doing. You have no idea what he has suffered in the past to get there or the road that lies ahead. He may need all that he has just to make it over the next hump and may have little else on the other side. Worry about you.

Follow Others' Stories, But Don't Live by Them—As I watched many stories of mega million-dollar deals from private equity and investment banking transactions with awe and a bit of inspiration, a lot of it was eventually found to be bad deals. The Wall Street to Main Street analysis that became so frequently talked about during the presidential election debates and town hall meetings blew the covers back on some of the most notoriously shady deals to ever be made. Corporate greed took over, and a lot of people lost everything along the way. It's okay to watch the stories for motivation, but don't get overly consumed in what you think is the fabulous life, because some of the people may turn out to be unscrupulous.

Networking Events—To some, they seem a total waste. Do yourself a favor, and only go to the ones that truly interest you. After a while, it gets old running to every event looking for an opportunity, and it's not free either. Some are expensive, while others just cost you your most precious asset of time; but even after attending ten events, you may feel that you've gained nothing. I assure you that you did, but it's probably not readily apparent. A huge point is you never know who sees you. After an event or two, you never know who may stop you. One thing is for sure, and that's if you don't get out there, nobody is coming to your house to get you and pull you to success. Don't pay a lot of attention to the guy who seems to be the biggest baller in the room. He may be good at looking good and that's it.

Books, Books, Books, and More Books—You've read about the books that I read while writing this book, but I never mentioned them all. You have to become a student of wealth and read about all the great business leaders. Know their stories and their struggles. Before long, you will use that knowledge to understand their success in other places and realize how some of their new relationships and other successful businesses were formed. By the way, you will become a source of knowledge, and people will start to ask you to become their guest or keynote speaker. When you're tired of reading books, magazines, and periodicals, turn to CNBC and watch the business profiles.

Courage to Speak with the Titans—For some reason, I'm not intimidated by hugely successful people, and I think that started at the Citadel. Regardless, don't be afraid to talk with the big boys. I've tried to introduce some people to those who have really done it or are out there doing it, and they chicken up faster than you can say run and hide. I don't get it at all and am not really interested in getting it. People put their pants on one leg at a time, so stop making them gods. If they give you recommendations for your problems, follow up on them, and then let them know you did and that you appreciate it. That will encourage them to keep spreading the wealth.

Be Prepared to Take a Financial Hit if Necessary—As you begin, continue, or restart your journey, you will not be able to control various factors, markets included. At some points, the economy will go up, and at others, it will go down. If you're not prepared to get your hind parts kicked, and I mean possibly slammed, you'd better tread very lightly. It's easy to stay motivated through a small setback, but when reaching for your goals costs you everything, are you prepared to keep fighting and keep reaching? Should you find yourself far away from the shoreline and not sure what to do, keep detailing the dream. Celebrate small wins as you move forward and it will help pass the time, but don't ever, ever give up or give in.

Exercise Your Faith—If you don't, frustration will run you right out of this game. You have to believe it's going to happen for you and believe it long before you see it. There is no such thing as some other higher power. There's God, and that's it. He created the heavens, earth, opportunity, success, and more. I could be wrong about all this (although I'm not), but what if you don't believe any of this and you're wrong? If you are wrong, I wouldn't want to be around when you find out. I never gave a lot of thought to daily horoscopes until a very successful man told me to respect the "ologies," as people have dedicated entire careers to them with the highest academic achievements one can gain. Shortly after I began feeling like I was coming out of my personal recession, the following horoscope was read to me by a friend:

> At some point over the last year or so, you got out of a bad situation. In your mind, you may even feel like you escaped. But you were in control the entire time, even though you probably felt fearful, trapped, and very stressed. Now, though, you're free. Yet you still feel nervous that what you left behind somehow poses a potential threat to your present life. It does *not*. In fact, it put you in a position to be in exactly the right place at the right time somewhere down the road. You're getting close to an opportunity that wouldn't have been if not for what you endured!

How on earth could a horoscope pull this together? It couldn't have been closer to the truth. I'm not saying replace God with horoscopes, but they are pretty darn spectacular apparently.

Exercising Fiscal Responsibility with Pricey Goals

When people see others living flamboyant lives, it's easy to get caught up in the moment and think of how you want and deserve a few pricey items for yourself. In some cases, a splurge on a pair of pricey shoes because you saw Oprah wearing a pair may feel justified. The thing you have to remember is Oprah's personal expense account is probably unlimited. If yours is not, then you have to remember the periodic expenses you are accountable for.

I have watched countless people think that because they see someone else with something, if they mimic the idea or concept, they should have instant success. I've watched men add golf memberships to already-strained budgets thinking that if they join these elite clubs, their money will multiply simply due to being in the crowd. Wouldn't it be so easy if that's all we had to do?

It is not happenstance that you earn within 20 percent of your closest friends, but that doesn't mean go out and befriend who you think is rich. You don't know what's on the other side of the shiny new Mercedes Benz. It could very well be a very high car payment with a very high interest rate that's all for show. Some people do legitimately have it together, but from my experience of being in affluent circles, more often than not, there is a lot of keeping up with the Joneses.

I recall one of my neighbors years ago doing everything he saw me doing. If I went to St. Regis Monarch Beach, he went. If I chartered a helicopter, he attempted to charter one. It simply did not matter what I did; he attempted to do the same thing. He finally stopped talking to me when I decided to upgrade homes. I believe his finances simply wouldn't allow that, so perhaps he found someone else to mimic. I would certainly hate to see his credit card balances before I left, however. Unfortunately for him, he didn't realize I had no credit card debt, so everything I did was paid for at the time I was doing it.

Your Family's Future

If you have a family, you have to take care of them while reaching for your dreams. Believe it or not, both things can happen simultaneously, provided your family operates on the same frequency. I've witnessed couples who made less than $100,000 a year who lived like kings and queens. The biggest reason I found was that they shared similar dreams or one bought into the dreams of the other.

1 + 1 = 3

There is a lot that can be said for synergy, or gaining more together than you can individually. If a couple have a goal of taking a three-week European vacation and they are in agreement on most things, their money stretches significantly further because their heads are in the same place. That can mean they are both researching travel sites simultaneously. It can also mean when one finds the price of a hotel and believes they have the best deal, the other now has a reference point. If they find a cheaper deal, they can let the other one know and move swiftly to take advantage of it. While one is gaining tourist knowledge, perhaps the other is checking the wear and tear on the luggage to see if something needs replacing before the trip. The possibilities there are endless, and so are the savings. Onlookers may think they are living at the top of the pile and in many ways they probably are, but they are doing it together.

Hey, Kids, Check This Out

If you have children, get them involved in your goals and dreams. Kids today are very savvy in terms of research and are perpetually plugged into this information age. You'd be surprised at how much they will get involved when they understand what the ultimate dream is. They may even want a piece of the dream. If it's a new car, they may envision themselves driving it to the prom, which doesn't necessarily mean they can do it but let them dream anyway.

I recall doing a bit of yacht research one boating season and figured I'd take the family to Miami to see some of the larger vessels. When we arrived, there was so much to see and do. I met with the broker, and we began touring some of the ones I'd selected that met my requirements. Even with having done a lot of research before going, the daylight passed us by before I could get to everything I needed to do. Because I'd promised them dinner on Miami's South Beach, I had to stick to my word and leave the yacht search behind. The next day, we were having lunch in Orlando with my real estate agent, and I simply couldn't squeeze everything in.

As we talked about the boats during lunch the next day, I thought about how much money I shelled out over the two-day weekend. The kids chimed in by saying, "The next time we can cut costs by staying at a hotel that includes breakfast." They apparently saw one on the way to the yacht show and realized it was cheaper. I don't think they were necessarily looking out for me, but they did get involved in the cost savings. They didn't think I noticed, but they were calculating costs for themselves to come back to Miami to browse the eye candy. Regardless of why, cost savings are costs savings.

Money Is No Object

The people who try to look the wealthiest tend to be the ones who are the poorest. I've witnessed on more than one occasion someone attempting to buy some high-priced item and when the salesperson asks what their budget is, they respond, "Money is no object," as if to suggest they have an unlimited checkbook. I don't think Warren Buffett would say something as absurd as this, and I've consulted him for his feedback on prosperity.

You do not impress people by telling them money is no object. If anything, you show them that you haven't done any homework and they can give you any number, as you won't know the difference. Donald Trump appears to be mean and nasty while during business, and in many ways he probably is. I don't think that is because he's a mean-spirited guy; but instead, he realizes that some people's objective is to get you to part with as much money as possible, and if you're not extremely cautious or let people know you mean business, they will take you for a ride.

Another very important aspect of getting those pricey items on your list is negotiation. Whether it's a car, home, or piece of jewelry, you have to be willing to negotiate your price. You never know what you can get for pennies on the dollar. Throughout my world travels, I see that Americans are least likely to do this, especially at the middle—to upper middle-class levels. Many tend to feel, "now that I've made it to a certain level, it is almost embarrassing to ask for a discount." The perception is if you're really doing well, then you don't need a discount. I can assure you that this mentality will allow you to spend the most money and people will be glad to see you coming. It seems to be a local mind-set, as everywhere else I've traveled in the world, people are quick to negotiate.

Managing Slide 68 Employees

Companies are not obligated to allow employees anything more than what they are paid to do. Managers within organizations should not be forced to deal with employees' outside interests. That being said, I think the innovative companies that will continue to grow and prosper the most are the ones that embrace the idea of nurturing outside interests. Take Google, for example. The cofounders of Google, both Sergey Brin and Larry Page, allowed engineers a 20-percent rule. Essentially, engineers could spend up to one day a week on something they were passionate about without even worrying if the idea would make money. They realized that when people pursued passionate interests, they were substantially more productive.

Google wasn't the only employer to take advantage of this fringe benefit; 3M also realized the value of it, and according to the book *The Google Story*, allowing employees to pursue other interests led to the creation of Post-it Notes, among other things. For Google, it led to the creation of Google News, which caught on like wildfire, and soon, millions of users were signing up for news alerts, which I'm sure led to plenty of revenue for the company. Having this extra time to do other things is clearly not for everyone. The company has to be well run, and the policy must be well understood by managers and employees alike. Some might want to abuse it, and others not use it at all. It's like anything else in that if it fits your environment, it is probably a real winner, but if not, it could turn out to be Pandora's box.

I can assure you that many of the jobs I previously held were good jobs and I actually learned a lot. The times where I was given full rein on a new technology were the times I prospered the most, but those times were few and far between. After several months of being on a leash, I realized I was not being as productive as I could be, and I believe employers have a lot to gain if they would nurture more of those opportunities. Some may feel that it is your job to show them all the skills you bring and it certainly can be, but if you're not managed in the right environment, top talent will blow right past your managers all day long.

Even if you list outside or passionate interests on your resume, most recruiters or hiring managers never even notice them, and few will have any conversation for it. Even with having my websites and entrepreneurial interests listed, only one recruiter ever even gave it any substantial conversation. He was pretty astute and not your typical recruiter, I might add. He had a previous background in finance and could easily see my skill set and where it might lead me. He asked the tough questions that no one else ever even contemplated.

I've observed many employees who either worked for me or around me spending significant time doing things that didn't amount to any employee productivity. Whether they were at the desk or not didn't matter, because their conversation or actions proved they were light-years away. Having an office space where employees become very chummy has shown to be very unproductive at times from my experience. I'm not suggesting people not be friendly, but I've seen that too much of the chumminess has even led to extramarital affairs, which no employer wants to deal with.

The Leadership Aspect

If you can sense how I felt dealing with the Slide 68 syndrome, imagine what that must be like for a manager. I have managed many technical teams in my career, and I have to admit that I have never managed anyone who was even close to showing they had any discontent for where they were. I am sure that some people wanted to change jobs, but the place I was in is considerably different from an ordinary job change. Let's think about all the managers who have to deal with individuals who are grossly out of place. How do they identify this, let alone manage it? My signs were blatantly obvious, and I had a smart manager who could see my time was limited. What happens when the managers are not so smart and cannot see what is just beneath the surface?

Even more direct, what happens when the manager is on Slide 200, while managing someone who is on Slide 2 and he realizes what it takes to grow the team or organization well beyond where it is? One shining example leads right back to Donahue Peebles, who sat on the board of the DC tax appeals business. He took over for a manager who was about to retire and wasn't the most fully engaged. Peebles, who was obviously on Slide 2, ran for chairman of the board and won the seat. Twenty-five years later, he sits on a $4 billion dollar empire. Would his destiny have eventually led him to entrepreneur status anyway, or could that have been managed and perhaps led him to a successful career in government management? Instead of supporting President Obama, he perhaps would have been the first black president himself. Who knows? One thing is for sure, he wasn't going to sit idle and be led by someone who wasn't actively engaged in the business.

From a business standpoint, I would surely hope this puts corporate America on alert that many of your people may not be happy where they are. Perhaps this can reenergize a training department or human resources staff to take a more intense look at exactly what it is you are seeing, as opposed to receiving in employee productivity. If the employees are saying they are happy but output is minimal, there may be a few Slide 68 employees in the ranks. When I was at my best on the job, it showed up in my productivity; and when I was less than my best, it showed up there also. This isn't anything new. In fact, there's probably nothing new under the sun. We just find ways to recycle the same things and spit them back out during different centuries in different countries so they appear new.

Somebody's Dying to Get Out of the Job You Swear That You Want

If all the reading you've done in this book is still not enough to convince you to take a hard look at where it is you are and where you ought to be if you are not happy with your nine-to-five, just consider the ability to live life itself. Shortly after famed R&B singer Gerald Levert died late in 2006, I decided to go to the doctor for a checkup. Levert was only forty years young, and I wasn't terribly far behind him in age. My guess was financially he was just fine. He came from a family of famed R&B singers and was the son of O'Jays singer Eddie Levert. I know nothing about his personal life, but I'm quite sure he'd seen and experienced some things that others will never even fathom.

Physically, I was fine. I exercised daily and rather enjoyed my gym workout. In fact, there were very few things that I would allow to interrupt it. I made exercise a serious priority. However, I knew I was growing unhappy at work. The doctor asked me how life was in general, and I told him I really wanted to change careers. I explained to him a few reasons why, and he adamantly told me to do it quickly.

"I have patients who are walking time bombs," he said. Confused, I asked him what he meant. He explained to me that many of his patients hated their jobs, bosses, commutes, careers or lack of them, and they felt trapped. They didn't have the belief that they could do anything else. With the financial responsibilities of families and livelihoods, they decided that they simply must continue doing what it was they did, even though it was killing them. He urged me to make a new start, as he urged many others. Unfortunately, many others didn't seem to heed the advice, and it was taking them to an early grave.

Don't let that be you. Time isn't forever, and as soon as you start realizing that you need to follow where it is you are truly supposed to be, make it a priority to get there.

When someone thinks you've been goofing off or not doing what you're supposed to do when you really are doing what you *need* to do, which may not be what they want you to do, just tell them, "I'm on Slide 68."

Which Slide Are You On?

It took me nearly eleven years to the day working a nine-to-five to realize I never belonged there in the first place. After I came to grips with where I wanted to be and realized the traditional day job wasn't going to get me there, I finally got fed up enough to vent my frustrations and committed to doing more about changing it, not that I was sitting idly by anyway. Still, I say there is nothing wrong with a day job if you really aren't sure where it is you want to be. In a nine-to-five is precisely where many want to be, and for them, I kindly say, "Enjoy, and I wish you the best." Some of the years I spent there were great, and I learned a lot. It was such a huge wake-up call to realize that I just wasn't going to get where I wanted to go on the path I was taking. The realization certainly didn't come overnight. I had to be there long enough to understand the system and my odds of making it, accept that this was not the be-all and end-all, and transform my mind out of it. That takes years to process.

This is not to say that I sat idly by and accepted everything, because I didn't. I was very aggressive in my approach in trying to get myself to where I thought I needed to be. Everything has a process, and things come in due season. You have to have experienced something to know whether you want more of it or not. Reading the magazines of the people at the top or who were working their way up the ladder was very appealing to me. I figured they had the reserved parking space at work, drove the nice cars, had beautiful families, and took nice vacations once a year. What I didn't see was the mandatory phone that they had to carry and the e-mails that they had to read even if they received the messages at 11:30 p.m. Still, I watched with envy and worked along the way to the best of my tolerance within the limited playground I was given.

Realizing that I wasn't getting the opportunities that I wanted was just an amazing, yet very frustrating, time. The traditional office catchphrases were driving me nucking futs. Every Monday, the elevator conversation was the same. "How was your weekend?" It was always followed with some derivative of not long enough. There was always some project that was being held up with a thoroughly decided and necessary step that was mandated much too long ago. We were waiting for some group or person of authority who just wanted to prove that nothing moved without him to bless it. I always thought the term "blessing" in this context was absurd. To me, blessings come from God, not some QA department.

In the meantime, I was never fed up enough to leave a meeting that I knew served little to no purpose in where I was trying to go. Thankfully, the meeting wasn't mandatory and had no bearing on my job performance. Still, everyone has a breaking point, and mine finally came on that day in a meeting on slide 68.

Slide 68 Mind-Set

Whenever possible, find someone who is willing to mentor you to help you achieve your goals and dreams. It doesn't have to be one person that you call every day or every week. It doesn't necessarily have to be someone older or younger or richer. It just has to be someone who provides you enough mental stimulation to want to continue doing better.

One day I received a call from my mentor, friend, and phenomenal investor Dr. Shirley Dominick. We really had no agenda except for me delivering her a few copies of my real estate investing book. When I delivered the books, we sat down and talked at length. Like so many times that we saw each other, our conversation was diverse. We spent quite a bit of time talking about her daughters and the ebb and flow of some of their most trying times in their teenage years. The baby girl wanted to climb every mountain that was ever formed. The oldest daughter wanted the top of Mt. Everest, but seemingly only wanted to get there partially through climbing and partially through ski lift. If I knew anything about Shirley and her husband John, I didn't see the ski lift in operation anytime soon.

As we sat there at the beautifully crafted, round kitchen table sipping V8 Splash and discussing the current falls in the market, Shirley, as usual, said some things that caused me to have deep thoughts. When she speaks, I tend to find myself in conflict. On the one hand, I try hard to listen intently. On the other, I'm trying hard to implement what she is saying while she is saying it, which of course makes it tough to listen.

She asked, "What slide do you need before you say enough? What do you want to be the optimal slide? Can you do this at slide 12? How many people leave slide 68 for another round of 50 slides?" We both understand that life is a process. Sometimes you simply have to go through some things to figure out where it is you want to be, but most importantly, where it is you should not be. Her oldest daughter was deciding that the Best Buy part-time job wasn't for her and perhaps she should just give it up.

I understood her concept, as she was gaining discontent in listening to her colleagues talk about how bad the job sucked. In the meantime, however, she didn't see the underlying opportunity that she was at the very forefront of technology. She could see the demands that customers needed to make themselves players in this digital age. Just the fact of being in a store that housed so much technology meant she could become an expert on many levels. She could have become the community technology consultant. In fact, she could have become that community consultant for anything that Best Buy sells. She could have purchased the software from the store at a discount and created her own business cards. Then she could have purchased legal software to form the entity that she needed for her business. Unfortunately, she saw none of those tremendous opportunities right before her eyes that could have rewarded her far better than a weekly Best Buy check could ever have.

Best Buy is the reason I have my own DVD. From concept to hard copy disk that plays in a DVD player, it all happened because a few-dollars-an-hour employee was savvy enough to explain to me which hardware and software I needed to make it all come alive. Within a few weeks, not only was I playing the DVD in my player, but I was also shipping it across the United States to people who purchased it online. Opportunity meets you where you are. You have to be willing to grow where you are planted until you reach a point that displays you are out of place. I don't think she reached that point, because I never heard where she explored the opportunities. The great thing about Shirley's daughters is they are going to make it big because they are destined to. It's in their blood. This is only a slump for the oldest daughter, and before long she will be off and running at speeds she never even imagined.

If you are prepared for it, success will come in many forms. If you are not prepared, it will only pass you by. The person sitting right next to you can take the same hand you were dealt and win big with it. There is nothing inherently wrong with that. It just means that you could be destined for something else. The point is to not let too many opportunities pass you by before you realize that you're on slide 200 and you feel too old and too weak, with little to no capability to do anything about it.

Slide 68 is movement. Are you onboard?

The Fleetwood: Brief Newsletters That Put People in Motion

"The Fleetwood" is a free monthly newsletter that I have been writing for years. Every month, it goes out, and every month feedback comes in. Here I have included a few of the ones that appear to have helped my readers and investors the most, based on what they have said. It is my intent that it inspire and help you as well. We recently celebrated our hundredth edition and hope to continue to help and inspire for years to come.

The Perfect Business Idea: You "Thought," and Someone Else "Executed"

Have you ever had the perfect business idea? It hit you in a restaurant, at home, behind the wheel? Oh, this one was big, your ideal moment—you were so deep on this one that you solved plate tectonics. It was going to make you rich and famous, your breakthrough moment even. Then you look up several years later only to find someone else doing it. Chances are this has happened to you on some level somewhere somehow.

Fellas, bear with me, I'm going to flash the ladies . . . with news, that is. Ladies, I know you don't know this, but men are nothing more than oversize little boys who may or may not grow up! Yes, yes, I know this is something you've often pondered, but I will admit there's some truth to it. Well actually, we're sure most of you knew that. If you don't mind, however, allow me to paint a picture.

There I was in the pricey Armani suit, Bentley watch, and Bruno Magli shoes as the construction crew broke ground on the project . . . . Ahh, what a great feeling after months of planning. As I was standing there probably a bit too close to the bulldozers, I watched the backhoe digger claw enough dirt to bury and hide a small car. Meanwhile, the front scoop was used to break hundreds of pounds of concrete with one fell swoop. Just a few yards away, a jackhammer was pounding the pavement into little rocks, while a crane off in the distance was lifting thousands of pounds of materials. I stood there in awe, just thinking wowwww, how cool it would be if I could do all of that with my bare hands while other men stood in admiration. Then I began to think, although I'm the guy deemed successful here, it sure would be cool to trade places with the construction guys for a spell. Right at that moment, the idea hit me. A gentlemen's playground—not the glass heels, adult version, but a real manly man's playground, a Tonka truck paradise for all of us who couldn't afford Tonka as kids!

I saw it so clearly, the acquisition of a few hundred acres of land filled with yellow Caterpillar-type equipment consisting of tractors, cranes, bulldozers, etc. This is a place men could spend hours building huge sand castles with their sons. And then, and then and then right, we could have a café at the top of the hill that serves meals, and then we could have a clothing shop that sold like Wrangler jeans and Timberland boots, etc. Man, oh man, was I into this as I watched the operation. Then the sun went down, and I quietly allowed the vision to just slip away while getting back to the business at hand.

Periodically on my long trips, I'd think about this again as something I might explore somewhere down the line, but no real hurry. That was until I was asked to come to London for a speaking engagement. I had been to the UK many times, but wasn't familiar with this area. As I searched for nearby attractions, I came across my idea in full operation. What the? Yep, they call it *Diggerland*, and it seems the business is doing quite well because this was their fourth location.

Why do we allow this to happen to us? "I don't have the money; I don't know anybody; I don't know where to start," is what we say, but I'm sure if you polled many successful operations, they knew next to nothing on the how, but they never let the lack of resources stop them. We put our plans and dreams on the shelves, or we share our thoughts with people who dwell in negativity and they kill our dreams. Our ideas face the experience we never wish on anyone, which is born, dead, and buried all in the same day. I keep these newsletters too short to fully explore this point like I'd like to, but just allow me to say don't allow this to keep happening to you, as one time is enough.

At the very least, you can go to your county SBA (Small Business Administration), and with $20 or less, depending on where you live, register a fictitious name and gain title to the business. While you can't patent an idea, at least you can begin receiving invites to the Chamber of Commerce as president of your new venture. You never know who may be just waiting to partner or help you write a solid business plan. This minimum investment of time and money is generally the biggest seemingly insurmountable obstacle to success. Can you imagine allowing a dream to vanish over $20? It happens all the time, I can assure you. While spring is in the air, dust those concepts off and add one more step. Stop making the graveyard the richest place on earth.

Being one to take my own advice, I was spending way too much money on architects who were adding things I didn't want to my dream house, so I figured nobody could better design for me what I wanted. I didn't have the pricey architectural software and just assumed I didn't know how to do it, although I had two years wrapped into the design. I decided to just go for it and buy the $3k software, but to my surprise, there was a free thirty-day download. After the install, I knew the clock was against me, so I worked nonstop for nearly twenty days and created my masterpiece. Some liked it so much they told me I should explore home design.

I began thinking if I took the idea further, I already had the name for the business. Then one night as I sat in deep thought, I decided I would at least register the name. By the next morning, I'd created a business plan, built a website, and made a trip to the county. I may or may not take it further, but at least **Palatial Designs, Inc**., won't be taken by someone else.

Powerful Bedfellows: The Genesis of Why Your Mortgage May Be in the Toilet

I couldn't quite get my head around it all. Even the Declaration of Independence originally stated life, liberty. and the pursuit of property. How in the world did we go from real estate boom to bust so fast? I talked to countless numbers of people who are upside down on their homes and simply can't get out. I suppose better to have one than not, but only in some cases, because the upside-down amounts are so astronomical some people may be better off without them. With those continual thoughts, I started digging. I didn't want to hear from CNN, MSNBC, FOX (FUX, as some call it), NBC, etc. I wanted to dig a little deeper, and boy did I find what I was looking for—or perhaps what I wasn't looking for, thanks to Charles Gasparino's *Bought and Paid For: The Unholy Alliance Between Barack Obama and Wall Street*.

Going back to 1998, I was twenty-four and had only recently become a homeowner. I never focused much on high-ranking lawmakers, although several of my Ivy League classmates told me I should get into politics. I did, however, recall President Clinton saying he wanted to increase home ownership in America from 60 to 70 percent. I figured that sounded really nice, and at a then number of 270 million people, about 100 million of them owning homes, a 10 percent increase would mean about 10 million more homes. When homes are bought, it puts people to work because homeowners go to Home Depot, Lowes, Wal-Mart, Bed, Bath & Beyond, etc.; but we're getting off track—you get the point. So Clinton created legislation that helped put people, especially minorities, in homes by guaranteeing home loans based on the full faith and credit of the USA, with the goal of increasing the American dream of home ownership. Wall Street salivated by saying, "Borrow the money from us so we can make huge fees." With organizations like Fannie Mae and Freddie Mac guaranteeing loans to help Little Suzzie who makes $18K a year become a homeowner, banks were much more willing to lend. What they didn't account for was every bank getting in on sweeps week and new mortgage companies popping up out of nowhere or the fact that Little Suzzie was being coerced into a $300K home.

With so many new homes being sold, it squeezed the competition, which drove prices through the roof. Meanwhile, back in Lower Manhattan, investors said, "I have another moneymaking idea. Since Suzzie has to pay $2K a month, or $24K a year (forget she only makes 18K annually for the moment), why don't I sell her stream of payments from her brick house to investors in another BRIC (Brazil, Russia, India, China) house. That way they will get 24K a year for thirty years. I'll sell it to them for let's say $100K. I will call the investment a mortgage-backed security, and China will be my biggest buyer."

A few years later, Jun Tao of China realized instead of getting $24K a year, Suzzie wasn't making all her payments and he was only getting $3K. Angry, he called back to Wall Street, and this is what he heard: "Doo-dooo-dooooo, I'm sorry, the number you have dialed has been temporarily disconnected. If you feel you have reached this recording in error . . ." Now Jun Tao wants to karaticize Goldman Sachs, JP Morgan, Bear Stearns, Bank of America, etc., but he's too late because they're protected under a clause called Too Big to Fail.

So we fast-forward a few years, and now it's Dubya Bush's helm. Instead of his administration putting a stop to the madness, his policies greased the skids in favor of the superrich; and as a final departing act, he wrote the code to bail out Wall Street of all those long-distance angry callers. That brings us to President Obama. In order for him to win the White House, he needed big money, which we all know he didn't have because, as I understand it now, First Lady Michelle was carrying the load. Big government-loving Wall Street didn't like Hillary Clinton because she wouldn't totally commit to them. John McCain "publicly" hated Wall Street, and they hated his brilliant running mate, who could spot Russia from her house. And that left super-intelligent, great orator of our time, Senator Obama. Stuck between a rock and a hard place, he allowed Wall Street to fund his campaign, as many politicians do—which essentially was making a deal with the devil unfortunately, but he did and he won. Today, the country and your mortgage is in a mess because Little Suzzie defaulted, the Wall Street greedy now sleep on Capitol Hill, and the banks got another round of billions. It was either that or have President Obama be responsible for the second Great Depression.

They were supposed to help Little Suzzie get her mortgage back in order, but since the government gave them billions of taxpayer dollars, they said, "Little Suzzie's living with her mother now so she doesn't need the money. We'll just give ourselves a few billion in bonuses, devalue our assets so we have to pay less taxes, and instead of helping out small businesses, which are the driving force of the economy, we're going to do something else. We will invest the money in ourselves again and say, 'Screw the cash cow, taxpaying middle and poor classes.' We borrowed government money at close to zero percent interest, so we're going to put the money into the Treasury bond market, where we'll get higher interest rates, which will fund our yachts. No, no, not that yacht; we paid for that one in 2004; this one, which has two helipads, is for our summer home, not the one in the Hamptons, the one in Monarch Beach, California, the place where we caused Orange County to go bankrupt in 1994 and now home to people like Kobe Bryant, who was a kid while the real ballers were balling."

"Okay, Mr. Mickle, that sounds great, but when the heck is my house going to come from underneath all this water so I can move?" Well, I'm not sure. What I can tell you is when you don't understand something, follow the money trail. That trail doesn't start on Wall Street; it starts in Washington, and regardless of how much they bash each other in public, they are a lot chummier than you may think. My best advice is to do what billionaire business mogul Ted Leonsis and I did, which is make a dream sheet and work diligently toward crossing off each item over time. Meanwhile, I have an upcoming meeting with the Wall Street elite to rap about riding the next wave before it hits the beach.

I like President Obama, but he's going to have to be even more astute about his Wall Street advisors if he wants another term. It's best that I stay away from politics because somebody might offer me a lot of money . . . and I might just take it:>).

As the Polo Paparazzi Snapped Wildly, I Officially Became an All-Star

We've all parked on grassy fields for outdoor events, but this grass was different. In fact, it was more beautiful than the grass at Pebble Beach, and we were only in the parking lot. Moments later, I was whisked away in a high-speed golf cart to the VIP section, where I briefly met Susan, a former executive of America's Most Wanted. She returned with flashing lights as the shutters started what would be the beginning of a "flash" flood afternoon. First it was a picture with the president of the polo club, then some political bigwigs. The conversations and pictures continued with cigarette boat racers and thoroughbred owners, lawyers and business moguls. "Von! Can I take a picture of you?" Huh! Are they talking to me?

Perhaps the most-blinding moments were the pictures with Adolfo Cambiaso, the number one polo player in the world, but he would have to take a backseat to the Stallones. You know, the Stallones, as in *Rambo* and *Rocky I–IV*. The entire time I spent with Frank, Sly's brother, and especially Kathleen Rhodes Stallone, Sly's stepmom, was great. I couldn't help thinking, "Man, y'all look like Rocky!" I'm not sure who people thought I was or why they admitted goggling me two minutes after introductions, but I liked it. Black, tall, decent personality, familiar look, or whatever the reason, I hadn't been the subject of that level of impromptu picture-taking since Beijing, and I felt officially, yet embarrassingly, like a rock star, or as the article suggests, all-star. It almost sounds like some made-up story, but actually it is all quite true.

That tantalizing introduction was a huge shocker, and while it exudes all-star status, it was not exactly the status I initially intended to portray. The intent was to distribute a brief note of thanks to all who follow this newsletter. Constant Contact has over 500,000 small business subscribers to date who market to customers in one form or another. Of that, only a select few receive their coveted, annual "all-star" award. For the second year in a row, *The Fleetwood* aka News from the Investment Forum has made the cut, and I just wanted to say thank you all sincerely. Why the name Fleetwood? It was the name of our double-wide mobile home manufacturer. When I said *from the mobile home to where moguls roam*, surely you didn't think I was kidding.

I would like to think this subscription provides content that is usable enough to make you *move* or at least strongly consider moving toward making your life a little more financially sound. The whole intent behind any forum has always been to bridge the gap between the haves and have-nots with the have-mores by removing the barriers of misunderstanding. Further, we look at eliminating the horrible amounts of bad investment advice and replacing it with real-life data from tangible, successful people, with a lighthearted twist. At least that's the intent anyway. The frequency is one message per month, leaving people's inboxes alone for other important content. I must take the opportunity to provide new readers an example of what I'm getting at.

Not long ago, I was explaining Washington's Merriweather Post Pavilion. In an attempt to provide further understanding of who she was, I figured, what better way to illustrate than via my favorite topic, exotic real estate? I explained that *Marjorie Merriweather Post* was the heiress of the Postum Cereal Company and once-wife of banking sensation E. F. Hutton. Hutton incidentally gave Washington Capital's owner, Ted Leonisis, one million dollars and the genesis of his platinum titanium billionaire status. Marjorie owned many properties, one of which was a posh estate named Mar-A-lago in Palm Beach, Florida, where other moguls like Rockefeller (Exxon-Mobile) and Carnegie (steel magnate) built mansions. After she died, her extravagant mansion near the Breakers hotel, owned by Henry Flager, Rockffeller's oil, rail and real estate tycoon partner, caught the eye of apprentice star and consummate real estate billionaire Donald Trump. He turned it into an exclusive tennis club.

I took a few less fortunate young men to Palm Beach as a way to illustrate wealth's far-reaching tentacles and show them life's possibilities. It was important that they understand lifestyles of sunshine and mansions fronting aqua blue water just beyond the golf-course-like lawns and Canary Island date palms are real. The floating, patented Double R's embedded in the center of the Phantom's wheels are real. Most of Palm Beach's eight-month-a-year settlers are very nice, hardworking-at-one-time people who received *God's favor*. Now some have "stupid" money and take aspirin daily to help decide between the Bentley and the Maserati, this yacht or that one. Most people will never earn salaries that will buy them a lifestyle like this, but a few great investments can change your life. The Investment Forum just wants to help cut through the voluminous mounds of bologna out there to keep people from making costly mistakes.

So as we celebrate another year of victory among the paparazzi and Hollywood A-List, it is only fitting that we end by a line from *Rocky IV*. I grew up in a pothole-filled trailer park, but "If I can change, and you can change, everybody can change!"

Reward Yourself Along the Way When Pursuing Aggressive Goals

Sitting on a white sand beach under a palm tree, I gazed out into the ocean, watching the sun rapidly sink into the horizon as I reflected on the aggressive effort put in to get things done on short notice. Now here I was finally getting the chance to slow up a bit. There was a pianist behind me, and a renowned vocalist about to sing. **Little Palm Island** was living up to its reputation as described to me by a former colleague as described to her by her parents. It was clearly one of the most fascinating experiences I had in a while. Although it was my first time there, the staff already knew my name and ushered me across the island to my table. There were a few other noteworthy items, one of which was the island was minutes from the southernmost tip of the United States. The others were that this place was only accessible by private plane or vessel. Perhaps that's why I was caught off guard when a pretty little baby deer walked up out of nowhere and tried to take my warm dinner rolls. Since when can deer swim across the Atlantic?

It reminded me of the time I landed in Lihue, Hawaii, and saw chickens roaming free all over the island. I'm not sure what storm blew these animals across the water, but here they were. Of all the guests, I was the only one there not celebrating some sort of anniversary, but that shouldn't be. I'm not pretending this place wasn't expensive, but when we grind toward aggressive goals, I think it's important to give yourself a little reward along the way, even if it's not some special occasion.

Why Was I Here?

Working on a home design project, I was trying to create the perfect rear decking. A former associate, who clearly didn't understand what I was doing, said, "I know you are not going all the way down there to see a deck." She didn't get it, and I wasn't about to waste a lot of time trying to sell it. I couldn't quite translate what I was envisioning, but I had seen it before in a magazine described as one of the most exotic homes built in 2010, but the issue was it was 930 miles away. I had just been informed it was going to be taken off the market in a number of hours, and the business day was already over. I couldn't let the opportunity slip by, so there I was with only one thing to do. *Activate guerilla grind mode.*

Current time: 8:00 p.m.

Hours remaining: 20

Hours to destination: 16

Vehicle: Car

I took a two-hour power nap, and at 10:00 p.m. hit the road with my R Kelly *This is the Life of a Go Getta*! superhero theme music. The hours of 2:00 to 6:00 a.m. separate the men from the boys on the highway, so I'd need Wale's *Bait* with super drum beats and the perpetual lyrics of Work! Work Work Work! in the dark of night. Upon arrival, I checked into my hotel, grabbed my tools, and went to work. With literally minutes to spare, I accomplished the mission as I ran into the new owner. Sitting out on the deck of this $22-million estate overlooking the Gulf of Mexico was worth it. It was hardly just a deck. It was a trilevel oceanfront observatory lined with concrete balusters, water features, hardwood ceilings, travertine tiles, and the like. After a night like this, anyone would deserve a nice break. These architectural features had created, by conservative estimates, a seven-figure net payoff from a property I conducted a fundamental investment analysis on earlier, so, yes, the trip was worth it.

At that point I realized I was four and a half hours from Little Palm Island and figured if I had traveled this far, it would only make sense to take it to the lim its of the land. I've watched people grind for success without taking a moment to breathe. If you're going to shoot for aggressive goals, ensure that you build in some rewards for yourself, and here is why:

1) Nobody cares about what you do like you.

2) Sometimes you have to act fast and travel far on short notice. Aggressive goals are not always groupie-friendly. Family and friends are immensely important, but they may have to catch you next trip.

3) If people criticize you because they lack understanding, don't invest a lot of time trying to convert them. Aggressive goal setters have no time to carry dead weight.

4) Rewarding yourself periodically gives you much-needed time to reflect on what could have been done better.

5) Don't burn yourself out, but if you don't live every day like it's your last, one day you'll wake up *dead* wrong!

My travels may sound fancy now in hindsight, but there were no shortcuts in any of this. As I boarded the vessel headed back to the mainland, I was the sole passenger with the entire crew at my beckoning call. Gazing at the sky so far south, I witnessed the unobstructed, pollution-free view, which made the stars sparkle like diamonds. Well-rested, I could now 86 the *Biggest Boss That You've Seen This Far* music and dawn the Sade *Lover's Live*. Facing the now 1200-mile, twenty-three-hour all uphill drive, I was well rested, but I still had a long road back. I figured maybe I'd spot my dad 18-wheeling the interstate along the way. My drive had to come from somewhere, but I'm the next generation, which means air travel. Where is that Diamond DA-42 twin engine plane when I need it?

Let's work!

Job Mastery Can Lead to Boredom Even After Millions Earned

I got a call from great friend and superior networker Jay Pendarvis. We discussed next steps after his inevitable liquidity event (i.e., Ca$h Me Out), which is essentially every entrepreneur's dream. I watched Jay's life transform literally overnight. We worked for the same firm several years ago as W-2 employees. He boldly and correctly calculated that not only could he do the same work for himself, but also that he could begin building an empire. Adding to his brilliance, he created a think tank and sent top billing invoices to his clients under the aptly noted name Cerebral Solutions. Over the years, his staff, presence, and revenues have grown substantially. That's worthy of celebration in itself, but the trouble is when you experience that type of growth, you may become a moving target, or even worse, unthinkable as it may seem, bored with success.

Many government clients in the Washington region are very difficult to penetrate. Cerebral Solutions' lucrative client base has proven that, which incidentally hasn't gone unnoticed by competing firms. They may find it easier to pierce the armor on an M-1 Abrams tank than break through certain government doors. It is for this reason that they target guys like Jay and ask him to sell his company. Such an acquisition provides instantaneous access. His employees remain employed, while the acquiring company instantly gains sought-after contracts. CEOs are paid based on incoming revenues, and one way to boost revenues is to buy existing businesses. The acquiring company may offer the targeted company several times their annual earnings or EBIT (Earnings Before Interest and Taxes), which can lead to millions of dollars in offerings and a seven-figure net payday for someone like Jay.

From CEO to DJ (Desk Junkie)

Normally after the dust settles and Jay is wired his millions, the acquiring company will ask him to come on board as a consultant. They may offer a salary of a few hundred thousand dollars a year, or it could be millions, depending on the revenue size. The problem is now you're back on the W-2 bandwagon, and boredom can quickly set in. Remember, Jay didn't gain this level of business acumen by being an employee. Due to his sale, he can't reenter the same line of business for a defined period, usually a year or two, due to noncompeting agreements. So now he's either in an office or a cube next to people who couldn't care less that his company was acquired or that he's the new resident expert.

In the interim, his homelife goes from affluent to fabulous, with new shoes for the whole family. His wife flies to Hollywood to get her signature Christian Louboutins personally autographed. His kids outbid all the other kids on eBay for the new Air Jordans Spike Lee gave to President Obama, and Jay gets what every other guy wants . . . a new car! So he dons his former BMW license plate that literally meant M5 BEAST, calls BMW of Sterling, Virginia, owner Thomas Moorehead, and asks what's in his new inventory. With a family of smiles, everybody's cool, right? Well, sort of. It's not that Jay's not happy, but he didn't exactly call to celebrate, so now what?

The "And Then What?" Factor

I hung my shingle out for investment consultancy, so I normally work on fundamental or technical analysis of real estate or equity investments. People usually want me to go into how much money they can make from this investment or that one, or they want advice on starting a business. I respond with a series of "and then what?" questions for three reasons. One, it ensures they are passionate about whatever it is they are trying to do. Two, it eliminates unnecessary steps. Three, it helps determine if you can do what you ultimately want to do tomorrow, today.

Passion

At Jay's level, and any of our levels for that matter, if you're not passionate about what you're doing, it will probably never work. In my case, just sending a monthly newsletter occasionally jerks me out of bed at 3:00 a.m., even if I'm scheduled to wake at 4:30. Sometimes I don't even want to wait until the next month, but because I'm busily drafting other things, I keep my **Fleetwood** passions from cluttering your inbox. I mentioned Thomas Moorehead for a reason, and that is because he is partial owner of a Marriott Hotel at Washington DC's National Harbor. That means even though he is a hugely successful automotive dealer, he too may be experiencing some of Jay's success woes and getting an early head start toward something else. I didn't personally ask him, so I'm not 100 percent sure. Telecom billionaire John Caudwell admits, "Business [success] gives you a massive high . . . . It's very addictive. But it doesn't last long."

Eliminating Steps

I built three personal residences and invested in countless others before I accepted the fact that I was only trying to build my dream home. Look at the monetary missteps behind those decisions. Whether it's an item you want to buy or a new career path, the same rules apply when you know what you want. If you can figure out your destination's direction now and be excited about it, chances are you can eliminate steps toward making that dream come alive.

Ultimately Happy Doing Tomorrow, Today

A new career direction is likely a treacherous cut in pay unless you're lucky. One way to eliminate that decision is by volunteering in the desired field and attending networking events. This gives you instant inside access to what your new life may be like. In addition, you may be able to do it part-time for limited pay now, which can lead to full-time pay later, especially after retirement. Studies show you live longer when your mind is actively engaged. I know people in their seventies who live very vibrant lives and make the most of doing what they love, so it never feels like work. It's nice to not need that bloated, pretax retirement account at age seventy and a half, when the government forces you to take it.

I was asked in a White House interview what my favorite song was. I could have said "I'm Proud to Be an American," but my answer was Maybach Music's own Rick Ross and Nicki Minaj's **"You the Boss"**! Perhaps I'll summon Jay and Ross to join me in South Florida for ownership conversations. It's there where we discuss hotels and Class A real estate among the sophisticates, which are my tomorrows and the things that keep me happy today. For now, Jay's the boss, so let's ensure he happily stays that way.

Helping a Friend Turn $75 into $500,000

Fair to say we've all heard of the international bestseller *Rich Dad Poor Dad*, but fairer to say we haven't a clue who the rich dad is or how he really made his money. We don't because the rich tend to keep their means to great financial wealth to themselves, and that just sickens me, to be honest. I was recently in an affluent community in South Florida, and one of the wealthiest guys there made his NFL neighbors pale in regard to wealth as he had just closed an international business deal netting him $30 million dollars, but I don't have a clue how. Not saying that he owed anyone an explanation and he doesn't, but just in general, I've been around enough wealthy folk to say they tend to be mysterious when it comes to their wealth and failures sustained along the way. They make it seem as if they've had it great their entire lives. I've tried not to follow that path.

When I had a recent conversation with a friend, he mentioned to me that he'd fallen into a financial slump. When I inquired further, he said that every pay period for the last several months, he'd come up short or only had $50 to $60 left. "If I only had about $2000, I'd be straight and could breathe a little bit."

I understood his frustrations, as we have all been there, but then asked him if he was taking advantage of his 401(k) contributions. He said, "Sadly I am not, and I know I should." I asked why he wasn't, and he responded that he didn't have the three to four hundred dollars a month to put in. It was at that very moment, I knew he was ill-informed. Let me give you a quick rundown on how I spent the next five minutes solving his problem.

This individual made $80K a year, which is twice the national average for a family of four. His taxable income after deductions and exemptions, and we know the 401(k) was not a part of that, was 80,000—20,000, or 25% federal tax, 3,200 or 4% state tax, 3,360 or 4.2 Social Security, 1,160 or 1.45 for Medicare, which totals $27,720; nearly 35 percent of his salary was gone. That left $52,280/12, or $4,356 a month. He said after all the current bills, there was absolutely no room for a 401(k) contribution. I said, "Let's try this again."

Since his employer matched contributions 100% for the first 3% of his salary, an advantageous approach would have added $2,400 (80K x.03) a year into his 401(k). His taxable income now starts at 77,600, since the contributions are tax-free. Instead of the former tax equation, this new one follows: 77,600—19,400 federal tax, 3,104 state tax, 3,259 Social Security, and 1,125 for Medicare, for a total of $26,888. You may notice the $832 (27,720—26,888) difference between the scenarios and say, "Big deal." Well, actually, it's a huge deal. For starters, the thought that he would have to contribute three to four hundred dollars a month is totally off. The 401(k) contributions equation leaves 4,426 (53,112/12) a month, which isn't even a $75 monthly difference.

The $2,400 a year he would have put in his 401(k) would be matched by the company, and at the end of two years after he's been on that job, he'd have over $10,000! The stock market generally returns 10 to 12%, but let's just say it's only 5% for the last two years since we're in a recession, which still means over $5,040 each year. I can assure you that a person who continues to find themselves with $50 at the end of the pay period is a person who probably does a lot of debit card swiping and little to no checkbook balancing and probably gets occasional overdraft fees. That means stronger balancing will ensure that they have more money at the end of the month because it will highlight inefficiencies like too many $4 trips to the frappolattay-mochachi-sweet hot drink hangout. I'm not suggesting that this person could have borrowed the $2,000 they needed from their 401(k), but at the very least, they could have seen it in an account whereas today it was nowhere to be found.

In addition, this person had federal student loans, which I suggested that they may want to defer for one year to make a temporary adjustment, which gives them an immediate $200 a month. I've stated many times that most people don't earn a dime until June, and people look at me like a deer in the headlights. Look back briefly at the $27,000 amount of taxes he is paying. Is that not six months of take-home pay eaten up by taxes? Oh, and incidentally, if he does his plan for the next thirty years, he will have $0 in his retirement account; if he does my plan for the next thirty years, he'll have over $500,000. The old adage says, "If you want what you have, do what you do; if you want what I have, do what I do." It's perfectly fine to be a millionaire, but being worth half a million ain't bad either. I know too many numbers in one message can rack a person's brain, so we'll stop there.

With the middle class being squeezed, people will be forced to make a choice. Either fall to the bottom and be among the poor, or claw to the top and be among the rich. Financial literacy says you can squeeze blood from a turnip when you know what to do. It took me five minutes to give this person that solution, but once he nails these principles, he'll begin generational wealth, and that to me is payback for a lifetime. Years ago, I used to give workshops on rocket science literally, but this stuff is hardly jet propulsion. I know the rich tend to pay less in taxes, but until you get there, you have to control the things you can control. Take emotions out of your wallet, and you can make reaching the moon a reality; but I will be the first to admit that it's not easy if you're influenced by the Macy's 40-percent-off sale. I could go on and on, but some of us need to pull out the ol' checkbook and account for that $50 we swiped at the gas station this morning, ignored the receipt, and are unaware that there is only $48 in the account.